DEFENSE, SECURITY AND STRATEGIES

# INFORMATION SECURITY TERMS

## GLOSSARY WITH ACRONYMS AND ABBREVIATIONS

# DEFENSE, SECURITY AND STRATEGIES

Additional books in this series can be found on Nova's website under the Series tab.

Additional E-books in this series can be found on Nova's website under the E-book tab.

DEFENSE, SECURITY AND STRATEGIES

# INFORMATION SECURITY TERMS

## GLOSSARY WITH ACRONYMS AND ABBREVIATIONS

DANIEL S. COX
AND
ERIC R. ELLIS
EDITORS

Nova Science Publishers, Inc.
*New York*

**Library of Congress Cataloging-in-Publication Data**

ISBN: 978-1-62100-787-6

*Published by Nova Science Publishers, Inc. + New York*

# CONTENTS

# PREFACE

This book includes a glossary of common security terms that have been extracted from NIST Federal Information Processing Standards (FIPS), the Special Publication (SP) 800 series, NIST Interagency Reports (NISTIRs), and from the Committee for National Security Systems Instruction 4009 (CNSSI-4009). The glossary includes most of the terms in the NIST publications. It also contains nearly all of the terms and definitions from CNSSI-4009. The glossary provides a central resource of terms and definitions most commonly used in NIST information security publications and in CNSS information assurance publications.

Chapter 1 - Authors have received numerous requests to provide a summary glossary for our publications and other relevant sources, and to make the glossary available to practitioners. As a result of these requests, this glossary of common security terms has been extracted from NIST Federal Information Processing Standards (FIPS), the Special Publication (SP) 800 series, NIST Interagency Reports (NISTIRs), and from the Committee for National Security Systems Instruction 4009 (CNSSI-4009). The glossary includes most of the terms in the NIST publications. It also contains nearly all of the terms and definitions from CNSSI-4009. The glossary provides a central resource of terms and definitions most commonly used in NIST information security publications and in CNSS information assurance publications. For a given term, authors do not include all definitions in NIST documents – especially not from the older NIST publications. Since draft documents are not stable, authors do not refer to terms/definitions in them.

Chapter 2 - This report contains a list of selected acronyms and abbreviations for system and network security terms with their generally accepted or preferred definitions. It is intended as a resource for federal agencies and other users of system and network security publications.

The capitalization, spelling, and definitions of acronyms and abbreviations frequently vary among publications. It is easy to understand why this happens. While some acronyms and abbreviations (e.g., WWW) have one universally recognized and understood definition within the domain of system and network security, others (e.g., IA, MAC) have multiple valid definitions depending upon the context in which they are used. Some acronyms bear little resemblance to their definitions, such as Modes of Operation Validation System for the Triple DES Algorithm (TMOVS). Others use unexpected capitalization or spelling (e.g., Electronic Business using eXtensible Markup Language [ebXML] and Organisation for Economic Co-operation and Development [OECD]). As a result, acronyms, abbreviations, and their definitions may be inaccurately or inconsistently defined by authors, perpetuating errors and confusing or misleading readers.

In: Information Security Terms
Editors: Daniel S. Cox and Eric R. Ellis

ISBN: 978-1-62100-787-6


*Chapter 1*

# GLOSSARY OF KEY INFORMATION SECURITY TERMS*

***Richard Kissel***

## INTRODUCTION

We have received numerous requests to provide a summary glossary for our publications and other relevant sources, and to make the glossary available to practitioners. As a result of these requests, this glossary of common security terms has been extracted from NIST Federal Information Processing Standards (FIPS), the Special Publication (SP) 800 series, NIST Interagency Reports (NISTIRs), and from the Committee for National Security Systems Instruction 4009 (CNSSI-4009). The glossary includes most of the terms in the NIST publications. It also contains nearly all of the terms and definitions from CNSSI-4009. The glossary provides a central resource of terms and definitions most commonly used in NIST information security publications and in CNSS information assurance publications. For a given term, we do not include all definitions in NIST documents – especially not from the older NIST publications. Since draft documents are not stable, we do not refer to terms/definitions in them.

Each entry in the glossary points to one or more source NIST publications, and/or CNSSI-4009, and/or supplemental sources where appropriate. A list of the supplemental (non-NIST) sources may be found on pages 210-211. As we are continuously refreshing our publication suite, terms included in the glossary come from our more recent publications. The NIST publications referenced are the most recent versions of those publications (as of the date of this document).

It is our intention to keep the glossary current by providing updates online. New definitions will be added to the glossary as required, and updated versions will be posted on the Computer Security Resource Center (CSRC) Web site at http://csrc.nist.gov/.

---

* This is an edited, reformatted and augmented version of the National Institute of Standards and Technology publication, NIST IR 7298, Revision 1, dated February 2011.

The Editor, Richard Kissel, would like to express special thanks to Ms. Tanya Brewer for her outstanding work in the design of the cover page and in the overall design and organization of the document. Special thanks are also given to Kelley Dempsey for her insightful review and comments which made this a much better document. Thanks also to all who provided comments during the public review period of this document. The Editor also expresses special thanks to the CNSS Glossary Working Group for encouraging the inclusion of CNSSI-4009 terms and definitions into this glossary.

Comments and suggestions on this publication should be sent to secglossary@nist.gov.

| | |
|---|---|
| Access – | Ability to make use of any information system (IS) resource.<br>SOURCE: SP 800-32<br>Ability and means to communicate with or otherwise interact with a system, to use system resources to handle information, to gain knowledge of the information the system contains, or to control system components and functions.<br>SOURCE: CNSSI-4009 |
| Access Authority – | An entity responsible for monitoring and granting access privileges for other authorized entities.<br>SOURCE: CNSSI-4009 |
| Access Control – | The process of granting or denying specific requests to: 1) obtain and use information and related information processing services; and 2) enter specific physical facilities (e.g., federal buildings, military establishments, border crossing entrances).<br>SOURCE: FIPS 201; CNSSI-4009 |
| Access Control List (ACL) – | 1. A list of permissions associated with an object. The list specifies who or what is allowed to access the object and what operations are allowed to be performed on the object.<br>2. A mechanism that implements access control for a system resourceby enumerating the system entities that are permitted to access the resource and stating, either implicitly or explicitly, the access modes granted to each entity.<br>SOURCE: CNSSI-4009 |
| Access Control Lists (ACLs) – | A register of:<br>1. users (including groups, machines, processes) who have been given permission to use a particular system resource, and<br>2. the types of access they have been permitted.<br>SOURCE: SP 800-12 |
| Access Control Mechanism – | Security safeguards (i.e., hardware and software features, physical controls, operating procedures, management procedures, and various combinations of these) designed to detect and deny unauthorized access and permit authorized access to an information system.<br>SOURCE: CNSSI-4009 |
| Access Level – | A category within a given security classification limiting entry or system connectivity to only authorized persons.<br>SOURCE: CNSSI-4009 |

**Access List** – Roster of individuals authorized admittance to a controlled area.
SOURCE: CNSSI-4009

**Access Point** – A device that logically connects wireless client devices operating in infrastructure to one another and provides access to a distribution system, if connected, which is typically an organization's enterprise wired network.
SOURCE: SP 800-48; SP 800-121

**Access Profile** – Association of a user with a list of protected objects the user may access.
SOURCE: CNSSI-4009

**Access Type** – Privilege to perform action on an object. Read, write, execute, append, modify, delete, and create are examples of access types. Seewrite.
SOURCE: CNSSI-4009

**Account Management, User** – Involves
1)the process of requesting, establishing, issuing, and closing user accounts;
2)tracking users and their respective access authorizations; and
3)managing these functions.
SOURCE: SP 800-12

**Accountability** – The security goal that generates the requirement for actions of an entity to be traced uniquely to that entity. This supports non-repudiation, deterrence, fault isolation, intrusion detection and prevention, and after-action recovery and legal action.
SOURCE: SP 800-27

Principle that an individual is entrusted to safeguard and control equipment, keying material, and information and is answerable to proper authority for the loss or misuse of that equipment or information.
SOURCE: CNSSI-4009

**Accounting Legend Code (ALC)** – Numeric code used to indicate the minimum accounting controls required for items of accountable communications security (COMSEC) material within the COMSEC Material Control System.
SOURCE: CNSSI-4009

**Accounting Number** – Number assigned to an item of COMSEC material to facilitate its control.
SOURCE: CNSSI-4009

**Accreditation** – See Authorization.

**Accreditation Authority** – See Authorizing Official.

**Accreditation Boundary** – See Authorization Boundary.

**Accreditation Package** – Product comprised of a System Security Plan (SSP) and a report documenting the basis for the accreditation decision.
SOURCE: CNSSI-4009

| | |
|---|---|
| Accrediting Authority – | Synonymous with Designated Accrediting Authority (DAA). See also Authorizing Official.<br>SOURCE: CNSSI-4009 |
| Activation Data – | Private data, other than keys, that are required to access cryptographic modules.<br>SOURCE: SP 800-32 |
| Active Attack – | An attack that alters a system or data.<br>SOURCE: CNSSI-4009 |
| Active Content – | Electronic documents that can carry out or trigger actions automatically on a computer platform without the intervention of a user.<br>SOURCE: SP 800-28<br>Software in various forms that is able to automatically carry out or trigger actions on a computer platform without the intervention of a user.<br>SOURCE: CNSSI-4009 |
| Active Security Testing – | Security testing that involves direct interaction with a target, such assending packets to a target.<br>SOURCE: SP 800-115 |
| Activities – | An assessment object that includes specific protection-related pursuits or actions supporting an information system that involve people (e.g., conducting system backup operations, monitoring network traffic).<br>SOURCE: SP 800-53A |
| Add-on Security – | Incorporation of new hardware, software, or firmware safeguards in an operational information system.<br>SOURCE: CNSSI-4009 |
| Adequate Security – | Security commensurate with the risk and the magnitude of harm resulting from the loss, misuse, or unauthorized access to or modification of information.<br>SOURCE: SP 800-53; FIPS 200; OMB Circular A-130, App. III<br>Security commensurate with the risk and magnitude of harm resultingfrom the loss, misuse, or unauthorized access to or modification of information.<br>Note: This includes assuring that information systems operate effectively and provide appropriate confidentiality, integrity, and availability, through the use of cost-effective management, personnel,operational, and technical controls.<br>SOURCE: CNSSI-4009; SP 800-37 |
| Administrative Account – | A user account with full privileges on a computer.<br>SOURCE: SP 800-69 |
| Administrative Safeguards – | Administrative actions, policies, and procedures to manage the selection, development, implementation, and maintenance of security measures to protect electronic health information and |

to manage the conduct of the covered entity's workforce in relation to protecting that information.
SOURCE: SP 800-66

**Advanced Encryption Standard – (AES)** The Advanced Encryption Standard specifies a U.S. government-approved cryptographic algorithm that can be used to protect electronic data. The AES algorithm is a symmetric block cipher that can encrypt (encipher) and decrypt (decipher) information. This standard specifies the Rijndaelalgorithm, a symmetric block cipher that can process data blocksof 128 bits, using cipher keys with lengths of 128, 192, and 256 bits.
SOURCE: FIPS 197

A U.S. government-approved cryptographic algorithm that can be used to protect electronic data. The AES algorithm is a symmetric block cipher that can encrypt (encipher) and decrypt (decipher) information.
SOURCE: CNSSI-4009

**Advanced Key Processor (AKP) –** A cryptographic device that performs all cryptographic functions for a management client node and contains the interfaces to 1) exchange information with a client platform, 2) interact with fill devices, and 3)connect a client platform securely to the primary services node (PRSN).
SOURCE: CNSSI-4009

**Advisory –** Notification of significant new trends or developments regarding the threat to the information systems of an organization. This notification may include analytical insights into trends, intentions, technologies, or tactics of an adversary targeting information systems.
SOURCE: CNSSI-4009

**Agency –** Any executive department, military department, government corporation, government-controlled corporation, or other establishment in the executive branch of the government (including the Executive Office of the President), or any independent regulatoryagency, but does not include: 1) the Government Accountability Office; 2) the Federal Election Commission; 3) the governments of the District of Columbia and of the territories and possessions of the United States, and their various subdivisions; or 4) government-owned contractor-operated facilities, including laboratories engaged in national defense research and production activities.
SOURCE: FIPS 200; 44 U.S.C., Sec. 3502
ALSO See Executive Agency.

**Agency Certification Authority – (CA)** A CA that acts on behalf of an agency and is under the operational control of an agency.
SOURCE: SP 800-32

| | |
|---|---|
| Agent – | A program used in distributed denial of service (DDoS) attacks that send malicious traffic to hosts based on the instructions of a handler. Also known as a bot.<br>SOURCE: SP 800-61<br>A program acting on behalf of a person or organization.<br>SOURCE: SP 800-95 |
| Alert – | Notification that a specific attack has been directed at an organization's information systems.<br>SOURCE: CNSSI-4009 |
| Allocation – | The process an organization employs to determine whether security controls are defined as system-specific, hybrid, or common.<br>The process an organization employs to assign security controls to specific information system components responsible for providing a particular security capability (e.g., router, server, remote sensor).<br>SOURCE: SP 800-37 |
| Alternate COMSEC Custodian – | Individual designated by proper authority to perform the duties of the COMSEC custodian during the temporary absence of the COMSEC custodian.<br>SOURCE: CNSSI-4009 |
| Alternate Work Site – | Governmentwide, national program allowing federal employees to work at home or at geographically convenient satellite offices for partof the work week (e.g., telecommuting).<br>SOURCE: CNSSI-4009 |
| Analysis – | The examination of acquired data for its significance and probative value to the case.<br>SOURCE: SP 800-72 |
| Anomaly-Based Detection – | The process of comparing definitions of what activity is considered normal against observed events to identify significant deviations.<br>SOURCE: SP 800-94 |
| Anti-jam – | Countermeasures ensuring that transmitted information can be received despite deliberate jamming attempts.<br>SOURCE: CNSSI-4009 |
| Anti-spoof – | Countermeasures taken to prevent the unauthorized use of legitimate Identification & Authentication (I&A) data, however it was obtained, to mimic a subject different from the attacker.<br>SOURCE: CNSSI-4009 |
| Antispyware Software – | A program that specializes in detecting both malware and non-malware forms of spyware.<br>SOURCE: SP 800-69 |
| Antivirus Software – | A program that monitors a computer or network to identify all major types of malware and prevent or contain malware incidents.<br>SOURCE: SP 800-83 |
| Applicant – | The subscriber is sometimes called an "applicant" after applying to a certification authority for a certificate, but before the certificate issuance procedure is completed.<br>SOURCE: SP 800-32 |

Application – A software program hosted by an information system.
SOURCE: SP 800-37
Software program that performs a specific function directly for a userand can be executed without access to system control, monitoring, or administrative privileges.
SOURCE: CNSSI-4009

Approval to Operate (ATO) – The official management decision issued by a DAA or PAA to authorize operation of an information system and to explicitly accept the residual risk to agency operations (including mission, functions, image, or reputation), agency assets, or individuals.
SOURCE: CNSSI-4009

Approved – Federal Information Processing Standard (FIPS)-approved or National Institute of Standards and Technology (NIST)-recommended. An algorithm or technique that is either 1)specified in a FIPS or NIST Recommendation, or 2)adopted in a FIPS or NIST Recommendation.
SOURCE: FIPS 201

Approved – FIPS-approved and/or NIST-recommended.
SOURCE: FIPS 140-2
FIPS-approved and/or NIST-recommended. An algorithm or technique that is either 1) specified in a FIPS or NIST Recommendation, 2) adopted in a FIPS or NIST Recommendation, or 3) specified in a list of NIST-approved security functions.
SOURCE: FIPS 186

Approved Mode of Operation – A mode of the cryptographic module that employs only Approved security functions (not to be confused with a specific mode of an Approved security function, e.g., Data Encryption Standard Cipher-Block Chaining (DES CBC) mode).
SOURCE: FIPS 140-2

Approved Security Function – A security function (e.g., cryptographic algorithm, cryptographic key management technique, or authentication technique) that is either

a) specified in an Approved Standard;
b) adopted in an Approved Standard and specified either in an appendix of the Approved Standard or in a document referenced by the Approved Standard; or
c) specified in the list of Approved security functions.
SOURCE: FIPS 140-2

Assessment – See Security Control Assessment.

Assessment Findings – Assessment results produced by the application of an assessment procedure to a security control or control enhancement to achieve an assessment objective; the execution of a determination statement within an assessment procedure by an assessor that results in either a *satisfied* or *other than satisfied* condition.
SOURCE: SP 800-53A

| | |
|---|---|
| Assessment Method – | One of three types of actions (i.e., examine, interview, test) taken by assessors in obtaining evidence during an assessment.<br>SOURCE: SP 800-53A |
| Assessment Object – | The item (i.e., specifications, mechanisms, activities, individuals) upon which an assessment method is applied during an assessment.<br>SOURCE: SP 800-53A |
| Assessment Objective – | A set of determination statements that expresses the desired outcome for the assessment of a security control or control enhancement.<br>SOURCE: SP 800-53A |
| Assessment Procedure – | A set of assessment objectives and an associated set of assessment methods and assessment objects.<br>SOURCE: SP 800-53A |
| Assessor – | See Security Control Assessor. |
| Asset – | A major application, general support system, high impact program, physical plant, mission critical system, personnel, equipment, or a logically related group of systems.<br>SOURCE: CNSSI-4009 |
| Assurance – | Grounds for confidence that the other four security goals (integrity, availability, confidentiality, and accountability) have been adequatelymet by a specific implementation. "Adequately met" includes (1) functionality that performs correctly, (2) sufficient protection against unintentional errors (by users or software), and (3) sufficient resistance to intentional penetration or by-pass.<br>SOURCE: SP 800-27<br>The grounds for confidence that the set of intended security controls in an information system are effective in their application.<br>SOURCE: SP 800-37; SP 800-53A<br>Measure of confidence that the security features, practices, procedures, and architecture of an information system accurately mediates and enforces the security policy.<br>SOURCE: CNSSI-4009 |
| Assurance Case – | A structured set of arguments and a body of evidence showing that aninformation system satisfies specific claims with respect to a given quality attribute.<br>SOURCE: SP 800-53A |
| Assured Information Sharing – | The ability to confidently share information with those who need it, when and where they need it, as determined by operational need and an acceptable level of security risk.<br>SOURCE: CNSSI-4009 |
| Assured Software – | Computer application that has been designed, developed, analyzed, and tested using processes, tools, and techniques that establish a level of confidence in it.<br>SOURCE: CNSSI-4009 |
| Asymmetric Cryptography – | See Public Key Cryptography.<br>SOURCE: CNSSI-4009 |

**Asymmetric Keys** – Two related keys, a public key and a private key that are used to perform complementary operations, such as encryption and decryption or signature generation and signature verification.
SOURCE: FIPS 201

**Attack** – An attempt to gain unauthorized access to system services, resources, or information, or an attempt to compromise system integrity.
SOURCE: SP 800-32
Any kind of malicious activity that attempts to collect, disrupt, deny, degrade, or destroy information system resources or the information itself.
SOURCE: CNSSI-4009

**Attack Sensing and Warning (AS&W)** – Detection, correlation, identification, and characterization of intentional unauthorized activity with notification to decision makers so that an appropriate response can be developed.
SOURCE: CNSSI-4009

**Attack Signature** – A specific sequence of events indicative of an unauthorized access attempt.
SOURCE: SP 800-12
A characteristic byte pattern used in malicious code or an indicator, or set of indicators, that allows the identification of malicious network activities.
SOURCE: CNSSI-4009

**Attribute Authority** – An entity, recognized by the Federal Public Key Infrastructure (PKI) Policy Authority or comparable agency body as having the authority to verify the association of attributes to an identity.
SOURCE: SP 800-32

**Attribute-Based Access Control** – Access control based on attributes associated with and about subjects,objects, targets, initiators, resources, or the environment. An access control rule set defines the combination of attributes under which an access may take place.
SOURCE: SP 800-53; CNSSI-4009

**Attribute-Based Authorization** – A structured process that determines when a user is authorized to access information, systems, or services based on attributes of the user and of the information, system, or service.
SOURCE: CNSSI-4009

**Audit** – Independent review and examination of records and activities to assess the adequacy of system controls, to ensure compliance with established policies and operational procedures, and to recommend necessary changes in controls, policies, or procedures.
SOURCE: SP 800-32
Independent review and examination of records and activities to assess the adequacy of system controls, to ensure compliance with established policies and operational procedures.
SOURCE: CNSSI-4009

| | |
|---|---|
| Audit Data – | Chronological record of system activities to enable the reconstruction and examination of the sequence of events and changes in an event.<br>SOURCE: SP 800-32 |
| Audit Log – | A chronological record of system activities. Includes records of system accesses and operations performed in a given period.<br>SOURCE: CNSSI-4009 |
| Audit Reduction Tools – | Preprocessors designed to reduce the volume of audit records to facilitate manual review. Before a security review, these tools can remove many audit records known to have little security significance.These tools generally remove records generated by specified classes of events, such as records generated by nightly backups.<br>SOURCE: SP 800-12; CNSSI-4009 |
| Audit Review – | The assessment of an information system to evaluate the adequacy of implemented security controls, assure that they are functioning properly, identify vulnerabilities, and assist in implementation of newsecurity controls where required. This assessment is conducted annually or whenever significant change has occurred and may lead to recertification of the information system.<br>SOURCE: CNSSI-4009 |
| Audit Trail – | A record showing who has accessed an Information Technology (IT) system and what operations the user has performed during a given period.<br>SOURCE: SP 800-47<br>A chronological record that reconstructs and examines the sequence of activities surrounding or leading to a specific operation, procedure,or event in a security relevant transaction from inception to final result.<br>SOURCE: CNSSI-4009 |
| Authenticate – | To confirm the identity of an entity when that identity is presented.<br>SOURCE: SP 800-32<br>To verify the identity of a user, user device, or other entity.<br>SOURCE: CNSSI-4009 |
| Authentication – | Verifying the identity of a user, process, or device, often as a prerequisite to allowing access to resources in an information system.<br>SOURCE: SP 800-53; SP 800-53A; SP 800-27; FIPS 200 |
| Authentication – | The process of establishing confidence of authenticity.<br>SOURCE: FIPS 201 |
| Authentication – | Encompasses identity verification, message origin authentication, andmessage content authentication.<br>SOURCE: FIPS 190 |
| Authentication – | A process that establishes the origin of information or determines an entity's identity.<br>SOURCE: SP 800-21 |

The process of verifying the identity or other attributes claimed by or assumed of an entity (user, process, or device), or to verify the source and integrity of data.
SOURCE: CNSSI-4009

Authentication Code – A cryptographic checksum based on an Approved security function (also known as a Message Authentication Code [MAC]).
SOURCE: FIPS 140-2

Authentication, Electronic – The process of establishing confidence in user identities electronically presented to an information system.
SOURCE: SP 800-63

Authentication Mechanism – Hardware-or software-based mechanisms that force users to prove their identity before accessing data on a device.
SOURCE: SP 800-72; SP 800-124
Hardware or software-based mechanisms that forces users, devices, or processes to prove their identity before accessing data on an information system.
SOURCE: CNSSI-4009

Authentication Mode – A block cipher mode of operation that can provide assurance of the authenticity and, therefore, the integrity of data.
SOURCE: SP 800-38B

Authentication Period – The maximum acceptable period between any initial authentication process and subsequent reauthentication processes during a single terminal session or during the period data is being accessed.
SOURCE: CNSSI-4009

Authentication Protocol – A well-specified message exchange process that verifies possession of a token to remotely authenticate a claimant. Some authentication protocols also generate cryptographic keys that are used to protect an entire session, so that the data transferred in the session is cryptographically protected.
SOURCE: SP 800-63
A well-specified message exchange process between a claimantand averifier that enables the verifier to confirm the claimant's identity.
SOURCE: CNSSI-4009

Authentication Tag – A pair of bit strings associated to data to provide assurance of its authenticity.
SOURCE: SP 800-38B

Authentication Token – Authentication information conveyed during an authentication exchange.
SOURCE: FIPS 196

Authenticator – The means used to confirm the identity of a user, process, or device (e.g., user password or token).
SOURCE: SP 800-53; CNSSI-4009

Authenticity – The property of being genuine and being able to be verified and trusted; confidence in the validity of a transmission, a message, or message originator. See Authentication.
SOURCE: SP 800-53; SP 800-53A; CNSSI-4009

Authority – Person(s) or established bodies with rights and responsibilities to exert control in an administrative sphere.
SOURCE: CNSSI-4009

Authorization – Access privileges granted to a user, program, or process or the act of granting those privileges.
SOURCE: CNSSI-4009

Authorization (to operate) – The official management decision given by a senior organizational official to authorize operation of an information system and to explicitly accept the risk to organizational operations (including mission, functions, image, or reputation), organizational assets, individuals, other organizations, and the Nation based on the implementation of an agreed-upon set of security controls.
SOURCE: SP 800-53; SP 800-53A; CNSSI-4009; SP 800-37

Authorization Boundary – All components of an information system to be authorized for operation by an authorizing official and excludes separately authorized systems, to which the information system is connected.
SOURCE: CNSSI-4009; SP 800-53; SP 800-53A; SP 800-37

Authorize Processing – See Authorization (to operate).

Authorized Vendor – Manufacturer of information assurance equipment authorized to produce quantities in excess of contractual requirements for direct sale to eligible buyers. Eligible buyers are typically U.S. governmentorganizations or U.S. government contractors.
SOURCE: CNSSI-4009

Authorized Vendor Program(AVP) – Program in which a vendor, producing an information systems security (INFOSEC) product under contract to NSA, is authorized to produce that product in numbers exceeding the contracted requirements for direct marketing and sale to eligible buyers. Eligible buyers are typically U.S. government organizations or U.S. government contractors. Products approved for marketing and sale through the AVP are placed on the Endorsed Cryptographic Products List (ECPL).
SOURCE: CNSSI-4009

Authorizing Official – Official with the authority to formally assume responsibility for operating an information system at an acceptable level of risk to agency operations (including mission, functions, image, or reputation), agency assets, or individuals. Synonymous with Accreditation Authority.
SOURCE: FIPS 200

Senior federal official or executive with the authority to formally assume responsibility for operating an information system at an acceptable level of risk to organizational operations (including mission, functions, image, or reputation), organizational assets, individuals, other organizations, and the Nation.
SOURCE: CNSSI-4009

| | |
|---|---|
| | A senior (federal) official or executive with the authority to formally assume responsibility for operating an information system at an acceptable level of risk to organizational operations (including mission, functions, image, or reputation), organizational assets, individuals, other organizations, and the Nation.<br>SOURCE: SP800-53;SP800-53A;SP800-37 |
| Authorizing Official Designated Representative – | An organizational official acting on behalf of an authorizing official in carrying out and coordinating the required activities associated with security authorization.<br>SOURCE: CNSSI-4009; SP 800-37; SP 800-53A |
| Automated Key Transport – | The transport of cryptographic keys, usually in encrypted form, usingelectronic means such as a computer network (e.g., key transport/agreement protocols).<br>SOURCE: FIPS 140-2 |
| Automated Password Generator – | An algorithm which creates random passwords that have no association with a particular user.<br>SOURCE: FIPS 181 |
| Automated Security Monitoring – | Use of automated procedures to ensure security controls are not circumvented or the use of these tools to track actions taken by subjects suspected of misusing the information system.<br>SOURCE: CNSSI-4009 |
| Automatic Remote Rekeying – | Procedure to rekey a distant crypto-equipment electronically without specific actions by the receiving terminal operator. See manual remote rekeying.<br>SOURCE: CNSSI-4009 |
| Autonomous System (AS) – | One or more routers under a single administration operating the same routing policy.<br>SOURCE: SP 800-54 |
| Availability – | Ensuring timely and reliable access to and use of information.<br>SOURCE: SP 800-53; SP 800-53A; SP 800-27; SP 800-60; SP 800-37; FIPS 200; FIPS 199; 44 U.S.C., Sec. 3542<br>The property of being accessible and useable upon demand by an authorized entity.<br>SOURCE: CNSSI-4009 |
| Awareness (Information Security) – | Activities which seek to focus an individual's attention on an (information security) issue or set of issues.<br>SOURCE: SP 800-50 |
| Back Door – | Typically unauthorized hidden software or hardware mechanism usedto circumvent security controls.<br>SOURCE: CNSSI-4009 |
| Backdoor – | An undocumented way of gaining access to a computer system.<br>SOURCE: SP 800-82 |
| Backup – | A copy of files and programs made to facilitate recovery, if necessary.<br>SOURCE: SP 800-34; CNSSI-4009 |

Banner – Display on an information system that sets parameters for system or data use.
SOURCE: CNSSI-4009

Banner Grabbing – The process of capturing banner information—such as application type and version—that is transmitted by a remote port when a connection is initiated.
SOURCE: SP 800-115

Baseline – Hardware, software, databases, and relevant documentation for an information system at a given point in time.
SOURCE: CNSSI-4009

Baseline Security – The minimum security controls required for safeguarding an IT system based on its identified needs for confidentiality, integrity, and/or availability protection.
SOURCE: SP 800-16

Baselining – Monitoring resources to determine typical utilization patterns so thatsignificant deviations can be detected.
SOURCE: SP 800-61

Basic Testing – A test methodology that assumes no knowledge of the internal structure and implementation detail of the assessment object. Also known as black box testing.
SOURCE: SP 800-53A

Bastion Host – A special-purpose computer on a network specifically designed and configured to withstand attacks.
SOURCE: CNSSI-4009

Behavioral Outcome – What an individual who has completed the specific training module is expected to be able to accomplish in terms of IT security-related job performance.
SOURCE: SP 800-16

Benign – Condition of cryptographic data that cannot be compromised by human access.
SOURCE: CNSSI-4009

Benign Environment – A non-hostile location protected from external hostile elements by physical, personnel, and procedural security countermeasures.
SOURCE: CNSSI-4009

Binding – Process of associating two related elements of information.
SOURCE: SP 800-32

Binding – An acknowledgement by a trusted third party that associates an entity's identity with its public key. This may take place through (1) a certification authority's generation of a public key certificate, (2) a security officer's verification of an entity's credentials and placementof the entity's public key and identifier in a secure database, or (3) ananalogous method.
SOURCE: SP 800-21

Process of associating a specific communications terminal with a specific cryptographic key or associating two related elements of information.
SOURCE: CNSSI-4009

Biometric – A physical or behavioral characteristic of a human being.
SOURCE: SP 800-32

Biometric – A measurable physical characteristic or personal behavioral trait usedto recognize the identity, or verify the claimed identity, of an applicant. Facial images, fingerprints, and iris scan samples are all examples of biometrics.
SOURCE: FIPS 201

Biometric Information – The stored electronic information pertaining to a biometric. This information can be in terms of raw or compressed pixels or in terms of some characteristic (e.g., patterns.)
SOURCE: FIPS 201

Biometric System – An automated system capable of:
1)capturing a biometric sample from an end user;
2)extracting biometric data from that sample;
3)comparing the extracted biometric data with data contained in oneor more references;
4)deciding how well they match; and
5)indicating whether or not an identification or verification of identity has been achieved.
SOURCE: FIPS 201

Biometrics – Measurable physical characteristics or personal behavioral traits used to identify, or verify the claimed identity, of an individual. Facial images, fingerprints, and handwriting samples are all examples of biometrics.
SOURCE: CNSSI-4009

Bit – A contraction of the term Binary Digit. The smallest unit of information in a binary system of notation.
SOURCE: CNSSI-4009

Bit Error Rate – Ratio between the number of bits incorrectly received and the total number of bits transmitted in a telecommunications system.
SOURCE: CNSSI-4009

BLACK – Designation applied to encrypted information and the information systems, the associated areas, circuits, components, and equipment processing that information. See also RED.
SOURCE: CNSSI-4009

Black Box Testing – See Basic Testing.

Black Core – A communication network architecture in which user data traversing a global Internet Protocol (IP) network is end-to-end encrypted at the IP layer. Related to striped core.
SOURCE: CNSSI-4009

**Blacklist** – A list of email senders who have previously sent span to a user.
SOURCE: SP 800-114
A list of discrete entities, such as hosts or applications, that have beenpreviously determined to be associated with malicious activity.
SOURCE: SP 800-94

**Blacklisting** – The process of the system invalidating a user ID based on the user's inappropriate actions. A blacklisted user ID cannot be used to log on to the system, even with the correct authenticator. Blacklisting and lifting of a blacklisting are both security-relevant events. Blacklisting also applies to blocks placed against IP addresses to prevent inappropriate or unauthorized use of Internet resources.
SOURCE: CNSSI-4009

**Blended Attack** – Malicious code that uses multiple methods to spread.
SOURCE: SP 800-61
A hostile action to spread malicious code via multiple methods.
SOURCE: CNSSI-4009

**Blinding** – Generating network traffic that is likely to trigger many alerts in a short period of time, to conceal alerts triggered by a "real" attack performed simultaneously.
SOURCE: SP 800-94

**Block** – Sequence of binary bits that comprise the input, output, State, and Round Key. The length of a sequence is the number of bits it contains. Blocks are also interpreted as arrays of bytes.
SOURCE: FIPS 197

**Block Cipher** – A symmetric key cryptographic algorithm that transforms a block of information at a time using a cryptographic key. For a block cipher algorithm, the length of the input block is the same as the length of the output block.
SOURCE: SP 800-90

**Block Cipher Algorithm** – A family of functions and their inverses that is parameterized by a cryptographic key; the function maps bit strings of a fixed length to bit strings of the same length.
SOURCE: SP 800-67

**Blue Team** – 1. The group responsible for defending an enterprise's use of information systems by maintaining its security posture against a group of mock attackers (i.e., the Red Team). Typically the Blue Team and its supporters must defend against real or simulated attacks 1) over a significant period of time, 2) in a representative operational context (e.g., as part of an operational exercise), and 3) according to rules established and monitored with the help of a neutral group refereeing the simulation or exercise (i.e., the White Team).
2. The term Blue Team is also used for defining a group of individuals that conduct operational network vulnerability evaluations and provide mitigation techniques to customers who havea need for an independent technical review of their network

security posture. The Blue Team identifies security threats and risks in the operating environment, and in cooperation with the customer, analyzes the network environment and its current state of security readiness. Based on the Blue Team findings and expertise, they provide recommendations that integrate into an overall community security solution to increase the customer's cyber securityreadiness posture. Often times a Blue Team is employed by itself or prior to a Red Team employment to ensure that the customer's networks are as secure as possible before having the Red Team test the systems.
SOURCE: CNSSI-4009

Body of Evidence (BoE) – The set of data that documents the information system's adherence to the security controls applied. The BoE will include a Requirements Verification Traceability Matrix (RVTM) delineating where the selected security controls are met and evidence to that fact can be found. The BoE content required by an Authorizing Official will be adjusted according to the impact levels selected.
SOURCE: CNSSI-4009

Boot Sector Virus – A virus that plants itself in a system's boot sector and infects the master boot record.
SOURCE: SP 800-61

Boundary – Physical or logical perimeter of a system.
SOURCE: CNSSI-4009

Boundary Protection – Monitoring and control of communications at the external boundary of an information system to prevent and detect malicious and other unauthorized communication, through the use of boundary protection devices (e.g., proxies, gateways, routers, firewalls, guards, encrypted tunnels).
SOURCE: SP 800-53; CNSSI-4009

Boundary Protection Device – A device with appropriate mechanisms that: (i) facilitates the adjudication of different interconnected system security policies (e.g.,controlling the flow of information into or out of an interconnected system); and/or (ii) provides information system boundary protection.
SOURCE: SP 800-53

A device with appropriate mechanisms that facilitates the adjudication of different security policies for interconnected systems.
SOURCE: CNSSI-4009

Browsing – Act of searching through information system storage or active content to locate or acquire information, without necessarily knowing the existence or format of information being sought.
SOURCE: CNSSI-4009

Brute Force Password Attack – A method of accessing an obstructed device through attempting multiple combinations of numeric and/or alphanumeric passwords.
SOURCE: SP 800-72

**Buffer Overflow** – A condition at an interface under which more input can be placed into a buffer or data holding area than the capacity allocated, overwriting other information. Attackers exploit such a condition to crash a system or to insert specially crafted code that allows them togain control of the system.
SOURCE: SP 800-28; CNSSI-4009

**Buffer Overflow Attack** – A method of overloading a predefined amount of space in a buffer, which can potentially overwrite and corrupt data in memory.
SOURCE: SP 800-72

**Bulk Encryption** – Simultaneous encryption of all channels of a multichannel telecommunications link.
SOURCE: CNSSI-4009

**Business Continuity Plan (BCP)** – The documentation of a predetermined set of instructions or procedures that describe how an organization's mission/business functions will be sustained during and after a significant disruption.
SOURCE: SP 800-34

The documentation of a predetermined set of instructions or procedures that describe how an organization's business functions will be sustained during and after a significant disruption.
SOURCE: CNSSI-4009

**Business Impact Analysis (BIA)** – An analysis of an information system's requirements, functions, andinterdependencies used to characterize system contingency requirements and priorities in the event of a significant disruption.
SOURCE: SP 800-34

An analysis of an enterprise's requirements, processes, and interdependencies used to characterize information system contingency requirements and priorities in the event of a significant disruption.
SOURCE: CNSSI-4009

**Call Back** – Procedure for identifying and authenticating a remote information system terminal, whereby the host system disconnects the terminal and reestablishes contact.
SOURCE: CNSSI-4009

**Canister** – Type of protective package used to contain and dispense keying material in punched or printed tape form.
SOURCE: CNSSI-4009

**Capture** – The method of taking a biometric sample from an end user.
SOURCE: FIPS 201

**Cardholder** – An individual possessing an issued Personal Identity Verification (PIV) card.
SOURCE: FIPS 201

**Cascading** – Downward flow of information through a range of security levels greater than the accreditation range of a system, network, or component.
SOURCE: CNSSI-4009

Category – Restrictive label applied to classified or unclassified information to limit access.
SOURCE: CNSSI-4009

CBC/MAC – See Cipher Block Chaining-Message Authentication Code.

CCM – See Counter with Cipher-Block Chaining-Message Authentication Code.

Central Office of Record (COR) – Office of a federal department or agency that keeps records of accountable COMSEC material held by elements subject to its oversight
SOURCE: CNSSI-4009

Central Services Node (CSN) – The Key Management Infrastructure core node that provides central security management and data management services.
SOURCE: CNSSI-4009

Certificate – A digital representation of information which at least
1)identifies the certification authority issuing it,
2)names or identifies its subscriber,
3)contains the subscriber's public key,
4)identifies its operational period, and
5)is digitally signed by the certification authority issuing it.
SOURCE: SP 800-32

Certificate – A set of data that uniquely identifies an entity, contains the entity's public key and possibly other information, and is digitally signed by a trusted party, thereby binding the public key to the entity. Additional information in the certificate could specify how the key isused and its cryptoperiod.
SOURCE: SP 800-21

the authority issuing it, 2) identifies the subscriber, 3) identifies its valid operational period (date issued / expiration date). In the information assurance (IA) community, certificate usually implies public key certificate and can have the following types:
cross certificate – a certificate issued from a CA that signs the public key of another CA not within its trust hierarchy that establishes a trust relationship between the two CAs.
encryption certificate – a certificate containing a public key that can encrypt or decrypt electronic messages, files, documents, or data transmissions, or establish or exchange a session key for these same purposes. Key management sometimes refers to the process of storing, protecting, and escrowing the private component of the key pair associated with the encryption certificate.
identity certificate – a certificate that provides authentication of the identity claimed. Within the National Security Systems (NSS) PKI, identity certificates may be used only for authentication or may be used for both authentication and digital signatures.
SOURCE: CNSSI-4009

A set of data that uniquely identifies a key pair and an owner that is authorized to use the key pair. The certificate contains the owner's

| | |
|---|---|
| | public key and possibly other information, and is digitally signed by a Certification Authority (i.e., a trusted party), thereby binding the public key to the owner.<br>SOURCE: FIPS 186 |
| Certificate Management – | Process whereby certificates (as defined above) are generated, stored,protected, transferred, loaded, used, and destroyed.<br>SOURCE: CNSSI-4009 |
| Certificate Management Authority – (CMA) | A Certification Authority (CA) or a Registration Authority (RA).<br>SOURCE: SP 800-32 |
| Certificate Policy (CP) – | A specialized form of administrative policy tuned to electronic transactions performed during certificate management. A Certificate Policy addresses all aspects associated with the generation, production, distribution, accounting, compromise recovery, and administration of digital certificates. Indirectly, a certificate policy can also govern the transactions conducted using a communications system protected by a certificate-based security system. By controlling critical certificate extensions, such policies and associatedenforcement technology can support provision of the security services required by particular applications.<br>SOURCE: CNSSI-4009; SP 800-32 |
| Certificate-Related Information – | Information, such as a subscriber's postal address, that is not includedin a certificate. May be used by a Certification Authority (CA) managing certificates.<br>SOURCE: SP 800-32<br>Data, such as a subscriber's postal address that is not included in a certificate. May be used by a Certification Authority (CA) managing certificates.<br>SOURCE: CNSSI-4009 |
| Certificate Revocation List (CRL) – | A list of revoked public key certificates created and digitally signed by a Certification Authority.<br>SOURCE: SP 800-63; FIPS 201 |
| Certificate Revocation List – | A list of revoked but un-expired certificates issued by a CA.<br>SOURCE: SP 800-21<br>A list of revoked public key certificates created and digitally signed by a Certification Authority.<br>SOURCE: CNSSI-4009 |
| Certificate Status Authority – | A trusted entity that provides online verification to a Relying Party ofa subject certificate's trustworthiness, and may also provide additional attribute information for the subject certificate.<br>SOURCE: SP 800-32; CNSSI-4009 |
| Certification – | A comprehensive assessment of the management, operational, and technical security controls in an information system, made in support of security accreditation, to determine the extent to which the controls are implemented correctly, operating as intended, and |

producing the desired outcome with respect to meeting the security requirements for the system.
SOURCE: FIPS 200

Certification – The process of verifying the correctness of a statement or claim and issuing a certificate as to its correctness.
SOURCE: FIPS 201
Comprehensive evaluation of the technical and nontechnical security safeguards of an information system to support the accreditation process that establishes the extent to which a particular design and implementation meets a set of specified security requirements. See security control assessment.
SOURCE: CNSSI-4009

Certification Analyst – The independent technical liaison for all stakeholders involved in theC&A process responsible for objectively and independently evaluating a system as part of the risk management process. Based on the security requirements documented in the security plan, performs a technical and non-technical review of potential vulnerabilities in the system and determines if the security controls (management, operational, and technical) are correctly implemented and effective.
SOURCE: CNSSI-4009

Certification Authority (CA) – A trusted entity that issues and revokes public key certificates.
SOURCE: FIPS 201

Certification Authority – The entity in a public key infrastructure (PKI) that is responsible for issuing certificates and exacting compliance to a PKI policy.
SOURCE: SP 800-21; FIPS 186
1. For Certification and Accreditation (C&A) (C&A Assessment): Official responsible for performing the comprehensive evaluation of the security features of an information system and determining the degree to which it meets its security requirements
2. For Public Key Infrastructure (PKI): A trusted third party that issues digital certificates and verifies the identity of the holder of the digital certificate.
SOURCE: CNSSI-4009

Certification Authority Facility – The collection of equipment, personnel, procedures and structures that are used by a Certification Authority to perform certificate issuance and revocation.
SOURCE: SP 800-32

Certification Authority Workstation (CAW) – Commercial off-the-shelf (COTS) workstation with a trusted operating system and special-purpose application software that is used to issue certificates
SOURCE: CNSSI-4009

Certification Package – Product of the certification effort documenting the detailed results of the certification activities.
SOURCE: CNSSI-4009

| | |
|---|---|
| Certification Practice Statement – (CPS) | A statement of the practices that a Certification Authority employs in issuing, suspending, revoking, and renewing certificates and providing access to them, in accordance with specific requirements (i.e., requirements specified in this Certificate Policy, or requirementsspecified in a contract for services).<br>SOURCE: SP 800-32; CNSSI-4009 |
| Certification Test and Evaluation – (CT&E) | Software and hardware security tests conducted during development of an information system.<br>SOURCE: CNSSI-4009 |
| Certified TEMPEST Technical Authority (CTTA) – | An experienced, technically qualified U.S. government employee who has met established certification requirements in accordance with CNSS-approved criteria and has been appointed by a U.S. government department or agency to fulfill CTTA responsibilities.<br>SOURCE: CNSSI-4009 |
| Certifier – | Individual responsible for making a technical judgment of the system's compliance with stated requirements, identifying and assessing the risks associated with operating the system, coordinating the certification activities, and consolidating the final certification and accreditation packages.<br>SOURCE: CNSSI-4009 |
| Chain of Custody – | A process that tracks the movement of evidence through its collection, safeguarding, and analysis lifecycle by documenting each person who handled the evidence, the date/time it was collected or transferred, and the purpose for the transfer.<br>SOURCE: SP 800-72; CNSSI-4009 |
| Chain of Evidence – | A process and record that shows who obtained the evidence; where and when the evidence was obtained; who secured the evidence; and who had control or possession of the evidence. The "sequencing" of the chain of evidence follows this order: collection and identification;analysis; storage; preservation; presentation in court; return to owner.<br>SOURCE: CNSSI-4009 |
| Challenge and Reply Authentication – | Prearranged procedure in which a subject requests authentication of another and the latter establishes validity with a correct reply.<br>SOURCE: CNSSI-4009 |
| Challenge-Response Protocol – | An authentication protocol where the verifier sends the claimant a challenge (usually a random value or a nonce) that the claimant combines with a shared secret (often by hashing the challenge and secret together) to generate a response that is sent to the verifier. The verifier knows the shared secret and can independently compute the response and compare it with the response generated by the claimant.If the two are the same, the claimant is considered to have successfully authenticated himself. When the shared secret is a cryptographic key, such protocols are generally secure against eavesdroppers. When the shared secret is a password, an eavesdropper does not directly intercept the password itself, but the |

| | |
|---|---|
| | eavesdropper may be able to find the password with an off-line password guessing attack.<br>SOURCE: SP 800-63 |
| Check Word – | Cipher text generated by cryptographic logic to detect failures in cryptography.<br>SOURCE: CNSSI-4009 |
| Checksum – | Value computed on data to detect error or manipulation.<br>SOURCE: CNSSI-4009 |
| Chief Information Officer (CIO) – | Agency official responsible for:<br>1)Providing advice and other assistance to the head of the executiveagency and other senior management personnel of the agency to ensure that information technology is acquired and information resources are managed in a manner that is consistent with laws, Executive Orders, directives, policies, regulations, and priorities established by the head of the agency;<br>2)Developing, maintaining, and facilitating the implementation of a sound and integrated information technology architecture for the agency; and<br>3)Promoting the effective and efficient design and operation of all major information resources management processes for the agency, including improvements to work processes of the agency.<br>SOURCE: FIPS 200; Public Law 104-106, Sec. 5125(b)<br>Agency official responsible for: 1) providing advice and other assistance to the head of the executive agency and other senior management personnel of the agency to ensure that information systems are acquired and information resources are managed in a manner that is consistent with laws, Executive Orders, directives, policies, regulations, and priorities established by the head of the agency; 2) developing, maintaining, and facilitating the implementation of a sound and integrated information system architecture for the agency; and 3) promoting the effective and efficient design and operation of all major information resources management processes for the agency, including improvements to work processes of the agency.<br>Note: Organizations subordinate to federal agencies may use the term Chief Information Officer to denote individuals filling positionswith similar security responsibilities to agency-level Chief Information Officers.<br>SOURCE: CNSSI-4009; SP 800-53 |
| Chief Information Security Officer – (CISO) | See Senior Agency Information Security Officer. |
| Cipher – | Series of transformations that converts plaintext to ciphertext using the Cipher Key.<br>SOURCE: FIPS 197 |

|  |  |
|---|---|
| | Any cryptographic system in which arbitrary symbols or groups of symbols, represent units of plain text, or in which units of plain text are rearranged, or both.<br>SOURCE: CNSSI-4009 |
| Cipher Block Chaining-Message Authentication Code – (CBC-MAC) | A secret-key block-cipher algorithm used to encrypt data and to generate a Message Authentication Code (MAC) to provide assurance that the payload and the associated data are authentic.<br>SOURCE: SP 800-38C |
| Cipher Suite – | Negotiated algorithm identifiers. Cipher suites are identified in human-readable form using a pneumonic code.<br>SOURCE: SP 800-52 |
| Cipher Text Auto-Key (CTAK) – | Cryptographic logic that uses previous cipher text to generate a key stream.<br>SOURCE: CNSSI-4009 |
| Ciphertext – | Data output from the Cipher or input to the Inverse Cipher.<br>SOURCE: FIPS 197<br>Data in its enciphered form.<br>SOURCE: SP 800-56B |
| Ciphertext/Cipher Text – | Data in its encrypted form.<br>SOURCE: SP 800-21; SP 800-57; CNSSI-4009 |
| Ciphony – | Process of enciphering audio information, resulting in encrypted speech.<br>SOURCE: CNSSI-4009 |
| Claimant – | A party whose identity is to be verified using an authentication protocol.<br>SOURCE: SP 800-63; FIPS 201 |
| Claimant – | An entity which is or represents a principal for the purposes of authentication, together with the functions involved in an authentication exchange on behalf of that entity. A claimant acting onbehalf of a principal must include the functions necessary for engaging in an authentication exchange. (e.g., a smartcard [claimant] can act on behalf of a human user [principal])<br>SOURCE: FIPS 196<br>An entity (user, device or process) whose assertion is to be verified using an authentication protocol.<br>SOURCE: CNSSI-4009 |
| Classified Information – | Information that has been determined pursuant to Executive Order (E.O.) 13292 or any predecessor order to require protection against unauthorized disclosure and is marked to indicate its classified status when in documentary form.<br>SOURCE: SP 800-60; E.O. 13292<br>See classified national security information.<br>SOURCE: CNSSI-4009<br>Information that has been determined: (i) pursuant to Executive Order 12958 as amended by Executive Order 13292, or any |

| | |
|---|---|
| | predecessor Order, to be classified national security information; or (ii) pursuant to the Atomic Energy Act of 1954, as amended, to be Restricted Data (RD).<br>SOURCE: SP 800-53 |
| Classified Information Spillage – | Security incident that occurs whenever classified data is spilled eitheronto an unclassified information system or to an information system with a lower level of classification.<br>SOURCE: CNSSI-4009 |
| Classified National Security Information – | Information that has been determined pursuant to Executive Order 13526 or any predecessor order to require protection against unauthorized disclosure and is marked to indicate its classified status when in documentary form.<br>SOURCE: CNSSI-4009 |
| Clear – | To use software or hardware products to overwrite storage space on the media with nonsensitive data. This process may include overwriting not only the logical storage location of a file(s) (e.g., file allocation table) but also may include all addressable locations. See comments on clear/purge convergence.<br>SOURCE: SP 800-88 |
| Clear Text – | Information that is not encrypted.<br>SOURCE: SP 800-82 |
| Clearance – | Formal certification of authorization to have access to classified information other than that protected in a special access program (including SCI). Clearances are of three types: confidential, secret, and top secret. A top secret clearance permits access to top secret, secret, and confidential material; a secret clearance, to secret and confidential material; and a confidential clearance, to confidential material.<br>SOURCE: CNSSI-4009 |
| Clearing – | Removal of data from an information system, its storage devices, andother peripheral devices with storage capacity, in such a way that the data may not be reconstructed using common system capabilities (i.e., through the keyboard); however, the data may be reconstructed using laboratory methods.<br>SOURCE: CNSSI-4009 |
| Client – | Individual or process acting on behalf of an individual who makes requests of a guard or dedicated server. The client's requests to the guard or dedicated server can involve data transfer to, from, or through the guard or dedicated server.<br>SOURCE: CNSSI-4009 |
| Client (Application) – | A system entity, usually a computer process acting on behalf of a human user, that makes use of a service provided by a server.<br>SOURCE: SP 800-32 |
| Clinger-Cohen Act of 1996 – | Also known as Information Technology Management Reform Act. A statute that substantially revised the way that IT resources are managed and procured, including a requirement that each agency |

design and implement a process for maximizing the value and assessing and managing the risks of IT investments.
SOURCE: SP 800-64

**Closed Security Environment –** Environment providing sufficient assurance that applications and equipment are protected against the introduction of malicious logic during an information system life cycle. Closed security is based upon a system's developers, operators, and maintenance personnel having sufficient clearances, authorization, and configuration control.
SOURCE: CNSSI-4009

**Closed Storage –** Storage of classified information within an accredited facility, in General Services Administration-approved secure containers, while the facility is unoccupied by authorized personnel.
SOURCE: CNSSI-4009

**Cloud Computing –** A model for enabling on-demand network access to a shared pool of configurable IT capabilities/ resources (e.g., networks, servers, storage, applications, and services) that can be rapidly provisioned and released with minimal management effort or service provider interaction. It allows users to access technology-based services from the network cloud without knowledge of, expertise with, or control over the technology infrastructure that supports them. This cloud model is composed of five essential characteristics (on-demand self-service, ubiquitous network access, location independent resource pooling, rapid elasticity, and measured service); three service delivery models (Cloud Software as a Service [SaaS], Cloud Platformas a Service [PaaS], and Cloud Infrastructure as a Service [IaaS]); and four models for enterprise access (Private cloud, Community cloud, Public cloud, and Hybrid cloud).
Note: Both the user's data and essential security services may reside in and be managed within the network cloud.
SOURCE: CNSSI-4009

**Code –** System of communication in which arbitrary groups of letters, numbers, or symbols represent units of plain text of varying length.
SOURCE: CNSSI-4009

**Code Book –** Document containing plain text and code equivalents in a systematic arrangement, or a technique of machine encryption using a word substitution technique.
SOURCE: CNSSI-4009

**Code Group –** Group of letters, numbers, or both in a code system used to represent a plain text word, phrase, or sentence.
SOURCE: CNSSI-4009

**Code Vocabulary –** Set of plain text words, numerals, phrases, or sentences for which code equivalents are assigned in a code system.
SOURCE: CNSSI-4009

**Cold Site –** Backup site that can be up and operational in a relatively short time span, such as a day or two. Provision of services, such as telephone

lines and power, is taken care of, and the basic office furniture might be in place, but there is unlikely to be any computer equipment, even though the building might well have a network infrastructure and a room ready to act as a server room. In most cases, cold sites provide the physical location and basic services.
SOURCE: CNSSI-4009
A backup facility that has the necessary electrical and physical components of a computer facility, but does not have the computer equipment in place. The site is ready to receive the necessary replacement computer equipment in the event that the user has to move from their main computing location to an alternate site.
SOURCE: SP 800-34

Cold Start – Procedure for initially keying crypto-equipment.
SOURCE: CNSSI-4009

Collision – Two or more distinct inputs produce the same output.
SOURCE: SP 800-57

Command Authority – Individual responsible for the appointment of user representatives for a department, agency, or organization and their key ordering privileges.
SOURCE: CNSSI-4009

Commercial COMSEC Evaluation Program (CCEP) – Relationship between NSA and industry in which NSA provides the COMSEC expertise (i.e., standards, algorithms, evaluations, and guidance) and industry provides design, development, and productioncapabilities to produce a type 1 or type 2 product. Products developed under the CCEP may include modules, subsystems, equipment, systems, and ancillary devices.
SOURCE: CNSSI-4009

Commodity Service – An information system service (e.g., telecommunications service) provided by a commercial service provider typically to a large and diverse set of consumers. The organization acquiring and/or receiving the commodity service possesses limited visibility into the management structure and operations of the provider, and while the organization may be able to negotiate service-level agreements, the organization is typically not in a position to require that the provider implement specific security controls.
SOURCE: SP 800-53

Common Access Card (CAC) – Standard identification/smart card issued by the Department of Defense that has an embedded integrated chip storing public key infrastructure (PKI) certificates.
SOURCE: CNSSI-4009

Common Carrier – In a telecommunications context, a telecommunications company thatholds itself out to the public for hire to provide communications transmission services. Note: In the United States, such companies are usually subject to regulation by federal and state regulatory commissions.
SOURCE: SP 800-53

Common Control – A security control that is inherited by one or more organizational information systems. See Security Control Inheritance.
SOURCE: SP 800-53; SP 800-53A; SP 800-37; CNSSI-4009

Common Control Provider – An organizational official responsible for the development, implementation, assessment, and monitoring of common controls (i.e., security controls inherited by information systems).
SOURCE: SP 800-37; SP 800-53A

Common Criteria – Governing document that provides a comprehensive, rigorous method for specifying security function and assurance requirements for products and systems.
SOURCE: CNSSI-4009

Common Fill Device – One of a family of devices developed to read-in, transfer, or store key.
SOURCE: CNSSI-4009

Common Vulnerabilities and Exposures (CVE) – A dictionary of common names for publicly known information system vulnerabilities.
SOURCE: SP800-51;CNSSI-4009

Communications Cover – Concealing or altering of characteristic communications patterns to hide information that could be of value to an adversary.
SOURCE: CNSSI-4009

Communications Deception – Deliberate transmission, retransmission, or alteration of communications to mislead an adversary's interpretation of the communications.
SOURCE: CNSSI-4009

Communications Profile – Analytic model of communications associated with an organization or activity. The model is prepared from a systematic examination of communications content and patterns, the functions they reflect, and the communications security measures applied.
SOURCE: CNSSI-4009

Communications Security – (COMSEC) A component of Information Assurance that deals with measures andcontrols taken to deny unauthorized persons information derived from telecommunications and to ensure the authenticity of such telecommunications. COMSEC includes crypto security, transmission security, emissions security, and physical security of COMSEC material.
SOURCE: CNSSI-4009

Community of Interest (COI) – A collaborative group of users who exchange information in pursuit of their shared goals, interests, missions, or business processes, and who therefore must have a shared vocabulary for the information they exchange. The group exchanges information within and between systems to include security domains.
SOURCE: CNSSI-4009

Community Risk – Probability that a particular vulnerability will be exploited within an interacting population and adversely impact some members of that population.
SOURCE: CNSSI-4009

Comparison – The process of comparing a biometric with a previously stored reference.
SOURCE: FIPS 201

Compartmentalization – A nonhierarchical grouping of sensitive information used to control access to data more finely than with hierarchical security classification alone.
SOURCE: CNSSI-4009

Compartmented Mode – Mode of operation wherein each user with direct or indirect access toa system, its peripherals, remote terminals, or remote hosts has all of the following: (1) valid security clearance for the most restricted information processed in the system; (2) formal access approval and signed nondisclosure agreements for that information which a user is to have access; and (3) valid need-to-know for information which a user is to have access.
SOURCE: CNSSI-4009

Compensating Security Control – A management, operational, and/or technical control (i.e., safeguard or countermeasure) employed by an organization in lieu of a recommended security control in the low, moderate, or high baselinesthat provides equivalent or comparable protection for an information system.
NIST SP 800-53: A management, operational, and technical control (i.e., safeguard or countermeasure) employed by an organization in lieu of the recommended control in the baselines described in NIST Special Publication 800-53 or in CNSS Instruction 1253, that provide equivalent or comparable protection for an information system.
SOURCE: CNSSI-4009

Compensating Security Controls – The management, operational, and technical controls (i.e., safeguards or countermeasures) employed by an organization in lieu of the recommended controls in the low, moderate, or high baselines described in NIST Special Publication 800-53, that provide equivalent or comparable protection for an information system.
SOURCE: SP 800-37
The management, operational, and technical controls (i.e., safeguards or countermeasures) employed by an organization in lieu of the recommended controls in the baselines described in NIST Special Publication 800-53 and CNSS Instruction 1253, that provide equivalent or comparable protection for an information system.
SOURCE: SP 800-53A; SP 800-53

| | |
|---|---|
| Comprehensive Testing – | A test methodology that assumes explicit and substantial knowledge of the internal structure and implementation detail of the assessment object. Also known as white box testing.<br>SOURCE: SP 800-53A |
| Compromise – | Disclosure of information to unauthorized persons, or a violation of the security policy of a system in which unauthorized intentional or unintentional disclosure, modification, destruction, or loss of an object may have occurred.<br>SOURCE: SP 800-32 |
| Compromise – | The unauthorized disclosure, modification, substitution, or use of sensitive data (including plaintext cryptographic keys and other CSPs).<br>SOURCE: FIPS 140-2<br>Disclosure of information to unauthorized persons, or a violation of the security policy of a system in which unauthorized intentional or unintentional disclosure, modification, destruction, or loss of an object may have occurred.<br>SOURCE: CNSSI-4009 |
| Compromising Emanations – | Unintentional signals that, if intercepted and analyzed, would disclose the information transmitted, received, handled, or otherwise processed by information systems equipment. See TEMPEST.<br>SOURCE: CNSSI-4009 |
| Computer Abuse – | Intentional or reckless misuse, alteration, disruption, or destruction ofinformation processing resources.<br>SOURCE: CNSSI-4009 |
| Computer Cryptography – | Use of a crypto-algorithm program by a computer to authenticate or encrypt/decrypt information.<br>SOURCE: CNSSI-4009 |
| Computer Forensics – | The practice of gathering, retaining, and analyzing computer-related data for investigative purposes in a manner that maintains the integrity of the data.<br>SOURCE: SP 800-61; CNSSI-4009 |
| Computer Incident Response Team – (CIRT) | Group of individuals usually consisting of Security Analysts organized to develop, recommend, and coordinate immediate mitigation actions for containment, eradication, and recovery resulting from computer security incidents. Also called a Computer Security Incident Response Team (CSIRT) or a CIRC (Computer Incident Response Center, Computer Incident Response Capability, or Cyber Incident Response Team).<br>SOURCE: CNSSI-4009 |
| Computer Network Attack (CNA) – | Actions taken through the use of computer networks to disrupt, deny, degrade, or destroy information resident in computers and computer networks, or the computers and networks themselves.<br>SOURCE: CNSSI-4009 |

| | |
|---|---|
| Computer Network Defense(CND) – | Actions taken to defend against unauthorized activity within computer networks. CND includes monitoring, detection, analysis (such as trend and pattern analysis), and response and restoration activities.<br>SOURCE: CNSSI-4009 |
| Computer Network Exploitation – (CNE) | Enabling operations and intelligence collection capabilities conducted through the use of computer networks to gather data from target or adversary information systems or networks.<br>SOURCE: CNSSI-4009 |
| Computer Network Operations – (CNO) | Comprised of computer network attack, computer network defense, and related computer network exploitation enabling operations.<br>SOURCE: CNSSI-4009 |
| Computer Security (COMPUSEC) – | Measures and controls that ensure confidentiality, integrity, and availability of information system assets including hardware, software, firmware, and information being processed, stored, and communicated.<br>SOURCE: CNSSI-4009 |
| Computer Security Incident – | See Incident. |
| Computer Security Incident Response Team (CSIRT) – | A capability set up for the purpose of assisting in responding to computer security-related incidents; also called a Computer Incident Response Team (CIRT) or a CIRC (Computer Incident Response Center, Computer Incident Response Capability).<br>SOURCE: SP 800-61 |
| Computer Security Object (CSO) – | A resource, tool, or mechanism used to maintain a condition of security in a computerized environment. These objects are defined in terms of attributes they possess, operations they perform or are performed on them, and their relationship with other objects.<br>SOURCE: FIPS 188; CNSSI-4009 |
| Computer Security Objects Register – | A collection of Computer Security Object names and definitions keptby a registration authority.<br>SOURCE: FIPS 188; CNSSI-4009 |
| Computer Security Subsystem – | Hardware/software designed to provide computer security features ina larger system environment.<br>SOURCE: CNSSI-4009 |
| Computer Virus – | See Virus. |
| Computing Environment – | Workstation or server (host) and its operating system, peripherals, and applications.<br>SOURCE: CNSSI-4009 |
| COMSEC – | Communications Security.<br>SOURCE: CNSSI-4009 |
| COMSEC Account – | Administrative entity, identified by an account number, used to maintain accountability, custody, and control of COMSEC material.<br>SOURCE: CNSSI-4009 |

| | |
|---|---|
| COMSEC Account Audit – | Examination of the holdings, records, and procedures of a COMSEC account ensuring all accountable COMSEC material is properly handled and safeguarded.<br>SOURCE: CNSSI-4009 |
| COMSEC Aid – | COMSEC material that assists in securing telecommunications and isrequired in the production, operation, or maintenance of COMSEC systems and their components. COMSEC keying material, callsign/frequency systems, and supporting documentation, such as operating and maintenance manuals, are examples of COMSEC aids.<br>SOURCE: CNSSI-4009 |
| COMSEC Assembly – | Group of parts, elements, subassemblies, or circuits that are removable items of COMSEC equipment.<br>SOURCE: CNSSI-4009 |
| COMSEC Boundary – | Definable perimeter encompassing all hardware, firmware, and software components performing critical COMSEC functions, such as key generation, handling, and storage.<br>SOURCE: CNSSI-4009 |
| COMSEC Chip Set – | Collection of NSA-approved microchips.<br>SOURCE: CNSSI-4009 |
| COMSEC Control Program – | Computer instructions or routines controlling or affecting the externally performed functions of key generation, key distribution, message encryption/decryption, or authentication.<br>SOURCE: CNSSI-4009 |
| COMSEC Custodian – | Individual designated by proper authority to be responsible for the receipt, transfer, accounting, safeguarding, and destruction of COMSEC material assigned to a COMSEC account.<br>SOURCE: CNSSI-4009 |
| COMSEC Demilitarization – | Process of preparing COMSEC equipment for disposal by extracting all CCI, classified, or cryptographic (CRYPTO) marked components for their secure destruction, as well as defacing and disposing of the remaining equipment hulk.<br>SOURCE: CNSSI-4009 |
| COMSEC Element – | Removable item of COMSEC equipment, assembly, or subassembly; normally consisting of a single piece or group of replaceable parts.<br>SOURCE: CNSSI-4009 |
| COMSEC End-item – | Equipment or combination of components ready for use in a COMSEC application.<br>SOURCE: CNSSI-4009 |
| COMSEC Equipment – | Equipment designed to provide security to telecommunications by converting information to a form unintelligible to an unauthorized interceptor and, subsequently, by reconverting such information to its original form for authorized recipients; also, equipment designed specifically to aid in, or as an essential element of, the conversion |

process. COMSEC equipment includes crypto-equipment, crypto-ancillary equipment, cryptographic production equipment, and authentication equipment.
SOURCE: CNSSI-4009

COMSEC Facility – Authorized and approved space used for generating, storing, repairing, or using COMSEC material.
SOURCE: CNSSI-4009

COMSEC Incident – Occurrence that potentially jeopardizes the security of COMSEC material or the secure electrical transmission of national security information or information governed by 10 U.S.C. Section 2315.
SOURCE: CNSSI-4009

COMSEC Insecurity – COMSEC incident that has been investigated, evaluated, and determined to jeopardize the security of COMSEC material or the secure transmission of information.
SOURCE: CNSSI-4009

COMSEC Manager – Individual who manages the COMSEC resources of an organization.
SOURCE: CNSSI-4009

COMSEC Material – Item designed to secure or authenticate telecommunications. COMSEC material includes, but is not limited to key, equipment, devices, documents, firmware, or software that embodies or describescryptographic logic and other items that perform COMSEC functions.
SOURCE: CNSSI-4009

COMSEC Material Control System (CMCS) – Logistics and accounting system through which COMSEC material marked "CRYPTO" is distributed, controlled, and safeguarded. Included are the COMSEC central offices of record, crypto logistic depots, and COMSEC accounts. COMSEC material other than key may be handled through the CMCS.
SOURCE: CNSSI-4009

COMSEC Modification – See Information Systems Security Equipment Modification.
SOURCE: CNSSI-4009

COMSEC Module – Removable component that performs COMSEC functions in a telecommunications equipment or system.
SOURCE: CNSSI-4009

COMSEC Monitoring – Act of listening to, copying, or recording transmissions of one's own official telecommunications to analyze the degree of security.
SOURCE: CNSSI-4009

COMSEC Profile – Statement of COMSEC measures and materials used to protect a given operation, system, or organization.
SOURCE: CNSSI-4009

COMSEC Survey – Organized collection of COMSEC and communications information relative to a given operation, system, or organization.
SOURCE: CNSSI-4009

| | |
|---|---|
| COMSEC System Data – | Information required by a COMSEC equipment or system to enable itto properly handle and control key.<br>SOURCE: CNSSI-4009 |
| COMSEC Training – | Teaching of skills relating to COMSEC accounting, use of COMSEC aids, or installation, use, maintenance, and repair of COMSEC equipment.<br>SOURCE: CNSSI-4009 |
| Concept of Operations (CONOP) – | See Security Concept of Operations.<br>SOURCE: CNSSI-4009 |
| Confidentiality – | Preserving authorized restrictions on information access and disclosure, including means for protecting personal privacy and proprietary information.<br>SOURCE: SP 800-53; SP 800-53A; SP 800-18; SP 800-27; SP 800-60; SP 800-37; FIPS 200; FIPS 199; 44 U.S.C., Sec. 3542 |
| Confidentiality – | The property that sensitive information is not disclosed to unauthorized individuals, entities, or processes.<br>SOURCE: FIPS 140-2<br>The property that information is not disclosed to system entities (users, processes, devices) unless they have been authorized to accessthe information.<br>SOURCE: CNSSI-4009 |
| Configuration Control – | Process of controlling modifications to hardware, firmware, software,and documentation to protect the information system against improper modification prior to, during, and after system implementation.<br>SOURCE: CNSSI-4009;SP800-37;SP 800-53 |
| Configuration Control Board – (CCB) | A group of qualified people with responsibility for the process of regulating and approving changes to hardware, firmware, software, and documentation throughout the development and operational life cycle of an information system.<br>SOURCE: CNSSI-4009 |
| Confinement Channel – | See Covert Channel.<br>SOURCE: CNSSI-4009 |
| Container – | The file used by a virtual disk encryption technology to encompass and protect other files.<br>SOURCE: SP 800-111 |
| Contamination – | Type of incident involving the introduction of data of one security classification or security category into data of a lower security classification or different security category.<br>SOURCE: CNSSI-4009 |
| Content Filtering – | The process of monitoring communications such as email and Web pages, analyzing them for suspicious content, and preventing the delivery of suspicious content to users.<br>SOURCE: SP 800-114 |

Contingency Key – Key held for use under specific operational conditions or in support of specific contingency plans. See reserve keying material.
SOURCE: CNSSI-4009

Contingency Plan – Management policy and procedures used to guide an enterprise response to a perceived loss of mission capability. The Contingency Plan is the first plan used by the enterprise risk managers to determine what happened, why, and what to do. It may point to the Continuity of Operations Plan (COOP) or Disaster Recovery Plan for major disruptions.
SOURCE: CNSSI-4009
See also Information System Contingency Plan.

Continuity of Government (COG) – A coordinated effort within the federal government's executive branch to ensure that national essential functions continue to be performed during a catastrophic emergency.
SOURCE: CNSSI-4009

Continuity of Operations Plan – (COOP) A predetermined set of instructions or procedures that describe how an organization's mission-essential functions will be sustained within 12 hours and for up to 30 days as a result of a disaster event before returning to normal operations.
SOURCE: SP 800-34
Management policy and procedures used to guide an enterprise response to a major loss of enterprise capability or damage to its facilities. The COOP is the third plan needed by the enterprise risk managers and is used when the enterprise must recover (often at an alternate site) for a specified period of time. Defines the activities of individual departments and agencies and their sub-components to ensure that their essential functions are performed. This includes plans and procedures that delineate essential functions; specifies succession to office and the emergency delegation of authority; provide for the safekeeping of vital records and databases; identify alternate operating facilities; provide for interoperable communications, and validate the capability through tests, training, and exercises. See also Disaster Recovery Plan and Contingency Plan.
SOURCE: CNSSI-4009

Continuous Monitoring – The process implemented to maintain a current security status for one or more information systems or for the entire suite of information systems on which the operational mission of the enterprise depends. The process includes: 1) he development of a strategy to regularly evaluate selected IA controls/metrics, 2) Recording and evaluating IArelevant events and the effectiveness of the enterprise in dealing with those events, 3) Recording changes to IA controls, or changes that affect IA risks, and 4) Publishing the current security status to enable information-sharing decisions involving the enterprise.
SOURCE: CNSSI-4009

| | |
|---|---|
| Control Information – | Information that is entered into a cryptographic module for the purposes of directing the operation of the module.<br>SOURCE: FIPS 140-2 |
| Controlled Access Area – | Physical area (e.g., building, room, etc.) to which only authorized personnel are granted unrestricted access. All other personnel are either escorted by authorized personnel or are under continuous surveillance.<br>SOURCE: CNSSI-4009 |
| Controlled Access Protection – | Minimum set of security functionality that enforces access control onindividual users and makes them accountable for their actions through login procedures, auditing of security-relevant events, and resource isolation.<br>SOURCE: CNSSI-4009 |
| Controlled Area – | Any area or space for which the organization has confidence that the physical and procedural protections provided are sufficient to meet the requirements established for protecting the information and/or information system.<br>SOURCE: SP800-53 |
| Controlled Cryptographic Item – (CCI) | Secure telecommunications or information system, or associated cryptographic component, that is unclassified and handled through the COMSEC Material Control System (CMCS), an equivalent material control system, or a combination of the two that provides accountability and visibility. Such items are marked "Controlled Cryptographic Item," or, where space is limited, "CCI".<br>SOURCE: CNSSI-4009 |
| Controlled Cryptographic Item (CCI) Assembly – | Device embodying a cryptographic logic or other COMSEC design that NSA has approved as a Controlled Cryptographic Item (CCI). It performs the entire COMSEC function, but depends upon the host equipment to operate.<br>SOURCE: CNSSI-4009 |
| Controlled Cryptographic Item (CCI) Component – | Part of a Controlled Cryptographic Item (CCI) that does not perform the entire COMSEC function but depends upon the host equipment, or assembly, to complete and operate the COMSEC function.<br>SOURCE: CNSSI-4009 |
| Controlled Cryptographic Item (CCI) Equipment – | Telecommunications or information handling equipment that embodies a Controlled Cryptographic Item (CCI) component or CCI assembly and performs the entire COMSEC function without dependence on host equipment to operate.<br>SOURCE: CNSSI-4009 |
| Controlled Interface – | A boundary with a set of mechanisms that enforces the security policies and controls the flow of information between interconnected information systems.<br>SOURCE: CNSSI-4009; SP 800-37 |
| Controlled Space – | Three-dimensional space surrounding information system equipment,within which unauthorized individuals are denied unrestricted access and are either escorted by authorized individuals |

or are under continuous physical or electronic surveillance.
SOURCE: CNSSI-4009

Controlled Unclassified Information (CUI) – A categorical designation that refers to unclassified information that does not meet the standards for National Security Classification under Executive Order 12958, as amended, but is (i) pertinent to the national interests of the United States or to the important interests of entities outside the federal government, and (ii) under law or policy requires protection from unauthorized disclosure, special handling safeguards, or prescribed limits on exchange or dissemination. Henceforth, the designation CUI replaces "Sensitive But Unclassified" (SBU).
SOURCE: SP 800-53; SP 800-53A

Controlling Authority – Official responsible for directing the operation of a cryptonet and for managing the operational use and control of keying material assignedto the cryptonet.
SOURCE: CNSSI-4009

Cookie – A piece of state information supplied by a Web server to a browser, in a response for a requested resource, for the browser to store temporarily and return to the server on any subsequent visits or requests.
SOURCE: SP 800-28

Data exchanged between an HTTP server and a browser (a client of the server) to store state information on the client side and retrieve it later for server use.
SOURCE: CNSSI-4009

Cooperative Key Generation – Electronically exchanging functions of locally generated, random components, from which both terminals of a secure circuit construct traffic encryption key or key encryption key for use on that circuit. See per-call key.
SOURCE: CNSSI-4009

Cooperative Remote Rekeying – Synonymous with manual remote rekeying.
SOURCE: CNSSI-4009

Correctness Proof – A mathematical proof of consistency between a specification and its implementation.
SOURCE: CNSSI-4009

Counter with Cipher Block Chaining-Message Authentication Code (CCM) – A mode of operation for a symmetric key block cipher algorithm. It combines the techniques of the Counter (CTR) mode and the Cipher Block Chaining-Message Authentication Code (CBC-MAC) algorithm to provide assurance of the confidentiality and the authenticity of computer data.
SOURCE: SP 800-38C

Countermeasure – Actions, devices, procedures, or techniques that meet or oppose (i.e., counters) a threat, a vulnerability, or an attack by eliminating or preventing it, by minimizing the harm it can cause,

| | |
|---|---|
| | or by discovering and reporting it so that corrective action can be taken.<br>SOURCE: CNSSI-4009 |
| Countermeasures – | Actions, devices, procedures, techniques, or other measures that reduce the vulnerability of an information system. Synonymous with security controls and safeguards.<br>SOURCE: SP 800-53; SP 800-37; FIPS 200 |
| Cover-Coding – | A technique to reduce the risks of eavesdropping by obscuring the information that is transmitted.<br>SOURCE: SP 800-98 |
| Coverage – | An attribute associated with an assessment method that addresses the scope or breadth of the assessment objects included in the assessment(e.g., types of objects to be assessed and the number of objects to be assessed by type). The values for the coverage attribute, hierarchically from less coverage to more coverage, are basic, focused, and comprehensive.<br>SOURCE: SP 800-53A |
| Covert Channel – | An unauthorized communication path that manipulates a communications medium in an unexpected, unconventional, or unforeseen way in order to transmit information without detection by anyone other than the entities operating the covert channel.<br>SOURCE: CNSSI-4009 |
| Covert Channel Analysis – | Determination of the extent to which the security policy model and subsequent lower-level program descriptions may allow unauthorizedaccess to information.<br>SOURCE: CNSSI-4009 |
| Covert Storage Channel – | Covert channel involving the direct or indirect writing to a storage location by one process and the direct or indirect reading of the storage location by another process. Covert storage channels typically involve a finite resource (e.g., sectors on a disk) that is shared by two subjects at different security levels.<br>SOURCE: CNSSI-4009 |
| Covert Testing – | Testing performed using covert methods and without the knowledge of the organization's IT staff, but with the full knowledge and permission of upper management.<br>SOURCE: SP 800-115 |
| Covert Timing Channel – | Covert channel in which one process signals information to another process by modulating its own use of system resources (e.g., central processing unit time) in such a way that this manipulation affects the real response time observed by the second process.<br>SOURCE: CNSSI-4009 |
| Credential – | An object that authoritatively binds an identity (and optionally, additional attributes) to a token possessed and controlled by a person.<br>SOURCE: SP 800-63 |

| | |
|---|---|
| Credential – | Evidence attesting to one's right to credit or authority.<br>SOURCE: FIPS 201<br>Evidence or testimonials that support a claim of identity or assertion of an attribute and usually are intended to be used more than once.<br>SOURCE: CNSSI-4009 |
| Credentials Service Provider – (CSP) | A trusted entity that issues or registers subscriber tokens and issues electronic credentials to subscribers. The CSP may encompass Registration Authorities and verifiers that it operates. A CSP may be an independent third party, or may issue credentials for its own use.<br>SOURCE: SP 800-63 |
| Critical Infrastructure – | System and assets, whether physical or virtual, so vital to the U.S. that the incapacity or destruction of such systems and assets would have a debilitating impact on security, national economic security, national public health or safety, or any combination of those matters. [Critical Infrastructures Protection Act of 2001, 42 U.S.C. 5195c(e)]<br>SOURCE: CNSSI-4009 |
| Critical Security Parameter (CSP) – | Security-related information (e.g., secret and private cryptographic keys, and authentication data such as passwords and Personal Identification Numbers [PINs]) whose disclosure or modification can compromise the security of a cryptographic module.<br>SOURCE: FIPS 140-2; CNSSI-4009 |
| Criticality – | A measure of the degree to which an organization depends on the information or information system for the success of a mission or of a business function.<br>SOURCE: SP 800-60 |
| Criticality Level – | Refers to the (consequences of) incorrect behavior of a system. The more serious the expected direct and indirect effects of incorrect behavior, the higher the criticality level.<br>SOURCE: CNSSI-4009 |
| Cross-Certificate – | A certificate used to establish a trust relationship between two Certification Authorities.<br>SOURCE: SP 800-32; CNSSI-4009 |
| Cross-Domain Capabilities – | The set of functions that enable the transfer of information between security domains in accordance with the policies of the security domains involved.<br>SOURCE: CNSSI-4009 |
| Cross-Domain Solution (CDS) – | A form of controlled interface that provides the ability to manually and/or automatically access and/or transfer information between different security domains.<br>SOURCE: CNSSI-4009; SP 800-37 |
| Cryptanalysis – | 1)Operations performed in defeating cryptographic protection without an initial knowledge of the key employed in providing theprotection. |

| | |
|---|---|
| | 2)The study of mathematical techniques for attempting to defeat cryptographic techniques and information system security. This includes the process of looking for errors or weaknesses in the implementation of an algorithm or of the algorithm itself.<br>SOURCE: SP 800-57; CNSSI-4009 |
| Crypto Officer – | An operator or process (subject), acting on behalf of the operator, performing cryptographic initialization or management functions.<br>SOURCE: FIPS 140-2 |
| Cryptographic – | Pertaining to, or concerned with, cryptography.<br>SOURCE: CNSSI-4009 |
| Cryptographic Alarm – | Circuit or device that detects failures or aberrations in the logic or operation of crypto-equipment. Crypto-alarm may inhibit transmission or may provide a visible and/or audible alarm.<br>SOURCE: CNSSI-4009 |
| Cryptographic Algorithm – | A well-defined computational procedure that takes variable inputs, including a cryptographic key, and produces an output.<br>SOURCE: SP 800-21; CNSSI-4009 |
| Cryptographic Ancillary Equipment – | Equipment designed specifically to facilitate efficient or reliable operation of cryptographic equipment, without performing cryptographic functions itself.<br>SOURCE: CNSSI-4009 |
| Cryptographic Binding – | Associating two or more related elements of information using cryptographic techniques.<br>SOURCE: CNSSI-4009 |
| Cryptographic Boundary – | An explicitly defined continuous perimeter that establishes the physical bounds of a cryptographic module and contains all the hardware, software, and/or firmware components of a cryptographic module.<br>SOURCE: FIPS 140-2 |
| Cryptographic Component – | Hardware or firmware embodiment of the cryptographic logic. A cryptographic component may be a modular assembly, a printed wiring assembly, a microcircuit, or a combination of these items.<br>SOURCE: CNSSI-4009 |
| Cryptographic Equipment – | Equipment that embodies a cryptographic logic.<br>SOURCE: CNSSI-4009 |
| Cryptographic Hash Function – | A function that maps a bit string of arbitrary length to a fixed length bit string. Approved hash functions satisfy the following properties:<br>1)(One-way) It is computationally infeasible to find any input whichmaps to any pre-specified output, and<br>2)(Collision resistant) It is computationally infeasible to find any two distinct inputs that map to the same output.<br>SOURCE: SP 800-21 |
| Cryptographic Ignition Key (CIK) – | Device or electronic key used to unlock the secure mode of crypto-equipment.<br>SOURCE: CNSSI-4009 |

Cryptographic Initialization – Function used to set the state of a cryptographic logic prior to key generation, encryption, or other operating mode.
SOURCE: CNSSI-4009

Cryptographic Key – A value used to control cryptographic operations, such as decryption,encryption, signature generation, or signature verification.
SOURCE: SP 800-63
A binary string used as a secret parameter by a cryptographic algorithm.
SOURCE: SP 800-108

Cryptographic Key – A parameter used in conjunction with a cryptographic algorithm that determines the specific operation of that algorithm.
SOURCE: FIPS 201; FIPS 198

Cryptographic Key – A parameter used in conjunction with a cryptographic algorithm that determines

- the transformation of plaintext data into ciphertext data,
- the transformation of ciphertext data into plaintext data,
- a digital signature computed from data,
- the verification of a digital signature computed from data,
- an authentication code computed from data, or
- an exchange agreement of a shared secret.

SOURCE: FIPS 140-2

Cryptographic Logic – The embodiment of one (or more) cryptographic algorithm(s) along with alarms, checks, and other processes essential to effective and secure performance of the cryptographic process(es).
SOURCE: CNSSI-4009

Cryptographic Material – (slang CRYPTO) COMSEC material used to secure or authenticate information.
SOURCE: CNSSI-4009

Cryptographic Module – The set of hardware, software, firmware, or some combination thereof that implements cryptographic logic or processes, including cryptographic algorithms, and is contained within the cryptographic boundary of the module.
SOURCE: SP 800-32; FIPS 196

Cryptographic Module – The set of hardware, software, and/or firmware that implements Approved security functions (including cryptographic algorithms andkey generation) and is contained within the cryptographic boundary.
SOURCE: FIPS 140-2

Cryptographic Module Security Policy – A precise specification of the security rules under which a cryptographic module will operate, including the rules derived from the requirements of this standard (FIPS 140-2) and additional rules imposed by the vendor.
SOURCE: FIPS 140-2

| | |
|---|---|
| Cryptographic Module Validation Program (CMVP) – | Validates cryptographic modules to Federal Information Processing Standard (FIPS) 140-2 and other cryptography-based standards. The CMVP is a joint effort between National Institute of Standards and Technology (NIST) and the Communications Security Establishment (CSE) of the government of Canada. Products validated as conforming to FIPS 140-2 are accepted by the federal agencies of both countries for the protection of sensitive information (United States) or Designated Information (Canada). The goal of the CMVP is to promote the use of validated cryptographic modules and provide federal agencies with a security metric to use in procuring equipment containing validated cryptographic modules.<br>SOURCE: FIPS 140-2 |
| Cryptographic Net – | Stations holding a common key.<br>SOURCE: CNSSI-4009 |
| Cryptographic Period – | Time span during which each key setting remains in effect.<br>SOURCE: CNSSI-4009 |
| Cryptographic Product – | A cryptographic key (public, private, or shared) or public key certificate, used for encryption, decryption, digital signature, or signature verification; and other items, such as compromised key lists(CKL) and certificate revocation lists (CRL), obtained by trusted means from the same source which validate the authenticity of keys or certificates. Protected software which generates or regenerates keys or certificates may also be considered a cryptographic product.<br>SOURCE: CNSSI-4009 |
| Cryptographic Randomization – | Function that randomly determines the transmit state of a cryptographic logic.<br>SOURCE: CNSSI-4009 |
| Cryptographic Security – | Component of COMSEC resulting from the provision of technically sound cryptographic systems and their proper use.<br>SOURCE: CNSSI-4009 |
| Cryptographic Strength – | A measure of the expected number of operations required to defeat a cryptographic mechanism.<br>SOURCE: SP 800-63 |
| Cryptographic Synchronization – | Process by which a receiving decrypting cryptographic logic attains the same internal state as the transmitting encrypting logic.<br>SOURCE: CNSSI-4009 |
| Cryptographic System – | Associated information assurance items interacting to provide a single means of encryption or decryption.<br>SOURCE: CNSSI-4009 |
| Cryptographic System Analysis – | Process of establishing the exploitability of a cryptographic system, normally by reviewing transmitted traffic protected or secured by the system under study.<br>SOURCE: CNSSI-4009 |

**Cryptographic System Evaluation** – Process of determining vulnerabilities of a cryptographic system and recommending countermeasures.
SOURCE: CNSSI-4009

**Cryptographic System Review** – Examination of a cryptographic system by the controlling authority ensuring its adequacy of design and content, continued need, and proper distribution.
SOURCE: CNSSI-4009

**Cryptographic System Survey** – Management technique in which actual holders of a cryptographic system express opinions on the system's suitability and provide usageinformation for technical evaluations.
SOURCE: CNSSI-4009

**Cryptographic Token** – A token where the secret is a cryptographic key.
SOURCE: SP 800-63

A portable, user-controlled physical device (e.g., smart card or PCMCIA card) used to store cryptographic information and possibly also perform cryptographic functions.
SOURCE: CNSSI-4009

**Cryptography** – The discipline that embodies the principles, means, and methods for the transformation of data in order to hide their semantic content, prevent their unauthorized use, or prevent their undetected modification.
SOURCE: SP 800-59

**Cryptography** – The discipline that embodies principles, means, and methods for providing information security, including confidentiality, data integrity, non-repudiation, and authenticity.
SOURCE: SP 800-21

**Cryptography** – Is categorized as either secret key or public key. Secret key cryptography is based on the use of a single cryptographic key sharedbetween two parties. The same key is used to encrypt and decrypt data. This key is kept secret by the two parties. Public key cryptography is a form of cryptography which makes use of two keys: a public key and a private key. The two keys are related but have the property that, given the public key, it is computationally infeasible to derive the private key [FIPS 140-1]. In a public key cryptosystem, each party has its own public/private key pair. The public key can be known by anyone; the private key is kept secret.
SOURCE: FIPS 191

Art or science concerning the principles, means, and methods for rendering plain information unintelligible and for restoring encrypted information to intelligible form.
SOURCE: CNSSI-4009

**Cryptology** – The science that deals with hidden, disguised, or encrypted communications. It includes communications security and communications intelligence.
SOURCE: SP 800-60

| | |
|---|---|
| | The mathematical science that deals with cryptanalysis and cryptography.<br>SOURCE: CNSSI-4009 |
| CVE – | See Common Vulnerabilities and Exposures. |
| Cyber Attack – | An attack, via cyberspace, targeting an enterprise's use of cyberspace for the purpose of disrupting, disabling, destroying, or maliciously controlling a computing environment/infrastructure; or destroying theintegrity of the data or stealing controlled information.<br>SOURCE: CNSSI-4009 |
| Cyber Incident – | Actions taken through the use of computer networks that result in an actual or potentially adverse effect on an information system and/or the information residing therein. See incident.<br>SOURCE: CNSSI-4009 |
| Cyber Infrastructure – | Includes electronic information and communications systems and services and the information contained in these systems and services. Information and communications systems and services are composed of all hardware and software that process, store, and communicate information, or any combination of all of these elements. Processing includes the creation, access, modification, and destruction of information. Storage includes paper, magnetic, electronic, and all other media types. Communications include sharing and distribution of information. For example: computer systems; control systems (e.g., supervisory control and data acquisition–SCADA); networks, such as the Internet; and cyber services (e.g., managed security services) are part of cyber infrastructure.<br>SOURCE: NISTIR 7628 |
| Cybersecurity – | The ability to protect or defend the use of cyberspace from cyber attacks.<br>SOURCE: CNSSI-4009 |
| Cyberspace – | A global domain within the information environment consisting of the interdependent network of information systems infrastructures including the Internet, telecommunications networks, computer systems, and embedded processors and controllers.<br>SOURCE: CNSSI-4009 |
| Cyclical Redundancy Check – (CRC) | A method to ensure data has not been altered after being sent througha communication channel.<br>SOURCE: SP 800-72<br>Error checking mechanism that verifies data integrity by computing apolynomial algorithm based checksum.<br>SOURCE: CNSSI-4009 |
| Data – | A subset of information in an electronic format that allows it to be retrieved or transmitted.<br>SOURCE: CNSSI-4009 |

| | |
|---|---|
| Data Aggregation – | Compilation of individual data systems and data that could result in the totality of the information being classified, or classified at a higher level, or of beneficial use to an adversary.<br>SOURCE: CNSSI-4009 |
| Data Asset – | 1. Any entity that is comprised of data. For example, a database is a data asset that is comprised of data records. A data asset may be a system or application output file, database, document, or Web page. A data asset also includes a service that may be provided to access data from an application. For example, a service that returns individual records from a database would be a data asset. Similarly, a Web site that returns data in response to specific queries (e.g., www.weather.com) would be a data asset.<br>2. An information-based resource.<br>SOURCE: CNSSI-4009 |
| Data Element – | A basic unit of information that has a unique meaning and subcategories (data items) of distinct value. Examples of data elements include gender, race, and geographic location.<br>SOURCE: SP 800-47; CNSSI-4009 |
| Data Encryption Algorithm (DEA) – | The cryptographic engine that is used by the Triple Data Encryption Algorithm (TDEA).<br>SOURCE: SP 800-67 |
| Data Encryption Standard (DES) – | Cryptographic algorithm designed for the protection of unclassified data and published by the National Institute of Standards and Technology (NIST) in Federal Information Processing Standard (FIPS) Publication 46. (FIPS 46-3 withdrawn 19 May 2005) See Triple DES.<br>SOURCE: CNSSI-4009 |
| Data Flow Control – | Synonymous with information flow control.<br>SOURCE: CNSSI-4009 |
| Data Integrity – | The property that data has not been altered in an unauthorized manner. Data integrity covers data in storage, during processing, andwhile in transit.<br>SOURCE: SP 800-27<br>The property that data has not been changed, destroyed, or lost in an unauthorized or accidental manner.<br>SOURCE: CNSSI-4009 |
| Data Origin Authentication – | The process of verifying that the source of the data is as claimed and that the data has not been modified.<br>SOURCE: CNSSI-4009 |
| Data Security – | Protection of data from unauthorized (accidental or intentional) modification, destruction, or disclosure.<br>SOURCE: CNSSI-4009 |
| Data Transfer Device (DTD) – | Fill device designed to securely store, transport, and transfer electronically both COMSEC and TRANSEC key, designed to be backward compatible with the previous generation of COMSEC |

common fill devices, and programmable to support modern missionsystems.
SOURCE: CNSSI-4009

Decertification – Revocation of the certification of an information system item or equipment for cause.
SOURCE: CNSSI-4009

Decipher – Convert enciphered text to plain text by means of a cryptographic system.
SOURCE: CNSSI-4009

Decode – Convert encoded text to plain text by means of a code.
SOURCE: CNSSI-4009

Decrypt – Generic term encompassing decode and decipher.
SOURCE: CNSSI-4009

Decryption – The process of transforming ciphertext into plaintext.
SOURCE: SP 800-67

Decryption – The process of changing ciphertext into plaintext using a cryptographic algorithm and key.
SOURCE: SP 800-21

Decryption – Conversion of ciphertext to plaintext through the use of a cryptographic algorithm.
SOURCE: FIPS 185

Dedicated Mode – Information systems security mode of operation wherein each user, with direct or indirect access to the system, its peripherals, remote terminals, or remote hosts, has all of the following: 1. valid security clearance for all information within the system, 2. formal access approval and signed nondisclosure agreements for all the information stored and/or processed (including all compartments, subcompartments, and/or special access programs), and 3. valid need-to-know for all information contained within the information system. When in the dedicated security mode, a system is specifically and exclusively dedicated to and controlled for the processing of one particular type or classification of information, either for full-time operation or for a specified period of time.
SOURCE: CNSSI-4009

Default Classification – Classification reflecting the highest classification being processed in an information system. Default classification is included in the caution statement affixed to an object.
SOURCE: CNSSI-4009

Defense-in-Breadth – A planned, systematic set of multidisciplinary activities that seek to identify, manage, and reduce risk of exploitable vulnerabilities at every stage of the system, network, or sub-component life cycle (system, network, or product design and development; manufacturing; packaging; assembly; system integration; distribution; operations; maintenance; and retirement).
SOURCE: CNSSI-4009

Defense-in-Depth – Information security strategy integrating people, technology, and operations capabilities to establish variable barriers across multiple layers and dimensions of the organization.
SOURCE: CNSSI-4009; SP 800-53

Degauss – Procedure that reduces the magnetic flux to virtual zero by applying areverse magnetizing field. Also called demagnetizing.
SOURCE: CNSSI-4009

Delegated Development Program – INFOSEC program in which the Director, NSA, delegates, on a case-by-case basis, the development and/or production of an entire telecommunications product, including the INFOSEC portion, to a lead department or agency.
SOURCE: CNSSI-4009

Deleted File – A file that has been logically, but not necessarily physically, erased from the operating system, perhaps to eliminate potentially incriminating evidence. Deleting files does not always necessarily eliminate the possibility of recovering all or part of the original data.
SOURCE: SP 800-72

Demilitarized Zone (DMZ) – An interface on a routing firewall that is similar to the interfaces found on the firewall's protected side. Traffic moving between the DMZ and other interfaces on the protected side of the firewall still goes through the firewall and can have firewall protection policies applied.
SOURCE: SP 800-41

A host or network segment inserted as a "neutral zone" between an organization's private network and the Internet.
SOURCE: SP 800-45

Perimeter network segment that is logically between internal and external networks. Its purpose is to enforce the internal network's Information Assurance policy for external information exchange and to provide external, untrusted sources with restricted access to releasable information while shielding the internal networks from outside attacks.
SOURCE: CNSSI-4009

Denial of Service (DoS) – An attack that prevents or impairs the authorized use of networks, systems, or applications by exhausting resources.
SOURCE: SP 800-61

The prevention of authorized access to resources or the delaying of time-critical operations. (Time-critical may be milliseconds or it maybe hours, depending upon the service provided.)
SOURCE: CNSSI-4009

Depth – An attribute associated with an assessment method that addresses the rigor and level of detail associated with the application of the method. The values for the depth attribute, hierarchically from less depth to more depth, are basic, focused, and comprehensive.
SOURCE: SP 800-53A

| | |
|---|---|
| Descriptive Top-Level Specification (DTLS) – | A natural language descriptive of a system's security requirements, an informal design notation, or a combination of the two.<br>SOURCE: CNSSI-4009 |
| Designated Approval Authority – (DAA) | Official with the authority to formally assume responsibility for operating a system at an acceptable level of risk. This term is synonymous with authorizing official, designated accrediting authority, and delegated accrediting authority.<br>SOURCE: CNSSI-4009 |
| Designated Approving (Accrediting) Authority – | See Authorizing Official |
| Device Distribution Profile – | An approval-based Access Control List (ACL) for a specific product that 1) names the user devices in a specific key management infrastructure (KMI) Operating Account (KOA) to which PRSNs distribute the product, and 2) states conditions of distribution for eachdevice.<br>SOURCE: CNSSI-4009 |
| Device Registration Manager – | The management role that is responsible for performing activities related to registering users that are devices.<br>SOURCE: CNSSI-4009 |
| Dial Back – | Synonymous with call back.<br>SOURCE: CNSSI-4009 |
| Differential Power Analysis – (DPA) | An analysis of the variations of the electrical power consumption of a cryptographic module, using advanced statistical methods and/or other techniques, for the purpose of extracting information correlated to cryptographic keys used in a cryptographic algorithm.<br>SOURCE: FIPS 140-2 |
| Digital Evidence – | Electronic information stored or transferred in digital form.<br>SOURCE: SP 800-72 |
| Digital Forensics – | The application of science to the identification, collection, examination, and analysis of data while preserving the integrity of theinformation and maintaining a strict chain of custody for the data.<br>SOURCE: SP 800-86 |
| Digital Signature – | An asymmetric key operation where the private key is used to digitally sign an electronic document and the public key is used to verify the signature. Digital signatures provide authentication and integrity protection.<br>SOURCE: SP 800-63 |
| Digital Signature – | A nonforgeable transformation of data that allows the proof of the source (with non-repudiation) and the verification of the integrity of that data.<br>SOURCE: FIPS 196 |

Digital Signature – The result of a cryptographic transformation of data which, when properly implemented, provides the services of:
1.origin authentication,
2.data integrity, and
3.signer non-repudiation.
SOURCE: FIPS 140-2
The result of a cryptographic transformation of data that, when properly implemented, provides a mechanism for verifying origin authentication, data integrity, and signatory non-repudiation.
SOURCE: FIPS 186
The result of a cryptographic transformation of data that, when properly implemented, provides origin authentication, data integrity, and signatory non-repudiation.
SOURCE: SP 800-89
Cryptographic process used to assure data object originator authenticity, data integrity, and time stamping for prevention of replay.
SOURCE: CNSSI-4009

Digital Signature Algorithm – Asymmetric algorithms used for digitally signing data.
SOURCE: SP 800-49

Direct Shipment – Shipment of COMSEC material directly from NSA to user COMSECaccounts.
SOURCE: CNSSI-4009

Disaster Recovery Plan (DRP) – A written plan for recovering one or more information systems at an alternate facility in response to a major hardware or software failure or destruction of facilities.
SOURCE: SP 800-34
Management policy and procedures used to guide an enterprise response to a major loss of enterprise capability or damage to its facilities. The DRP is the second plan needed by the enterprise risk managers and is used when the enterprise must recover (at its originalfacilities) from a loss of capability over a period of hours or days. See Continuity of Operations Plan and Contingency Plan.
SOURCE: CNSSI-4009

Disconnection – The termination of an interconnection between two or more IT systems. A disconnection may be planned (e.g., due to changed business needs) or unplanned (i.e., due to an attack or other contingency).
SOURCE: SP 800-47

Discretionary Access Control – The basis of this kind of security is that an individual user, or program operating on the user's behalf, is allowed to specify explicitly the types of access other users (or programs executing on their behalf) may have to information under the user's control.
SOURCE: FIPS 191

| | |
|---|---|
| | A means of restricting access to objects (e.g., files, data entities) based on the identity and need-to-know of subjects (e.g., users, processes) and/or groups to which the object belongs. The controls are discretionary in the sense that a subject with a certain access permission is capable of passing that permission (perhaps indirectly) on to any other subject (unless restrained by mandatory access control).<br>SOURCE: CNSSI-4009 |
| Disk Imaging – | Generating a bit-for-bit copy of the original media, including free space and slack space.<br>SOURCE: SP 800-86 |
| Disruption – | An unplanned event that causes the general system or major application to be inoperable for an unacceptable length of time (e.g., minor or extended power outage, extended unavailable network, or equipment or facility damage or destruction).<br>SOURCE: CNSSI-4009<br>An unplanned event that causes an information system to be inoperable for a length of time (e.g., minor or extended power outage,extended unavailable network, or equipment or facility damage or destruction).<br>SOURCE: SP 800-34 |
| Distinguished Name (DN) – | A unique name or character string that unambiguously identifies an entity according to the hierarchical naming conventions of X.500 directory service.<br>SOURCE: CNSSI-4009 |
| Distinguishing Identifier – | Information which unambiguously distinguishes an entity in the authentication process.<br>SOURCE: FIPS 196; CNSSI-4009 |
| Distributed Denial of Service – (DDoS) | A Denial of Service technique that uses numerous hosts to perform the attack.<br>SOURCE: SP 800-61; CNSSI-4009 |
| DMZ – | SeeDemilitarized Zone. |
| Domain – | A set of subjects, their information objects, and a common security policy.<br>SOURCE: SP 800-27<br>An environment or context that includes a set of system resources and a set of system entities that have the right to access the resources as defined by a common security policy, security model, or security architecture. See Security Domain.<br>SOURCE: CNSSI-4009; SP 800-53; SP 800-37 |
| Drop Accountability – | Procedure under which a COMSEC account custodian initially receipts for COMSEC material, and provides no further accounting for it to its central office of record. Local accountability of the COMSEC material may continue to be required. See accounting legend code.<br>SOURCE: CNSSI-4009 |

| | |
|---|---|
| Dual-Use Certificate – | A certificate that is intended for use with both digital signature and data encryption services.<br>SOURCE: SP 800-32 |
| Due Care – | The responsibility that managers and their organizations have a duty to provide for information security to ensure that the type of control, the cost of control, and the deployment of control are appropriate for the system being managed.<br>SOURCE: SP 800-30 |
| Duplicate Digital Evidence – | A duplicate is an accurate digital reproduction of all data objects contained on the original physical item and associated media.<br>SOURCE: SP 800-72 |
| Duration – | A field within a certificate that is composed of two subfields; "date ofissue" and "date of next issue."<br>SOURCE: SP 800-32 |
| Dynamic Subsystem – | A subsystem that is not continually present during the execution phase of an information system. Service-oriented architectures and cloud computing architectures are examples of architectures that employ dynamic subsystems.<br>SOURCE: SP 800-37 |
| E-Government (e-gov) – | The use by the U.S. government of Web-based Internet applications and other information technology.<br>SOURCE: CNSSI-4009 |
| Easter Egg – | Hidden functionality within an application program, which becomes activated when an undocumented, and often convoluted, set of commands and keystrokes are entered. Easter eggs are typically used to display the credits for the development team and are intended to benonthreatening.<br>SOURCE: SP 800-28 |
| Education (Information Security) – | Education integrates all of the security skills and competencies of the various functional specialties into a common body of knowledge . . . and strives to produce IT security specialists and professionals capable of vision and proactive response.<br>SOURCE: SP 800-50 |
| Egress Filtering – | Filtering of outgoing network traffic.<br>SOURCE: SP 800-41<br>The process of blocking outgoing packets that use obviously false Internet Protocol (IP) addresses, such as source addresses from internal networks.<br>SOURCE: SP 800-61 |
| Electronic Authentication – (E-authentication) | The process of establishing confidence in user identities electronically presented to an information system.<br>SOURCE: SP 800-63; CNSSI-4009 |
| Electronic Business (e-business) – | Doing business online.<br>SOURCE: CNSSI-4009 |

| | |
|---|---|
| Electronic Credentials – | Digital documents used in authentication that bind an identity or an attribute to a subscriber's token.<br>SOURCE: SP 800-63; CNSSI-4009 |
| Electronic Evidence – | Information and data of investigative value that is stored on or transmitted by an electronic device.<br>SOURCE: SP 800-72 |
| Electronic Key Entry – | The entry of cryptographic keys into a cryptographic module using electronic methods such as a smart card or a key-loading device. (Theoperator of the key may have no knowledge of the value of the key being entered.)<br>SOURCE: FIPS 140-2 |
| Electronic Key Management System (EKMS) – | Interoperable collection of systems being developed by services and agencies of the U.S. government to automate the planning, ordering, generating, distributing, storing, filling, using, and destroying of electronic key and management of other types of COMSEC material.<br>SOURCE: CNSSI-4009 |
| Electronic Messaging Services – | Services providing interpersonal messaging capability; meeting specific functional, management, and technical requirements; and yielding a business-quality electronic mail service suitable for the conduct of official government business.<br>SOURCE: CNSSI-4009 |
| Electronic Signature – | The process of applying any mark in electronic form with the intent to sign a data object. See also digital signature.<br>SOURCE: CNSSI-4009 |
| Electronically Generated Key – | Key generated in a COMSEC device by introducing (either mechanically or electronically) a seed key into the device and then using the seed, together with a software algorithm stored in the device, to produce the desired key.<br>SOURCE: CNSSI-4009 |
| Emanations Security (EMSEC) – | Protection resulting from measures taken to deny unauthorized individuals information derived from intercept and analysis of compromising emissions from crypto-equipment or an information system. See TEMPEST.<br>SOURCE: CNSSI-4009 |
| Embedded Computer – | Computer system that is an integral part of a larger system.<br>SOURCE: CNSSI-4009 |
| Embedded Cryptographic System – | Cryptosystem performing or controlling a function as an integral element of a larger system or subsystem.<br>SOURCE: CNSSI-4009 |
| Embedded Cryptography – | Cryptography engineered into an equipment or system whose basic function is not cryptographic.<br>SOURCE: CNSSI-4009 |

| | |
|---|---|
| Encipher – | Convert plain text to cipher text by means of a cryptographic system.<br>SOURCE: CNSSI-4009 |
| Enclave – | Collection of information systems connected by one or more internal networks under the control of a single authority and security policy. The systems may be structured by physical proximity or by function, independent of location.<br>SOURCE: CNSSI-4009 |
| Enclave Boundary – | Point at which an enclave's internal network service layer connects toan external network's service layer, i.e., to another enclave or to a Wide Area Network (WAN).<br>SOURCE: CNSSI-4009 |
| Encode – | Convert plain text to cipher text by means of a code.<br>SOURCE: CNSSI-4009 |
| Encrypt – | Generic term encompassing encipher and encode.<br>SOURCE: CNSSI-4009 |
| Encrypted Key – | A cryptographic key that has been encrypted using an Approved security function with a key encrypting key, a PIN, or a password in order to disguise the value of the underlying plaintext key.<br>SOURCE: FIPS 140-2 |
| Encrypted Network – | A network on which messages are encrypted (e.g., using DES, AES, or other appropriate algorithms) to prevent reading by unauthorized parties.<br>SOURCE: SP 800-32 |
| Encryption – | Conversion of plaintext to ciphertext through the use of a cryptographic algorithm.<br>SOURCE: FIPS 185 |
| Encryption – | The process of changing plaintext into ciphertext for the purpose of security or privacy.<br>SOURCE: SP 800-21; CNSSI-4009 |
| Encryption Algorithm – | Set of mathematically expressed rules for rendering data unintelligible by executing a series of conversions controlled by a key.<br>SOURCE: CNSSI-4009 |
| Encryption Certificate – | A certificate containing a public key that is used to encrypt electronic messages, files, documents, or data transmissions, or to establish or exchange a session key for these same purposes.<br>SOURCE: SP 800-32 |
| End-Item Accounting – | Accounting for all the accountable components of a COMSEC equipment configuration by a single short title.<br>SOURCE: CNSSI-4009 |
| End Cryptographic Unit (ECU) – | Device that (1) performs cryptographic functions, (2) typically is partof a larger system for which the device provides security services, and (3) from the viewpoint of a supporting security infrastructure (e.g., a key management system), is the lowest level |

of identifiable component with which a management transaction can be conducted.
SOURCE: CNSSI-4009

**End-to-End Encryption** – Communications encryption in which data is encrypted when being passed through a network, but routing information remains visible.
SOURCE: SP 800-12
Encryption of information at its origin and decryption at its intended destination without intermediate decryption.
SOURCE: CNSSI-4009

**End-to-End Security** – Safeguarding information in an information system from point of origin to point of destination.
SOURCE: CNSSI-4009

**Enrollment Manager** – The management role that is responsible for assigning user identities to management and non-management roles.
SOURCE: CNSSI-4009

**Enterprise** – An organization with a defined mission/goal and a defined boundary,using information systems to execute that mission, and with responsibility for managing its own risks and performance. An enterprise may consist of all or some of the following business aspects: acquisition, program management, financial management (e.g., budgets), human resources, security, and information systems, information and mission management.
SOURCE: CNSSI-4009

**Enterprise Architecture (EA)** – The description of an enterprise's entire set of information systems: how they are configured, how they are integrated, how they interface to the external environment at the enterprise's boundary, how they are operated to support the enterprise mission, and how they contribute to the enterprise's overall security posture.
SOURCE: CNSSI-4009

**Enterprise Risk Management** – The methods and processes used by an enterprise to manage risks to its mission and to establish the trust necessary for the enterprise to support shared missions. It involves the identification of mission dependencies on enterprise capabilities, the identification and prioritization of risks due to defined threats, the implementation of countermeasures to provide both a static risk posture and an effective dynamic response to active threats; and it assesses enterprise performance against threats and adjusts countermeasures as necessary.
SOURCE: CNSSI-4009

**Enterprise Service** – A set of one or more computer applications and middleware systems hosted on computer hardware that provides standard information systems capabilities to end users and hosted mission applications and services.
SOURCE: CNSSI-4009

Entity – Either a subject (an active element that operates on information or thesystem state) or an object (a passive element that contains or receives information).
SOURCE: SP 800-27

Entity – An active element in an open system.
SOURCE: FIPS 188

Entity – Any participant in an authentication exchange; such a participant maybe human or nonhuman, and may take the role of a claimant and/or verifier.
SOURCE: FIPS 196

Entrapment – Deliberate planting of apparent flaws in an IS for the purpose of detecting attempted penetrations.
SOURCE: CNSSI-4009

Entropy – A measure of the amount of uncertainty that an attacker faces to determine the value of a secret.
SOURCE: SP 800-63

Environment – Aggregate of external procedures, conditions, and objects affecting the development, operation, and maintenance of an information system.
SOURCE: FIPS 200; CNSSI-4009

Environment of Operation – The physical surroundings in which an information system processes, stores, and transmits information.
SOURCE: SP 800-37; SP 800-53A

Ephemeral Key – A cryptographic key that is generated for each execution of a key establishment process and that meets other requirements of the key type (e.g., unique to each message or session).
SOURCE: SP 800-57

Erasure – Process intended to render magnetically stored information irretrievable by normal means.
SOURCE: CNSSI-4009

Error Detection Code – A code computed from data and comprised of redundant bits of information designed to detect, but not correct, unintentional changes in the data.
SOURCE: FIPS 140-2; CNSSI-4009

Escrow – Something (e.g., a document, an encryption key) that is "delivered to a third person to be given to the grantee only upon the fulfillment of acondition."
SOURCE: FIPS 185

Evaluation Products List (EPL) – List of validated products that have been successfully evaluated under the National Information Assurance Partnership (NIAP) Common Criteria Evaluation and Validation Scheme (CCEVS).
SOURCE: CNSSI-4009

Evaluation Assurance Level (EAL) – Set of assurance requirements that represent a point on the Common Criteria predefined assurance scale.
SOURCE: CNSSI-4009

| | |
|---|---|
| Event – | Any observable occurrence in a network or system.<br>SOURCE: SP 800-61<br>Any observable occurrence in a system and/or network. Events sometimes provide indication that an incident is occurring.<br>SOURCE: CNSSI-4009 |
| Examination – | A technical review that makes the evidence visible and suitable for analysis; tests performed on the evidence to determine the presence or absence of specific data.<br>SOURCE: SP 800-72 |
| Examine – | A type of assessment method that is characterized by the process of checking, inspecting, reviewing, observing, studying, or analyzing one or more assessment objects to facilitate understanding, achieve clarification, or obtain evidence, the results of which are used to support the determination of security control effectiveness over time.<br>SOURCE: SP 800-53A |
| Exculpatory Evidence – | Evidence that tends to decrease the likelihood of fault or guilt.<br>SOURCE: SP 800-72 |
| Executive Agency – | An executive department specified in 5 United States Code (U.S.C.), Sec. 101; a military department specified in 5 U.S.C., Sec. 102; an independent establishment as defined in 5 U.S.C., Sec. 104(1); and a wholly owned government corporation fully subject to the provisions of 31 U.S.C., Chapter 91.<br>SOURCE: SP 800-53; SP 800-37; FIPS 200; FIPS 199; 41 U.S.C., Sec. 403; CNSSI-4009 |
| Exercise Key – | Cryptographic key material used exclusively to safeguard communications transmitted over-the-air during military or organized civil training exercises.<br>SOURCE: CNSSI-4009 |
| Exploit Code – | A program that allows attackers to automatically break into a system.<br>SOURCE: SP 800-40 |
| Exploitable Channel – | Channel that allows the violation of the security policy governing an information system and is usable or detectable by subjects external to the trusted computing base. See covert channel.<br>SOURCE: CNSSI-4009 |
| External Information System (or Component) – | An information system or component of an information system that isoutside of the authorization boundary established by the organization and for which the organization typically has no direct control over theapplication of required security controls or the assessment of security control effectiveness.<br>SOURCE: SP 800-37; SP 800-53; CNSSI-4009 |
| External Information System Service – | An information system service that is implemented outside of the authorization boundary of the organizational information system (i.e., a service that is used by, but not a part of, the organizational information system) and for which the organization typically has no |

direct control over the application of required security controls or the assessment of security control effectiveness.
SOURCE: SP 800-53; SP 800-37; CNSSI-4009

External Information System Service Provider – A provider of external information system services to an organizationthrough a variety of consumer-producer relationships, including but not limited to: joint ventures; business partnerships; outsourcing arrangements (i.e., through contracts, interagency agreements, lines of business arrangements); licensing agreements; and/or supply chainexchanges.
SOURCE: SP 800-37; SP 800-53

External Network – A network not controlled by the organization.
SOURCE: SP800-53;CNSSI-4009

External Security Testing – Security testing conducted from outside the organization's security perimeter.
SOURCE: SP 800-115

Extraction Resistance – Capability of crypto-equipment or secure telecommunications equipment to resist efforts to extract key.
SOURCE: CNSSI-4009

Extranet – A private network that uses Web technology, permitting the sharing of portions of an enterprise's information or operations with suppliers, vendors, partners, customers, or other enterprises.
SOURCE: CNSSI-4009

Fail Safe – Automatic protection of programs and/or processing systems when hardware or software failure is detected.
SOURCE: CNSSI-4009

Fail Soft – Selective termination of affected nonessential processing when hardware or software failure is determined to be imminent.
SOURCE: CNSSI-4009

Failover – The capability to switch over automatically (typically without human intervention or warning) to a redundant or standby information system upon the failure or abnormal termination of the previously active system.
SOURCE: SP 800-53; CNSSI-4009

Failure Access – Type of incident in which unauthorized access to data results from hardware or software failure.
SOURCE: CNSSI-4009

Failure Control – Methodology used to detect imminent hardware or software failure and provide fail safe or fail soft recovery.
SOURCE: CNSSI-4009

False Acceptance – When a biometric system incorrectly identifies an individual or incorrectly verifies an impostor against a claimed identity
SOURCE: SP 800-76

In biometrics, the instance of a security system incorrectly verifying or identifying an unauthorized person. It typically is considered the most serious of biometric security errors as it gives unauthorized

| | |
|---|---|
| | users access to systems that expressly are trying to keep them out. SOURCE: CNSSI-4009 |
| False Acceptance Rate (FAR) – | The probability that a biometric system will incorrectly identify an individual or will fail to reject an impostor. The rate given normally assumes passive impostor attempts. SOURCE: SP 800-76<br>The measure of the likelihood that the biometric security system will incorrectly accept an access attempt by an unauthorized user. A system's false acceptance rate typically is stated as the ratio of the number of false acceptances divided by the number of identification attempts. SOURCE: CNSSI-4009 |
| False Positive – | An alert that incorrectly indicates that malicious activity is occurring. SOURCE: SP 800-61 |
| False Rejection – | When a biometric system fails to identify an applicant or fails to verify the legitimate claimed identity of an applicant. SOURCE: SP 800-76<br>In biometrics, the instance of a security system failing to verify or identify an authorized person. It does not necessarily indicate a flaw in the biometric system; for example, in a fingerprint-based system, an incorrectly aligned finger on the scanner or dirt on the scanner canresult in the scanner misreading the fingerprint, causing a false rejection of the authorized user. SOURCE: CNSSI-4009 |
| False Rejection Rate (FRR) – | The probability that a biometric system will fail to identify an applicant, or verify the legitimate claimed identity of an applicant. SOURCE: SP 800-76<br>The measure of the likelihood that the biometric security system will incorrectly reject an access attempt by an authorized user. A system's false rejection rate typically is stated as the ratio of the number of false rejections divided by the number of identification attempts. SOURCE: CNSSI-4009 |
| Federal Agency – | See Agency, See Executive Agency. |
| Federal Bridge Certification Authority (FBCA) – | The Federal Bridge Certification Authority consists of a collection ofPublic Key Infrastructure components (Certificate Authorities, Directories, Certificate Policies and Certificate Practice Statements) that are used to provide peer-to-peer interoperability among Agency Principal Certification Authorities. SOURCE: SP 800-32; CNSSI-4009 |
| Federal Bridge Certification Authority Membrane – | The Federal Bridge Certification Authority Membrane consists of a collection of Public Key Infrastructure components including a variety of Certification Authority PKI products, Databases, CA |

| | |
|---|---|
| | specific Directories, Border Directory, Firewalls, Routers, Randomizers, etc.<br>SOURCE: SP 800-32 |
| Federal Bridge Certification Authority Operational Authority – | The Federal Bridge Certification Authority Operational Authority is the organization selected by the Federal Public Key Infrastructure Policy Authority to be responsible for operating the Federal Bridge Certification Authority.<br>SOURCE: SP 800-32 |
| Federal Enterprise Architecture – | A business-based framework for governmentwide improvement developed by the Office of Management and Budget that is intended to facilitate efforts to transform the federal government to one that is citizen-centered, results-oriented, and market-based.<br>SOURCE: SP800-53;SP800-18;SP800-60;CNSSI-4009 |
| Federal Information Processing Standard (FIPS) – | A standard for adoption and use by federal departments and agencies that has been developed within the Information Technology Laboratory and published by the National Institute of Standards and Technology, a part of the U.S. Department of Commerce. A FIPS covers some topic in information technology in order to achieve a common level of quality or some level of interoperability.<br>SOURCE: FIPS 201 |
| Federal Information Security Management Act (FISMA) – | A statute (Title III, P.L. 107-347) that requires agencies to assess risk to information systems and provide information security protections commensurate with the risk. FISMA also requires that agencies integrate information security into their capital planning and enterprise architecture processes, conduct annual information systemssecurity reviews of all programs and systems, and report the results of those reviews to OMB.<br>SOURCE: CNSSI-4009 |
| Federal Information System – | An information system used or operated by an executive agency, by a contractor of an executive agency, or by another organization on behalf of an executive agency.<br>SOURCE: SP 800-53; FIPS 200; FIPS 199; 40 U.S.C., Sec. 11331; CNSSI-4009 |
| Federal Information Systems Security Educators' Association – (FISSEA) | An organization whose members come from federal agencies, industry, and academic institutions devoted to improving the IT security awareness and knowledge within the federal government and its related external workforce.<br>SOURCE: SP 800-16 |
| Federal Public Key Infrastructure Policy Authority (FPKI PA) – | The Federal PKI Policy Authority is a federal government body responsible for setting, implementing, and administering policy decisions regarding interagency PKI interoperability that uses the FBCA.<br>SOURCE: SP 800-32 |

| | |
|---|---|
| File Encryption – | The process of encrypting individual files on a storage medium and permitting access to the encrypted data only after proper authentication is provided.<br>SOURCE: SP 800-111 |
| File Infector Virus – | A virus that attaches itself to a program file, such as a word processor, spreadsheet application, or game.<br>SOURCE: SP 800-61 |
| File Integrity Checker – | Software that generates, stores, and compares message digests for files to detect changes to the files.<br>SOURCE: SP 800-61 |
| File Name Anomaly – | 1. A mismatch between the internal file header and its external extension; or<br>2. A file name inconsistent with the content of the file (e.g., renaming a graphics file with a non-graphical extension.<br>SOURCE: SP 800-72 |
| File Protection – | Aggregate of processes and procedures designed to inhibit unauthorized access, contamination, elimination, modification, or destruction of a file or any of its contents.<br>SOURCE: CNSSI-4009 |
| File Security – | Means by which access to computer files is limited to authorized users only.<br>SOURCE: CNSSI-4009 |
| Fill Device – | COMSEC item used to transfer or store key in electronic form or to insert key into a cryptographic equipment.<br>SOURCE: CNSSI-4009 |
| FIPS – | See Federal Information Processing Standard. |
| FIPS-Approved Security Method – | A security method (e.g., cryptographic algorithm, cryptographic keygeneration algorithm or key distribution technique, random number generator, authentication technique, or evaluation criteria) that is either a) specified in a FIPS, or b) adopted in a FIPS.<br>SOURCE: FIPS 196 |
| FIPS-Validated Cryptography – | A cryptographic module validated by the Cryptographic Module Validation Program (CMVP) to meet requirements specified in FIPS 140-2 (as amended). As a prerequisite to CMVP validation, the cryptographic module is required to employ a cryptographic algorithm implementation that has successfully passed validation testing by the Cryptographic Algorithm Validation Program (CAVP). See NSA-Approved Cryptography.<br>SOURCE: SP 800-53 |
| FIPS PUB – | An acronym for Federal Information Processing Standards Publication. FIPS publications (PUB) are issued by NIST after approval by the Secretary of Commerce.<br>SOURCE: SP 800-64 |
| FIREFLY – | Key management protocol based on public key cryptography.<br>SOURCE: CNSSI-4009 |

Firewall – A gateway that limits access between networks in accordance with local security policy.
SOURCE: SP 800-32
A hardware/software capability that limits access between networks and/or systems in accordance with a specific security policy.
SOURCE: CNSSI-4009
A device or program that controls the flow of network traffic betweennetworks or hosts that employ differing security postures.
SOURCE: SP 800-41

Firewall Control Proxy – The component that controls a firewall's handling of a call. The firewall control proxy can instruct the firewall to open specific ports that are needed by a call, and direct the firewall to close these ports at call termination.
SOURCE: SP 800-58

Firmware – The programs and data components of a cryptographic module that are stored in hardware within the cryptographic boundary and cannot be dynamically written or modified during execution.
SOURCE: FIPS 140-2
Computer programs and data stored in hardware - typically in read-only memory (ROM) or programmable read-only memory (PROM) - such that the programs and data cannot be dynamically written or modified during execution of the programs.
SOURCE: CNSSI-4009

FISMA – See Federal Information Security Management Act.

Fixed COMSEC Facility – COMSEC facility located in an immobile structure or aboard a ship.
SOURCE: CNSSI-4009

Flaw – Error of commission, omission, or oversight in an information systemthat may allow protection mechanisms to be bypassed.
SOURCE: CNSSI-4009

Flaw Hypothesis Methodology – System analysis and penetration technique in which the specification and documentation for an information system are analyzed to produce a list of hypothetical flaws. This list is prioritized on the basis of the estimated probability that a flaw exists, on the ease of exploiting it, and on the extent of control or compromise it would provide. The prioritized list is used to perform penetration testing of a system.
SOURCE: CNSSI-4009

Flooding – An attack that attempts to cause a failure in a system by providing more input than the system can process properly.
SOURCE: CNSSI-4009

Focused Testing – A test methodology that assumes some knowledge of the internal structure and implementation detail of the assessment object. Also known as gray box testing.
SOURCE: SP 800-53A

| | |
|---|---|
| Forensic Copy – | An accurate bit-for-bit reproduction of the information contained on an electronic device or associated media, whose validity and integrityhas been verified using an accepted algorithm. SOURCE: SP 800-72; CNSSI-4009 |
| Forensic Specialist – | A professional who locates, identifies, collects, analyzes, and examines data while preserving the integrity and maintaining a strict chain of custody of information discovered. SOURCE: SP 800-72 |
| Forensics – | The practice of gathering, retaining, and analyzing computer-related data for investigative purposes in a manner that maintains the integrity of the data. SOURCE: CNSSI-4009 See Also Computer Forensics |
| Forensically Clean – | Digital media that is completely wiped of all data, including nonessential and residual data, scanned for malware, and verified before use. SOURCE: SP 800-86 |
| Formal Access Approval – | A formalization of the security determination for authorizing access to a specific type of classified or sensitive information, based on specified access requirements, a determination of the individual's security eligibility and a determination that the individual's official duties require the individual be provided access to the information. SOURCE: CNSSI-4009 |
| Formal Development Methodology – | Software development strategy that proves security design specifications. SOURCE: CNSSI-4009 |
| Formal Method – | Mathematical argument which verifies that the system satisfies a mathematically-described security policy. SOURCE: CNSSI-4009 |
| Formal Proof – | Complete and convincing mathematical argument presenting the full logical justification for each proof step and for the truth of a theorem or set of theorems. SOURCE: CNSSI-4009 |
| Formal Security Policy – | Mathematically-precise statement of a security policy. SOURCE: CNSSI-4009 |
| Formatting Function – | The function that transforms the payload, associated data, and nonce into a sequence of complete blocks. SOURCE: SP 800-38C |
| Forward Cipher – | One of the two functions of the block cipher algorithm that is determined by the choice of a cryptographic key. SOURCE: SP 800-67 |
| Frequency Hopping – | Repeated switching of frequencies during radio transmission according to a specified algorithm, to minimize unauthorized interception or jamming of telecommunications. SOURCE: CNSSI-4009 |

| | |
|---|---|
| Full Disk Encryption (FDE) – | The process of encrypting all the data on the hard disk drive used to boot a computer, including the computer's operating system, and permitting access to the data only after successful authentication withthe full disk encryption product.<br>SOURCE: SP 800-111 |
| Full Maintenance – | Complete diagnostic repair, modification, and overhaul of COMSEC equipment, including repair of defective assemblies by piece part replacement. See limited maintenance.<br>SOURCE: CNSSI-4009 |
| Functional Testing – | Segment of security testing in which advertised security mechanisms of an information system are tested under operational conditions.<br>SOURCE: CNSSI-4009 |
| Gateway – | Interface providing compatibility between networks by converting transmission speeds, protocols, codes, or security measures.<br>SOURCE: CNSSI-4009 |
| General Support System – | An interconnected set of information resources under the same direct management control that shares common functionality. It normally includes hardware, software, information, data, applications, communications, and people.<br>SOURCE: OMB Circular A-130, App. III<br>An interconnected set of information resources under the same directmanagement control which shares common functionality. A system normally includes hardware, software, information, data, applications, communications, and people. A system can be, for example, a local area network (LAN) including smart terminals that supports a branch office, an agency-wide backbone, a communications network, a departmental data processing center including its operating system and utilities, a tactical radio network, or a shared information processing service organization (IPSO).<br>SOURCE: CNSSI-4009 |
| Global Information Grid (GIG) – | The globally interconnected, end-to-end set of information capabilities for collecting, processing, storing, disseminating, and managing information on demand to warfighters, policy makers, and support personnel. The GIG includes owned and leased communications and computing systems and services, software (including applications), data, security services, other associated services, and National Security Systems. Non-GIG IT includes stand-alone, self-contained, or embedded IT that is not, and will not be, connected to the enterprise network.<br>SOURCE: CNSSI-4009 |
| Global Information Infrastructure – (GII) | Worldwide interconnections of the information systems of all countries, international and multinational organizations, and international commercial communications.<br>SOURCE: CNSSI-4009 |

| | |
|---|---|
| Graduated Security – | A security system that provides several levels (e.g., low, moderate, high) of protection based on threats, risks, available technology, support services, time, human concerns, and economics.<br>SOURCE: FIPS 201 |
| Gray Box Testing – | See Focused Testing. |
| Group Authenticator – | Used, sometimes in addition to a sign-on authenticator, to allow access to specific data or functions that may be shared by all members of a particular group.<br>SOURCE: CNSSI-4009 |
| Guard (System) – | A mechanism limiting the exchange of information between information systems or subsystems.<br>SOURCE: CNSSI-4009 |
| Guessing Entropy – | A measure of the difficulty that an attacker has to guess the average password used in a system. In this document, entropy is stated in bits.When a password has n-bits of guessing entropy then an attacker has as much difficulty guessing the average password as in guessing an n-bit random quantity. The attacker is assumed to know the actual password frequency distribution.<br>SOURCE: SP 800-63 |
| Hacker – | Unauthorized user who attempts to or gains access to an information system.<br>SOURCE: CNSSI-4009 |
| Handler – | A type of program used in DDoS attacks to control agents distributed throughout a network. Also refers to an incident handler, which refers to a person who performs incident response work.<br>SOURCE: SP 800-61 |
| Handshaking Procedures – | Dialogue between two information systems for synchronizing, identifying, and authenticating themselves to one another.<br>SOURCE: CNSSI-4009 |
| Hard Copy Key – | Physical keying material, such as printed key lists, punched or printed key tapes, or programmable, read-only memories (PROM).<br>SOURCE: CNSSI-4009 |
| Hardening – | Configuring a host's operating systems and applications to reduce thehost's security weaknesses.<br>SOURCE: SP 800-123 |
| Hardware – | The physical components of an information system. See software andfirmware.<br>SOURCE: CNSSI-4009 |
| Hardwired Key – | Permanently installed key.<br>SOURCE: CNSSI-4009 |
| Hash Function – | A function that maps a bit string of arbitrary length to a fixed length bit string. Approved hash functions satisfy the following properties:<br>1) One-Way. It is computationally infeasible to find any input that maps to any prespecified output. |

2) Collision Resistant. It is computationally infeasible to find any two distinct inputs that map to the same output.
SOURCE: SP 800-63; FIPS 201

**Hash Function –** A mathematical function that maps a string of arbitrary length (up to a predetermined maximum size) to a fixed length string.
SOURCE: FIPS 198

A function that maps a bit string of arbitrary length to a fixed length bit string. Approved hash functions are specified in FIPS 180 and are designed to satisfy the following properties:
1. (One-way) It is computationally infeasible to find any input that maps to any new prespecified output, and
2. (Collision resistant) It is computationally infeasible to find any twodistinct inputs that map to the same output.
SOURCE: FIPS 186

**Hash Total –** Value computed on data to detect error or manipulation. See checksum.
SOURCE: CNSSI-4009

**Hash Value –** The result of applying a cryptographic hash function to data (e.g., a message).
SOURCE: SP 800-106

**Hash Value/ Result –** See Message Digest.
SOURCE: FIPS186;CNSSI-4009

**Hash-based Message Authentication Code (HMAC) –** A symmetric key authentication method using hash functions.
SOURCE: SP 800-63

**Hash-based Message Authentication Code – (HMAC)** A message authentication code that uses a cryptographic key in conjunction with a hash function.
SOURCE: FIPS 201; CNSSI-4009

A message authentication code that utilizes a keyed hash.
SOURCE: FIPS 140-2

**Hashing –** The process of using a mathematical algorithm against data to produce a numeric value that is representative of that data.
SOURCE: SP 800-72; CNSSI-4009

**Hashword –** Memory address containing hash total.
SOURCE: CNSSI-4009

**High Assurance Guard (HAG) –** An enclave boundary protection device that controls access between a local area network that an enterprise system has a requirement to protect, and an external network that is outside the control of the enterprise system, with a high degree of assurance.
SOURCE: SP 800-32

A guard that has two basic functional capabilities: a Message Guard and a Directory Guard. The Message Guard provides filter service for message traffic traversing the Guard between adjacent security domains. The Director Guard provides filter service for directory

| | |
|---|---|
| | access and updates traversing the Guard between adjacent security domains.<br>SOURCE: CNSSI-4009 |
| High Availability – | A failover feature to ensure availability during device or component interruptions.<br>SOURCE: SP 800-113 |
| High Impact – | The loss of confidentiality, integrity, or availability that could be expected to have a severe or catastrophic adverse effect on organizational operations, organizational assets, individuals, other organizations, or the national security interests of the United States; (i.e., 1) causes a severe degradation in mission capability to an extentand duration that the organization is able to perform its primary functions, but the effectiveness of the functions is significantly reduced; 2) results in major damage to organizational assets; 3) results in major financial loss; or 4) results in severe or catastrophic harm to individuals involving loss of life or serious life threatening injuries).<br>SOURCE: FIPS 199; CNSSI-4009 |
| High-Impact System – | An information system in which at least one security objective (i.e., confidentiality, integrity, or availability) is assigned a FIPS 199 potential impact value of high.<br>SOURCE: SP 800-37; SP 800-53; SP 800-60; FIPS 200<br>An information system in which at least one security objective (i.e., confidentiality, integrity, or availability) is assigned a potential impact value of high.<br>SOURCE: CNSSI-4009 |
| Honeypot – | A system (e.g., a Web server) or system resource (e.g., a file on a server) that is designed to be attractive to potential crackers and intruders and has no authorized users other than its administrators.<br>SOURCE: CNSSI-4009 |
| Hot Site – | A fully operational offsite data processing facility equipped with hardware and software, to be used in the event of an information system disruption.<br>SOURCE: SP 800-34<br>Backup site that includes phone systems with the phone lines already connected. Networks will also be in place, with any necessary routersand switches plugged in and turned on. Desks will have desktop PCs installed and waiting, and server areas will be replete with the necessary hardware to support business-critical functions. Within a few hours, a hot site can become a fully functioning element of an organization.<br>SOURCE: CNSSI-4009 |
| Hot Wash – | A debrief conducted immediately after an exercise or test with the staff and participants.<br>SOURCE: SP 800-84 |

**Hybrid Security Control** – A security control that is implemented in an information system in part as a common control and in part as a system-specific control. See also Common Control and System-Specific Control.
SOURCE: SP 800-37; SP 800-53; SP 800-53A; CNSSI-4009

**IA Architecture** – A description of the structure and behavior for an enterprise's security processes, information security systems, personnel and organizational sub-units, showing their alignment with the enterprise's mission and strategic plans.
SOURCE: CNSSI-4009

**IA Infrastructure** – The underlying security framework that lies beyond an enterprise's defined boundary, but supports its IA and IA-enabled products, its security posture and its risk management plan.
SOURCE: CNSSI-4009

**IA Product** – Product whose primary purpose is to provide security services (e.g., confidentiality, authentication, integrity, access control, non-repudiation of data); correct known vulnerabilities; and/or provide layered defense against various categories of non-authorized or malicious penetrations of information systems or networks.
SOURCE: CNSSI-4009

**IA-Enabled Information Technology Product** – Product or technology whose primary role is not security, but which provides security services as an associated feature of its intended operating capabilities. Examples include such products as security-enabled Web browsers, screening routers, trusted operating systems,and security-enabled messaging systems.
SOURCE: CNSSI-4009

**IA-Enabled Product** – Product whose primary role is not security, but provides security services as an associated feature of its intended operating capabilities.
Note: Examples include such products as security-enabled Web browsers, screening routers, trusted operating systems, and security enabling messaging systems.
SOURCE: CNSSI-4009

**Identification** – The process of verifying the identity of a user, process, or device, usually as a prerequisite for granting access to resources in an IT system.
SOURCE: SP 800-47

**Identification** – The process of discovering the true identity (i.e., origin, initial history) of a person or item from the entire collection of similar persons or items.
SOURCE: FIPS 201
An act or process that presents an identifier to a system so that the system can recognize a system entity (e.g., user, process, or device) and distinguish that entity from all others.
SOURCE: CNSSI-4009

| | |
|---|---|
| Identifier – | Unique data used to represent a person's identity and associated attributes. A name or a card number are examples of identifiers.<br>SOURCE: FIPS 201<br>A data object - often, a printable, non-blank character string - that definitively represents a specific identity of a system entity, distinguishing that identity from all others.<br>SOURCE: CNSSI-4009 |
| Identity – | A unique name of an individual person. Since the legal names of persons are not necessarily unique, the identity of a person must include sufficient additional information to make the complete nameunique.<br>SOURCE: SP 800-63 |
| Identity – | The set of physical and behavioral characteristics by which an individual is uniquely recognizable.<br>SOURCE: FIPS 201<br>The set of attribute values (i.e., characteristics) by which an entity is recognizable and that, within the scope of an identity manager's responsibility, is sufficient to distinguish that entity from any other entity.<br>SOURCE: CNSSI-4009 |
| Identity-Based Access Control – | Access control based on the identity of the user (typically relayed as a characteristic of the process acting on behalf of that user) where access authorizations to specific objects are assigned based on user identity.<br>SOURCE: SP800-53;CNSSI-4009 |
| Identity-Based Security Policy – | A security policy based on the identities and/or attributes of the object (system resource) being accessed and of the subject (user, group of users, process, or device) requesting access.<br>SOURCE: SP 800-33 |
| Identity Binding – | Binding of the vetted claimed identity to the individual (through biometrics) according to the issuing authority.<br>SOURCE: FIPS 201 |
| Identity Proofing – | The process by which a Credentials Service Provider (CSP) and a Registration Authority (RA) validate sufficient information to uniquely identify a person.<br>SOURCE: SP 800-63 |
| Identity Proofing – | The process of providing sufficient information (e.g., identity history,credentials, documents) to a Personal Identity Verification Registrar when attempting to establish an identity.<br>SOURCE: FIPS 201 |
| Identity Registration – | The process of making a person's identity known to the Personal Identity Verification (PIV) system, associating a unique identifier with that identity, and collecting and recording the person's relevant attributes into the system.<br>SOURCE: FIPS 201; CNSSI-4009 |

| | |
|---|---|
| Identity Token – | Smart card, metal key, or other physical object used to authenticate identity.<br>SOURCE: CNSSI-4009 |
| Identity Validation – | Tests enabling an information system to authenticate users or resources.<br>SOURCE: CNSSI-4009 |
| Identity Verification – | The process of confirming or denying that a claimed identity is correct by comparing the credentials (something you know, something you have, something you are) of a person requesting access with those previously proven and stored in the PIV Card of system and associated with the identity being claimed.<br>SOURCE: FIPS 201 |
| Identity Verification – | The process of confirming or denying that a claimed identity is correct by comparing the credentials (something you know, something you have, something you are) of a person requesting access with those previously proven and stored in the PIV Card or system and associated with the identity being claimed.<br>SOURCE: SP 800-79 |
| Image – | An exact bit-stream copy of all electronic data on a device, performed in a manner that ensures that the information is not altered.<br>SOURCE: SP 800-72 |
| Imitative Communications Deception – | Introduction of deceptive messages or signals into an adversary's telecommunications signals. See communications deception and manipulative communications deception.<br>SOURCE: CNSSI-4009 |
| Impact – | The magnitude of harm that can be expected to result from the consequences of unauthorized disclosure of information, unauthorized modification of information, unauthorized destruction of information, or loss of information or information system availability.<br>SOURCE: SP 800-60 |
| Impact Level – | The magnitude of harm that can be expected to result from the consequences of unauthorized disclosure of information, unauthorized modification of information, unauthorized destruction of information, or loss of information or information system availability.<br>SOURCE: CNSSI-4009<br>High, Moderate, or Low security categories of an information systemestablished in FIPS 199 which classify the intensity of a potential impact that may occur if the information system is jeopardized.<br>SOURCE: SP 800-34 |
| Implant – | Electronic device or electronic equipment modification designed to gain unauthorized interception of information-bearing emanations.<br>SOURCE: CNSSI-4009 |

| | |
|---|---|
| Inadvertent Disclosure – | Type of incident involving accidental exposure of information to an individual not authorized access.<br>SOURCE: CNSSI-4009 |
| Inappropriate Usage – | A person who violates acceptable use of any network or computer policies.<br>SOURCE: SP 800-61 |
| Incident – | A violation or imminent threat of violation of computer security policies, acceptable use policies, or standard security practices.<br>SOURCE: SP 800-61 |
| Incident – | An occurrence that actually or potentially jeopardizes the confidentiality, integrity, or availability of an information system or the information the system processes, stores, or transmits or that constitutes a violation or imminent threat of violation of security policies, security procedures, or acceptable use policies.<br>SOURCE: FIPS 200; SP 800-53<br>An assessed occurrence that actually or potentially jeopardizes the confidentiality, integrity, or availability of an information system; orthe information the system processes, stores, or transmits; or that constitutes a violation or imminent threat of violation of security policies, security procedures, or acceptable use policies.<br>SOURCE: CNSSI-4009 |
| Incident Handling – | The mitigation of violations of security policies and recommended practices.<br>SOURCE: SP 800-61 |
| Incident Response Plan – | The documentation of a predetermined set of instructions or procedures to detect, respond to, and limit consequences of a malicious cyber attacks against an organization's information system(s).<br>SOURCE: SP 800-34<br>The documentation of a predetermined set of instructions or procedures to detect, respond to, and limit consequences of an incident against an organization's IT system(s).<br>SOURCE: CNSSI-4009 |
| Incomplete Parameter Checking – | System flaw that exists when the operating system does not check allparameters fully for accuracy and consistency, thus making the system vulnerable to penetration.<br>SOURCE: CNSSI-4009 |
| Inculpatory Evidence – | Evidence that tends to increase the likelihood of fault or guilt.<br>SOURCE: SP 800-72 |
| Independent Validation Authority – (IVA) | Entity that reviews the soundness of independent tests and system compliance with all stated security controls and risk mitigation actions. IVAs will be designated by the Authorizing Official as needed.<br>SOURCE: CNSSI-4009 |

| | |
|---|---|
| Independent Verification & Validation (IV&V) – | A comprehensive review, analysis, and testing (software and/or hardware) performed by an objective third party to confirm (i.e., verify) that the requirements are correctly defined, and to confirm (i.e., validate) that the system correctly implements the required functionality and security requirements.<br>SOURCE: CNSSI-4009 |
| Indication – | A sign that an incident may have occurred or may be currently occurring.<br>SOURCE: SP 800-61 |
| Indicator – | Recognized action, specific, generalized, or theoretical, that an adversary might be expected to take in preparation for an attack.<br>SOURCE: CNSSI-4009 |
| Individual – | A citizen of the United States or an alien lawfully admitted for permanent residence. Agencies may, consistent with individual practice, choose to extend the protections of the Privacy Act and E-Government Act to businesses, sole proprietors, aliens, etc.<br>SOURCE: SP 800-60 |
| Individual Accountability – | Ability to associate positively the identity of a user with the time, method, and degree of access to an information system.<br>SOURCE: CNSSI-4009 |
| Individuals – | An assessment object that includes people applying specifications, mechanisms, or activities.<br>SOURCE: SP 800-53A |
| Industrial Control System – | An information system used to control industrial processes such as manufacturing, product handling, production, and distribution. Industrial control systems include supervisory control and data acquisition systems (SCADA) used to control geographically dispersed assets, as well as distributed control systems (DCS) and smaller control systems using programmable logic controllers to control localized processes.<br>SOURCE: SP 800-53; SP 800-53A |
| Informal Security Policy – | Natural language description, possibly supplemented by mathematical arguments, demonstrating the correspondence of the functional specification to the high-level design.<br>SOURCE: CNSSI-4009 |
| Information – | An instance of an information type.<br>SOURCE: FIPS 200; FIPS 199; SP 800-60; SP 800-53; SP 800-37<br>Any communication or representation of knowledge such as facts, data, or opinions in any medium or form, including textual, numerical, graphic, cartographic, narrative, or audiovisual.<br>SOURCE: CNSSI-4009 |
| Information Assurance (IA) – | Measures that protect and defend information and information systems by ensuring their availability, integrity, authentication, confidentiality, and non-repudiation. These measures include |

| | |
|---|---|
| | providing for restoration of information systems by incorporating protection, detection, and reaction capabilities.<br>SOURCE: SP 800-59; CNSSI-4009 |
| Information Assurance Component – (IAC) | An application (hardware and/or software) that provides one or moreInformation Assurance capabilities in support of the overall security and operational objectives of a system.<br>SOURCE: CNSSI-4009 |
| Information Assurance Manager – (IAM) | See information systems security manager.<br>SOURCE: CNSSI-4009 |
| Information Assurance Officer – (IAO) | See information systems security officer.<br>SOURCE: CNSSI-4009 |
| Information Assurance (IA) Professional – | Individual who works IA issues and has real-world experience plus appropriate IA training and education commensurate with their level of IA responsibility.<br>SOURCE: CNSSI-4009 |
| Information Assurance Vulnerability Alert (IAVA) – | Notification that is generated when an Information Assurance vulnerability may result in an immediate and potentially severe threatto DoD systems and information; this alert requires corrective action because of the severity of the vulnerability risk.<br>SOURCE: CNSSI-4009 |
| Information Domain – | A three-part concept for information sharing, independent of, and across information systems and security domains that 1) identifies information sharing participants as individual members, 2) contains shared information objects, and 3) provides a security policy that identifies the roles and privileges of the members and the protections required for the information objects.<br>SOURCE: CNSSI-4009 |
| Information Environment – | Aggregate of individuals, organizations, and/or systems that collect, process, or disseminate information, also included is the information itself.<br>SOURCE: CNSSI-4009 |
| Information Flow Control – | Procedure to ensure that information transfers within an information system are not made in violation of the security policy.<br>SOURCE: CNSSI-4009 |
| Information Management – | The planning, budgeting, manipulating, and controlling of information throughout its life cycle.<br>SOURCE: CNSSI-4009 |
| Information Operations (IO) – | The integrated employment of the core capabilities of electronic warfare, computer network operations, psychological operations, military deception, and operations security, in concert with specified supporting and related capabilities, to influence, disrupt, corrupt, or usurp adversarial human and automated decision-making process, |

| | |
|---|---|
| | information, and information systems while protecting our own. SOURCE: CNSSI-4009 |
| Information Owner – | Official with statutory or operational authority for specified information and responsibility for establishing the controls for its generation, collection, processing, dissemination, and disposal. SOURCE: FIPS 200; SP 800-37; SP 800-53; SP 800-60; SP 800-18<br>Official with statutory or operational authority for specified information and responsibility for establishing the controls for its generation, classification, collection, processing, dissemination, and disposal. SOURCE: CNSSI-4009 |
| Information Resources – | Information and related resources, such as personnel, equipment, funds, and information technology. SOURCE: FIPS 200; FIPS 199; SP 800-53; SP 800-18; SP 800-60; 44 U.S.C., Sec. 3502; CNSSI-4009 |
| Information Resources Management (IRM) – | The planning, budgeting, organizing, directing, training, controlling, and management activities associated with the burden, collection, creation, use, and dissemination of information by agencies. SOURCE: CNSSI-4009 |
| Information Security – | The protection of information and information systems from unauthorized access, use, disclosure, disruption, modification, or destruction in order to provide confidentiality, integrity, and availability. SOURCE: SP 800-37; SP 800-53; SP 800-53A; SP 800-18; SP 800-60; CNSSI-4009; FIPS 200; FIPS 199; 44 U.S.C., Sec. 3542 |
| Information Security – | Protecting information and information systems from unauthorized access, use, disclosure, disruption, modification, or destruction in order to provide—<br>1)integrity, which means guarding against improper information modification or destruction, and includes ensuring information nonrepudiation and authenticity;<br>2)confidentiality, which means preserving authorized restrictions onaccess and disclosure, including means for protecting personal privacy and proprietary information; and<br>3)availability, which means ensuring timely and reliable access to and use of information.<br>SOURCE: SP 800-66; 44 U.S.C., Sec 3541 |
| Information Security Architect – | Individual, group, or organization responsible for ensuring that the information security requirements necessary to protect the organization's core missions and business processes are adequately addressed in all aspects of enterprise architecture including reference models, segment and solution architectures, and the resulting information systems supporting those missions and business processes. SOURCE: SP 800-37 |

| | |
|---|---|
| Information Security Policy – | Aggregate of directives, regulations, rules, and practices that prescribes how an organization manages, protects, and distributes information.<br>SOURCE: SP 800-53; SP 800-37; SP 800-18; CNSSI-4009 |
| Information Security Program Plan – | Formal document that provides an overview of the security requirements for an organization-wide information security program and describes the program management controls and common controls in place or planned for meeting those requirements.<br>SOURCE: SP 800-37; SP 800-53; SP 800-53A |
| Information Sharing – | The requirements for information sharing by an IT system with one or more other IT systems or applications, for information sharing to support multiple internal or external organizations, missions, or public programs.<br>SOURCE: SP 800-16 |
| Information Sharing Environment – | 1. An approach that facilitates the sharing of terrorism and homeland security information; or<br>2. ISE in its broader application enables those in a trusted partnershipto share, discover, and access controlled information.<br>SOURCE: CNSSI-4009 |
| Information Steward – | An agency official with statutory or operational authority for specified information and responsibility for establishing the controls for its generation, collection, processing, dissemination, and disposal.<br>SOURCE: CNSSI-4009<br>Individual or group that helps to ensure the careful and responsible management of federal information belonging to the Nation as a whole, regardless of the entity or source that may have originated, created, or compiled the information.<br>Information stewards provide maximum access to federal information to elements of the federal government and its customers, balanced by the obligation to protect the information in accordance with the provisions of FISMA and any associated security-related federal policies, directives, regulations, standards, and guidance.<br>SOURCE: SP 800-37 |
| nformation System – | A discrete set of information resources organized for the collection, processing, maintenance, use, sharing, dissemination, or disposition of information.<br>SOURCE: FIPS 200; FIPS 199; SP 800-53A; SP 800-37; SP 800-60; SP 800-18; 44 U.S.C., Sec. 3502; OMB Circular A-130, App. III<br>A discrete set of information resources organized for the collection, processing, maintenance, use, sharing, dissemination, or disposition of information.<br>[Note: Information systems also include specialized systems such as industrial/process controls systems, telephone switching and private |

| | |
|---|---|
| | branch exchange (PBX) systems, and environmental control systems.]<br>SOURCE: SP800-53;CNSSI-4009 |
| Information System Contingency Plan (ISCP) – | Management policy and procedures designed to maintain or restore business operations, including computer operations, possibly at an alternate location, in the event of emergencies, system failures, or disasters.<br>SOURCE: SP 800-34 |
| Information System Boundary – | See Authorization Boundary |
| Information System Life Cycle – | The phases through which an information system passes, typically characterized as initiation, development, operation, and termination (i.e., sanitization, disposal and/or destruction).<br>SOURCE: CNSSI-4009 |
| Information System Owner (or Program Manager) – | Official responsible for the overall procurement, development, integration, modification, or operation and maintenance of an information system.<br>SOURCE: SP 800-53; SP 800-53A; SP 800-18; SP 800-60 |
| Information System Owner – | Official responsible for the overall procurement, development, integration, modification, or operation and maintenance of an information system.<br>SOURCE: FIPS 200 |
| Information System Security Officer (ISSO) – | Individual with assigned responsibility for maintaining the appropriate operational security posture for an information system or program.<br>SOURCE: SP 800-37; SP 800-53<br>Individual assigned responsibility by the senior agency information security officer, authorizing official, management official, or information system owner for maintaining the appropriate operationalsecurity posture for an information system or program.<br>SOURCE: SP 800-53A; SP 800-60<br>Individual assigned responsibility by the senior agency information security officer, authorizing official, management official, or information system owner for ensuring that the appropriate operational security posture is maintained for an information system or program.<br>SOURCE: SP 800-18 |
| Information System-Related Security Risks – | Information system-related security risks are those risks that arise through the loss of confidentiality, integrity, or availability of information or information systems and consider impacts to the organization (including assets, mission, functions, image, or reputation), individuals, other organizations, and the Nation.<br>See *Risk*.<br>SOURCE: SP 800-37; SP 800-53A |

| | |
|---|---|
| Information Systems Security – (INFOSEC) | Protection of information systems against unauthorized access to or modification of information, whether in storage, processing, or transit, and against the denial of service to authorized users, includingthose measures necessary to detect, document, and counter such threats.<br>SOURCE: CNSSI-4009 |
| Information Systems Security Engineer (ISSE) – | Individual assigned responsibility for conducting information system security engineering activities.<br>SOURCE: SP800-37;CNSSI-4009 |
| Information Systems Security Engineering (ISSE) – | Process of capturing and refining information protection requirements to ensure their integration into information systems acquisition and information systems development through purposeful security design or configuration.<br>SOURCE: CNSSI-4009<br>Process that captures and refines information security requirements and ensures their integration into information technology component products and information systems through purposeful security design or configuration.<br>SOURCE: SP800-37 |
| Information Systems Security Equipment Modification – | Modification of any fielded hardware, firmware, software, or portion thereof, under NSA configuration control. There are three classes of modifications: mandatory (to include human safety); optional/specialmission modifications; and repair actions. These classes apply to elements, subassemblies, equipment, systems, and software packages performing functions such as key generation, key distribution, message encryption, decryption, authentication, or those mechanisms necessary to satisfy security policy, labeling, identification, or accountability.<br>SOURCE: CNSSI-4009 |
| Information Systems Security Manager (ISSM) – | Individual responsible for the information assurance of a program, organization, system, or enclave.<br>SOURCE: CNSSI-4009 |
| Information Systems Security Officer (ISSO) – | Individual assigned responsibility for maintaining the appropriate operational security posture for an information system or program.<br>SOURCE: CNSSI-4009 |
| Information Systems Security Product – | Item (chip, module, assembly, or equipment), technique, or service that performs or relates to information systems security.<br>SOURCE: CNSSI-4009 |
| Information Technology – | Any equipment or interconnected system or subsystem of equipment that is used in the automatic acquisition, storage, manipulation, management, movement, control, display, switching, interchange, transmission, or reception of data or information by the executive agency. For purposes of the preceding sentence, equipment is used byan executive agency if the equipment is used by the executive agency directly or is used by a contractor under a contract with the executive agency which— |

| | |
|---|---|
| | 1) requires the use of such equipment; or<br>2) requires the use, to a significant extent, of such equipment in the performance of a service or the furnishing of a product.<br>The term information technology includes computers, ancillary equipment, software, firmware and similar procedures, services (including support services), and related resources.<br>SOURCE: SP 800-53; SP 800-53A; SP 800-37; SP 800-18; SP 800-60; FIPS 200; FIPS 199; CNSSI-4009; 40 U.S.C., Sec. 11101 and Sec 1401 |
| Information Type – | A specific category of information (e.g., privacy, medical, proprietary, financial, investigative, contractor sensitive, security management), defined by an organization or in some instances, by a specific law, Executive Order, directive, policy, or regulation.<br>SOURCE: SP 800-53; SP 800-53A; SP 800-37; SP 800-18; SP 800-60; FIPS 200; FIPS 199; CNSSI-4009 |
| Information Value – | A qualitative measure of the importance of the information based upon factors such as: level of robustness of the Information Assurance controls allocated to the protection of information based upon: mission criticality, the sensitivity (e.g., classification and compartmentalization) of the information, releasability to other countries, perishability/longevity of the information (e.g., short life data versus long life intelligence source data), and potential impact ofloss of confidentiality and integrity and/or availability of the information.<br>SOURCE: CNSSI-4009 |
| Ingress Filtering – | The process of blocking incoming packets that use obviously false IP addresses, such as reserved source addresses.<br>SOURCE: SP 800-61 |
| Inheritance – | See Security Control Inheritance. |
| Initialization Vector (IV) – | A vector used in defining the starting point of an encryption process within a cryptographic algorithm.<br>SOURCE: FIPS 140-2 |
| Initialize – | Setting the state of a cryptographic logic prior to key generation, encryption, or other operating mode.<br>SOURCE: CNSSI-4009 |
| Initiator – | The entity that initiates an authentication exchange.<br>SOURCE: FIPS 196 |
| Inside Threat – | An entity with authorized access that has the potential to harm an information system through destruction, disclosure, modification of data, and/or denial of service.<br>SOURCE: SP 800-32 |
| Inside(r) Threat – | An entity with authorized access (i.e., within the security domain) that has the potential to harm an information system or enterprise through destruction, disclosure, modification of data, and/or denial ofservice.<br>SOURCE: CNSSI-4009 |

**Inspectable Space** – Three dimensional space surrounding equipment that processes classified and/or sensitive information within which TEMPEST exploitation is not considered practical or where legal authority to identify and remove a potential TEMPEST exploitation exists. Synonymous with zone of control.
SOURCE: CNSSI-4009

**Integrity** – Guarding against improper information modification or destruction, and includes ensuring information non-repudiation and authenticity.
SOURCE: SP 800-53; SP 800-53A; SP 800-18; SP 800-27; SP 800-37; SP 800-60; FIPS 200; FIPS 199; 44 U.S.C., Sec. 3542

**Integrity** – The property that sensitive data has not been modified or deleted in an unauthorized and undetected manner.
SOURCE: FIPS 140-2
The property whereby an entity has not been modified in an unauthorized manner.
SOURCE: CNSSI-4009

**Integrity Check Value** – Checksum capable of detecting modification of an information system.
SOURCE: CNSSI-4009

**Intellectual Property** – Useful artistic, technical, and/or industrial information, knowledge or ideas that convey ownership and control of tangible or virtual usage and/or representation.
SOURCE: SP 800-32
Creations of the mind such as musical, literary, and artistic works; inventions; and symbols, names, images, and designs used in commerce, including copyrights, trademarks, patents, and related rights. Under intellectual property law, the holder of one of these abstract "properties" has certain exclusive rights to the creative work,commercial symbol, or invention by which it is covered.
SOURCE: CNSSI-4009

**Interconnection Security Agreement (ISA)** – An agreement established between the organizations that own and operate connected IT systems to document the technical requirementsof the interconnection. The ISA also supports a Memorandum of Understanding or Agreement (MOU/A) between the organizations.
SOURCE: SP 800-47
A document that regulates security-relevant aspects of an intended connection between an agency and an external system. It regulates the security interface between any two systems operating under two different distinct authorities. It includes a variety of descriptive, technical, procedural, and planning information. It is usually preceded by a formal MOA/MOU that defines high-level roles and responsibilities in management of a cross-domain connection.
SOURCE: CNSSI-4009

| | |
|---|---|
| Interface – | Common boundary between independent systems or modules where interactions take place.<br>SOURCE: CNSSI-4009 |
| Interface Control Document – | Technical document describing interface controls and identifying the authorities and responsibilities for ensuring the operation of such controls. This document is baselined during the preliminary design review and is maintained throughout the information system life cycle.<br>SOURCE: CNSSI-4009 |
| Interim Approval to Operate – (IATO) | Temporary authorization granted by a DAA for an information system to process information based on preliminary results of a security evaluation of the system. (To be replaced by ATO and POA&M)<br>SOURCE: CNSSI-4009 |
| Interim Approval to Test (IATT) – | Temporary authorization to test an information system in a specified operational information environment within the time frame and under the conditions or constraints enumerated in the written authorization.<br>SOURCE: CNSSI-4009 |
| Intermediate Certification Authority (CA) – | A Certification Authority that is subordinate to another CA, and has a CA subordinate to itself.<br>SOURCE: SP 800-32 |
| Internal Network – | A network where: (i) the establishment, maintenance, and provisioning of security controls are under the direct control of organizational employees or contractors; or (ii) cryptographic encapsulation or similar security technology provides the same effect.An internal network is typically organization-owned, yet may be organization-controlled while not being organization-owned.<br>SOURCE: SP800-53<br>A network where 1) the establishment, maintenance, and provisioning of security controls are under the direct control of organizational employees or contractors; or 2) cryptographic encapsulation or similar security technology implemented between organization-controlled endpoints provides the same effect (at least with regard to confidentiality and integrity). An internal network is typically organization-owned, yet may be organization-controlled while not being organization-owned.<br>SOURCE: CNSSI-4009 |
| Internal Security Controls – | Hardware, firmware, or software features within an information system that restrict access to resources only to authorized subjects.<br>SOURCE: CNSSI-4009 |
| Internal Security Testing – | Security testing conducted from inside the organization's security perimeter.<br>SOURCE: SP 800-115 |
| Internet – | The Internet is the single, interconnected, worldwide system of commercial, governmental, educational, and other computer |

| | |
|---|---|
| | networks that share (a) the protocol suite specified by the Internet Architecture Board (IAB), and (b) the name and address spaces managed by the Internet Corporation for Assigned Names and Numbers (ICANN).<br>SOURCE: CNSSI-4009 |
| Internet Protocol (IP) – | Standard protocol for transmission of data from source to destinationsin packet-switched communications networks and interconnected systems of such networks.<br>SOURCE: CNSSI-4009 |
| Interoperability – | For the purposes of this standard, interoperability allows any government facility or information system, regardless of the PIV Issuer, to verify a cardholder's identity using the credentials on the PIV Card.<br>SOURCE: FIPS 201 |
| Interview – | A type of assessment method that is characterized by the process of conducting discussions with individuals or groups within an organization to facilitate understanding, achieve clarification, or lead to the location of evidence, the results of which are used to support the determination of security control effectiveness over time.<br>SOURCE: SP 800-53A |
| Intranet – | A private network that is employed within the confines of a given enterprise (e.g., internal to a business or agency).<br>SOURCE: CNSSI-4009 |
| Intrusion – | Unauthorized act of bypassing the security mechanisms of a system.<br>SOURCE: CNSSI-4009 |
| Intrusion Detection Systems (IDS) – | Hardware or software product that gathers and analyzes information from various areas within a computer or a network to identify possible security breaches, which include both intrusions (attacks from outside the organizations) and misuse (attacks from within the organizations.)<br>SOURCE: CNSSI-4009 |
| Intrusion Detection Systems (IDS) – (Host-Based) | IDSs which operate on information collected from within an individual computer system. This vantage point allows host-based IDSs to determine exactly which processes and user accounts are involved in a particular attack on the Operating System. Furthermore, unlike network-based IDSs, host-based IDSs can more readily "see" the intended outcome of an attempted attack, because they can directly access and monitor the data files and system processes usually targeted by attacks.<br>SOURCE: SP800-36;CNSSI-4009 |
| Intrusion Detection Systems (IDS) – (Network-Based) | IDSs which detect attacks by capturing and analyzing network packets. Listening on a network segment or switch, one network-based IDS can monitor the network traffic affecting multiple hosts that are connected to the network segment.<br>SOURCE: SP800-36;CNSSI-4009 |

| | |
|---|---|
| Intrusion Detection and Prevention System (IDPS) – | Software that automates the process of monitoring the events occurring in a computer system or network and analyzing them for signs of possible incidents and attempting to stop detected possible incidents.<br>SOURCE: SP 800-61 |
| Intrusion Prevention System(s) (IPS) – | System(s) which can detect an intrusive activity and can also attempt to stop the activity, ideally before it reaches its targets.<br>SOURCE: SP 800-36; CNSSI-4009 |
| Inverse Cipher – | Series of transformations that converts ciphertext to plaintext using the Cipher Key.<br>SOURCE: FIPS 197 |
| IP Security (IPsec) – | Suite of protocols for securing Internet Protocol (IP) communicationsat the network layer, layer 3 of the OSI model by authenticating and/or encrypting each IP packet in a data stream. IPsec also includes protocols for cryptographic key establishment.<br>SOURCE: CNSSI-4009 |
| IT-Related Risk – | The net mission/business impact considering<br>1)the likelihood that a particular threat source will exploit, or trigger, a particular information system vulnerability, and<br>2)the resulting impact if this should occur. IT-related risks arise from legal liability or mission/business loss due to, but not limitedto:<br>• Unauthorized (malicious, non-malicious, or accidental) disclosure, modification, or destruction of information;<br>• Non-malicious errors and omissions;<br>• IT disruptions due to natural or man-made disasters; or<br>• Failure to exercise due care and diligence in the implementation and operation of the IT.<br>SOURCE: SP 800-27 |
| IT Security Architecture – | A description of security principles and an overall approach for complying with the principles that drive the system design; i.e., guidelines on the placement and implementation of specific security services within various distributed computing environments.<br>SOURCE: SP 800-27 |
| IT Security Awareness – | The purpose of awareness presentations is simply to focus attention on security. Awareness presentations are intended to allow individuals to recognize IT security concerns and respond accordingly.<br>SOURCE: SP 800-50 |
| IT Security Awareness and Training Program – | Explains proper rules of behavior for the use of agency IT systems and information. The program communicates IT security policies andprocedures that need to be followed.<br>SOURCE: SP 800-50<br>Explains proper rules of behavior for the use of agency information systems and information. The program communicates IT security |

policies and procedures that need to be followed (i.e., NSTISSD 501, NIST SP 800-50).
SOURCE: CNSSI-4009

IT Security Education – IT Security Education seeks to integrate all of the security skills and competencies of the various functional specialties into a common body of knowledge, adds a multidisciplinary study of concepts, issues, and principles (technological and social), and strives to produce IT security specialists and professionals capable of vision and proactive response.
SOURCE: SP 800-50

IT Security Investment – An IT application or system that is solely devoted to security. For instance, intrusion detection systems (IDS) and public key infrastructure (PKI) are examples of IT security investments.
SOURCE: SP 800-65

IT Security Metrics – Metrics based on IT security performance goals and objectives.
SOURCE: SP 800-55

IT Security Policy – The "documentation of IT security decisions" in an organization. NIST SP 800-12 categorizes IT Security Policy into three basic types:
1) Program Policy—high-level policy used to create an organization's IT security program, define its scope within the organization, assign implementation responsibilities, establish strategic direction, and assign resources for implementation.
2) Issue-Specific Policies—address specific issues of concern to the organization, such as contingency planning, the use of a particularmethodology for systems risk management, and implementation of new regulations or law. These policies are likely to require more frequent revision as changes in technology and related factors take place.
3)System-Specific Policies—address individual systems, such as establishing an access control list or in training users as to what system actions are permitted. These policies may vary from system to system within the same organization. In addition, policymay refer to entirely different matters, such as the specific managerial decisions setting an organization's electronic mail (email) policy or fax security policy.
SOURCE: SP 800-35

IT Security Training – IT Security Training strives to produce relevant and needed security skills and competencies by practitioners of functional specialties other than IT security (e.g., management, systems design and development, acquisition, auditing). The most significant difference between training and awareness is that training seeks to teach skills, which allow a person to perform a specific function, while awareness seeks to focus an individual's attention on an issue or set of issues. The skills acquired during training are built upon the

wareness foundation, in particular, upon the security basics and literacy material.
SOURCE: SP 800-50

Jamming – An attack in which a device is used to emit electromagnetic energy on a wireless network's frequency to make it unusable.
SOURCE: SP 800-48
An attack that attempts to interfere with the reception of broadcast communications.
SOURCE: CNSSI-4009

Joint Authorization – Security authorization involving multiple authorizing officials.
SOURCE: SP 800-37

Kerberos – A widely used authentication protocol developed at the Massachusetts Institute of Technology (MIT). In "classic" Kerberos, users share a secret password with a Key Distribution Center (KDC). The user, Alice, who wishes to communicate with another user, Bob, authenticates to the KDC and is furnished a "ticket" by the KDC to use to authenticate with Bob. When Kerberos authentication is based on passwords, the protocol is known to be vulnerable to off-line dictionary attacks by eavesdroppers who capture the initial user-to-KDC exchange.
SOURCE: SP 800-63
A means of verifying the identities of principals on an open network. It accomplishes this without relying on the authentication, trustworthiness, or physical security of hosts while assuming all packets can be read, modified and inserted at will. It uses a trust broker model and symmetric cryptography to provide authentication and authorization of users and systems on the network.
SOURCE: SP 800-95

Key – A value used to control cryptographic operations, such as decryption,encryption, signature generation, or signature verification.
SOURCE: SP 800-63
A numerical value used to control cryptographic operations, such as decryption, encryption, signature generation, or signature verification.
SOURCE: CNSSI-4009
A parameter used in conjunction with a cryptographic algorithm that determines its operation.
Examples applicable to this Standard include:
1. The computation of a digital signature from data, and
2. The verification of a digital signature.
SOURCE: FIPS 186

Key Bundle – The three cryptographic keys (Key1, Key2, Key3) that are used with a Triple Data Encryption Algorithm mode.
SOURCE: SP 800-67

| | |
|---|---|
| Key Distribution Center (KDC) – | COMSEC facility generating and distributing key in electronic form.<br>SOURCE: CNSSI-4009 |
| Key Escrow – | A deposit of the private key of a subscriber and other pertinent information pursuant to an escrow agreement or similar contract binding upon the subscriber, the terms of which require one or more agents to hold the subscriber's private key for the benefit of the subscriber, an employer, or other party, upon provisions set forth in the agreement.<br>SOURCE: SP 800-32 |
| Key Escrow – | The processes of managing (e.g., generating, storing, transferring, auditing) the two components of a cryptographic key by two key component holders.<br>SOURCE: FIPS 185<br>1. The processes of managing (e.g., generating, storing, transferring, auditing) the two components of a cryptographic key by two key component holders.<br>2. A key recovery technique for storing knowledge of a cryptographickey, or parts thereof, in the custody of one or more third parties called "escrow agents," so that the key can be recovered and used in specified circumstances.<br>SOURCE: CNSSI-4009 |
| Key Escrow System – | A system that entrusts the two components comprising a cryptographic key (e.g., a device unique key) to two key component holders (also called "escrow agents").<br>SOURCE: FIPS 185; CNSSI-4009 |
| Key Establishment – | The process by which cryptographic keys are securely established among cryptographic modules using manual transport methods (e.g., key loaders), automated methods (e.g., key transport and/or key agreement protocols), or a combination of automated and manual methods (consists of key transport plus key agreement).<br>SOURCE: FIPS 140-2<br>The process by which cryptographic keys are securely established among cryptographic modules using key transport and/or key agreement procedures. See key distribution.<br>SOURCE: CNSSI-4009 |
| Key Exchange – | The process of exchanging public keys in order to establish secure communications.<br>SOURCE: SP 800-32<br>Process of exchanging public keys (and other information) in order toestablish secure communications.<br>SOURCE: CNSSI-4009 |
| Key Expansion – | Routine used to generate a series of Round Keys from the Cipher Key.<br>SOURCE: FIPS 197 |

| | |
|---|---|
| Key Generation Material – | Random numbers, pseudo-random numbers, and cryptographic parameters used in generating cryptographic keys.<br>SOURCE: SP 800-32; CNSSI-4009 |
| Key List – | Printed series of key settings for a specific cryptonet. Key lists may be produced in list, pad, or printed tape format.<br>SOURCE: CNSSI-4009 |
| Key Loader – | A self-contained unit that is capable of storing at least one plaintext or encrypted cryptographic key or key component that can be transferred, upon request, into a cryptographic module.<br>SOURCE: FIPS 140-2<br>A self-contained unit that is capable of storing at least one plaintext or encrypted cryptographic key or a component of a key that can be transferred, upon request, into a cryptographic module.<br>SOURCE: CNSSI-4009 |
| Key Logger – | A program designed to record which keys are pressed on a computer keyboard used to obtain passwords or encryption keys and thus bypass other security measures.<br>SOURCE: SP 800-82 |
| Key Management – | The activities involving the handling of cryptographic keys and other related security parameters (e.g., IVs and passwords) during the entire life cycle of the keys, including their generation, storage, establishment, entry and output, and zeroization.<br>SOURCE: FIPS 140-2; CNSSI-4009 |
| Key Management Device – | A unit that provides for secure electronic distribution of encryption keys to authorized users.<br>SOURCE: CNSSI-4009 |
| Key Management Infrastructure – (KMI) | All parts – computer hardware, firmware, software, and other equipment and its documentation; facilities that house the equipment and related functions; and companion standards, policies, procedures,and doctrine that form the system that manages and supports the ordering and delivery of cryptographic material and related information products and services to users.<br>SOURCE: CNSSI-4009 |
| Key Pair – | Two mathematically related keys having the properties that (1) one key can be used to encrypt a message that can only be decrypted using the other key, and 2) even knowing one key, it is computationally infeasible to discover the other key.<br>SOURCE: SP 800-32 |
| Key Pair – | A public key and its corresponding private key; a key pair is used with a public key algorithm.<br>SOURCE: SP 800-21; CNSSI-4009 |
| Key Production Key (KPK) – | Key used to initialize a keystream generator for the production of other electronically generated key.<br>SOURCE: CNSSI-4009 |

| | |
|---|---|
| Key Recovery – | Mechanisms and processes that allow authorized parties to retrieve the cryptographic key used for data confidentiality.<br>SOURCE: CNSSI-4009 |
| Key Stream – | Sequence of symbols (or their electrical or mechanical equivalents) produced in a machine or auto-manual cryptosystem to combine with plain text to produce cipher text, control transmission security processes, or produce key.<br>SOURCE: CNSSI-4009 |
| Key Tag – | Identification information associated with certain types of electronic key.<br>SOURCE: CNSSI-4009 |
| Key Tape – | Punched or magnetic tape containing key. Printed key in tape form is referred to as a key list.<br>SOURCE: CNSSI-4009 |
| Key Transport – | The secure transport of cryptographic keys from one cryptographic module to another module.<br>SOURCE: FIPS 140-2; CNSSI-4009 |
| Key Updating – | Irreversible cryptographic process for modifying key.<br>SOURCE: CNSSI-4009 |
| Key Wrap – | A method of encrypting keying material (along with associated integrity information) that provides both confidentiality and integrityprotection using a symmetric key algorithm.<br>SOURCE: SP 800-56A |
| Key-Auto-Key (KAK) – | Cryptographic logic using previous key to produce key.<br>SOURCE: CNSSI-4009 |
| Key-Encryption-Key (KEK) – | Key that encrypts or decrypts other key for transmission or storage.<br>SOURCE: CNSSI-4009 |
| Keyed-hash based message authentication code (HMAC) – | A message authentication code that uses a cryptographic key in conjunction with a hash function.<br>SOURCE: FIPS 198; CNSSI-4009 |
| Keying Material – | Key, code, or authentication information in physical, electronic, or magnetic form.<br>SOURCE: CNSSI-4009 |
| Keystroke Monitoring – | The process used to view or record both the keystrokes entered by a computer user and the computer's response during an interactive session. Keystroke monitoring is usually considered a special case ofaudit trails.<br>SOURCE: SP 800-12; CNSSI-4009 |
| KMI Operating Account (KOA) – | A KMI business relationship that is established 1) to manage the set of user devices that are under the control of a specific KMI customerorganization, and 2) to control the distribution of KMI products to those devices.<br>SOURCE: CNSSI-4009 |

KMI Protected Channel (KPC) – A KMI Communication Channel that provides 1) Information Integrity Service; 2) either Data Origin Authentication Service or Peer Entity Authentication Service, as is appropriate to the mode of communications; and 3) optionally, Information Confidentiality Service.
SOURCE: CNSSI-4009

KMI-Aware Device – A user device that has a user identity for which the registration has significance across the entire KMI (i.e., the identity's registration data is maintained in a database at the PRSN level of the system, rather than only at an MGC) and for which a product can be generated and wrapped by a PSN for distribution to the specific device.
SOURCE: CNSSI-4009

KOA Agent – A user identity that is designated by a KOA manager to access PRSNproduct delivery enclaves for the purpose of retrieving wrapped products that have been ordered for user devices that are assigned to that KOA.
SOURCE: CNSSI-4009

KOA Manager – The Management Role that is responsible for the operation of one or KOA's (i.e., manages distribution of KMI products to the end cryptographic units, fill devices, and ADPs that are assigned to the manager's KOA).
SOURCE: CNSSI-4009

KOA Registration Manager – The individual responsible for performing activities related to registering KOAs.
SOURCE: CNSSI-4009

Label – See Security Label.

Labeled Security Protections – Access control protection features of a system that use security labelsto make access control decisions.
SOURCE: CNSSI-4009

Laboratory Attack – Use of sophisticated signal recovery equipment in a laboratory environment to recover information from data storage media.
SOURCE: SP800-88;CNSSI-4009

Least Privilege – The security objective of granting users only those accesses they need to perform their official duties.
SOURCE: SP 800-12
The principle that a security architecture should be designed so that each entity is granted the minimum system resources and authorizations that the entity needs to perform its function.
SOURCE: CNSSI-4009

Least Trust – The principal that a security architecture should be designed in a way that minimizes 1) the number of components that require trust, and 2) the extent to which each component is trusted.
SOURCE: CNSSI-4009

Level of Concern – Rating assigned to an information system indicating the extent to which protection measures, techniques, and procedures must be

applied. High, Medium, and Basic are identified levels of concern. A separate Level-of-Concern is assigned to each information system for confidentiality, integrity, and availability.
SOURCE: CNSSI-4009

**Level of Protection** – Extent to which protective measures, techniques, and procedures must be applied to information systems and networks based on risk, threat, vulnerability, system interconnectivity considerations, and information assurance needs. Levels of protection are: 1. Basic: information systems and networks requiring implementation of standard minimum security countermeasures. 2. Medium: information systems and networks requiring layering of additional safeguards above the standard minimum security countermeasures. 3. High: information systems and networks requiring the most stringent protection and rigorous security countermeasures.
SOURCE: CNSSI-4009

**Likelihood of Occurrence** – In Information Assurance risk analysis, a weighted factor based on a subjective analysis of the probability that a given threat is capable of exploiting a given vulnerability.
SOURCE: CNSSI-4009

**Limited Maintenance** – COMSEC maintenance restricted to fault isolation, removal, and replacement of plug-in assemblies. Soldering or unsoldering usually is prohibited in limited maintenance. See full maintenance.
SOURCE: CNSSI-4009

**Line Conditioning** – Elimination of unintentional signals or noise induced or conducted ona telecommunications or information system signal, power, control, indicator, or other external interface line.
SOURCE: CNSSI-4009

**Line Conduction** – Unintentional signals or noise induced or conducted on a telecommunications or information system signal, power, control, indicator, or other external interface line.
SOURCE: CNSSI-4009

**Line of Business** – The following OMB-defined process areas common to virtually all federal agencies: Case Management, Financial Management, Grants Management, Human Resources Management, Federal Health Architecture, Information Systems Security, Budget Formulation and Execution, Geospatial, and IT Infrastructure.
SOURCE: SP 800-53

"Lines of business" or "areas of operation" describe the purpose of government in functional terms or describe the support functions that the government must conduct in order to effectively deliver services to citizens. *Lines of business* relating to the purpose of government and the mechanisms the government uses to achieve its purposes tendto be mission-based. *Lines of business* relating to support functions and resource management functions that are necessary to conduct government operations tend to be common to most agencies. The recommended information types provided in

NIST SP 800-60 are established from the "business areas" and "lines of business" from OMB's Business Reference Model (BRM) section of *Federal Enterprise Architecture (FEA) Consolidated Reference Model Document Version 2.3*
SOURCE: SP 800-60

Link Encryption – Link encryption encrypts all of the data along a communications path (e.g., a satellite link, telephone circuit, or T1 line). Since link encryption also encrypts routing data, communications nodes need to decrypt the data to continue routing.
SOURCE: SP 800-12
Encryption of information between nodes of a communications system.
SOURCE: CNSSI-4009

List-Oriented – Information system protection in which each protected object has a list of all subjects authorized to access it.
SOURCE: CNSSI-4009

Local Access – Access to an organizational information system by a user (or process acting on behalf of a user) communicating through a direct connection without the use of a network.
SOURCE: SP 800-53; CNSSI-4009

Local Authority – Organization responsible for generating and signing user certificates in a PKI-enabled environment.
SOURCE: CNSSI-4009

Local Management Device/Key Processor (LMD/KP) – EKMS platform providing automated management of COMSEC material and generating key for designated users.
SOURCE: CNSSI-4009

Local Registration Authority – (LRA) A Registration Authority with responsibility for a local community.
SOURCE: SP 800-32
A Registration Authority with responsibility for a local community ina PKI-enabled environment.
SOURCE: CNSSI-4009

Logic Bomb – A piece of code intentionally inserted into a software system that will set off a malicious function when specified conditions are met.
SOURCE: CNSSI-4009

Logical Completeness Measure – Means for assessing the effectiveness and degree to which a set of security and access control mechanisms meets security specifications.
SOURCE: CNSSI-4009

Logical Perimeter – A conceptual perimeter that extends to all intended users of the system, both directly and indirectly connected, who receive output from the system without a reliable human review by an appropriate authority. The location of such a review is commonly referred to as an "air gap."
SOURCE: CNSSI-4009

| | |
|---|---|
| Long Title – | Descriptive title of a COMSEC item.<br>SOURCE: CNSSI-4009 |
| Low Impact – | The loss of confidentiality, integrity, or availability that could be expected to have a limited adverse effect on organizational operations, organizational assets, individuals, other organizations, or the national security interests of the United States; (i.e., 1) causes a degradation in mission capability to an extent and duration that the organization is able to perform its primary functions, but the effectiveness of the functions is noticeably reduced; 2) results in minor damage to organizational assets; 3) results in minor financial loss; or 4) results in minor harm to individuals).<br>SOURCE: CNSSI-4009 |
| Low-Impact System – | An information system in which all three security objectives (i.e., confidentiality, integrity, and availability) are assigned a FIPS 199 potential impact value of low.<br>SOURCE: SP 800-37; SP 800-53; SP 800-60; FIPS 200<br>An information system in which all three security properties (i.e., confidentiality, integrity, and availability) are assigned a potential impact value of low.<br>SOURCE: CNSSI-4009 |
| Low Probability of Detection – | Result of measures used to hide or disguise intentional electromagnetic transmissions.<br>SOURCE: CNSSI-4009 |
| Low Probability of Intercept – | Result of measures to prevent the intercept of intentional electromagnetic transmissions. The objective is to minimize an adversary's capability of receiving, processing, or replaying an electronic signal.<br>SOURCE: CNSSI-4009 |
| Macro Virus – | A virus that attaches itself to documents and uses the macro programming capabilities of the document's application to execute and propagate.<br>SOURCE: SP 800-61; CNSSI-4009 |
| Magnetic Remanence – | Magnetic representation of residual information remaining on a magnetic medium after the medium has been cleared. See clearing.<br>SOURCE: CNSSI-4009 |
| Maintenance Hook – | Special instructions (trapdoors) in software allowing easy maintenance and additional feature development. Since maintenance hooks frequently allow entry into the code without the usual checks, they are a serious security risk if they are not removed prior to live implementation.<br>SOURCE: CNSSI-4009 |
| Maintenance Key – | Key intended only for in-shop use.<br>SOURCE: CNSSI-4009 |
| Major Application – | An application that requires special attention to security due to the risk and magnitude of harm resulting from the loss, misuse, or unauthorized access to or modification of the information in the |

application. Note: All federal applications require some level of protection. Certain applications, because of the information in them, however, require special management oversight and should be treatedas major. Adequate security for other applications should be provided by security of the systems in which they operate.
SOURCE: OMB Circular A-130, App. III

Major Information System – An information system that requires special management attention because of its importance to an agency mission; its high development, operating, or maintenance costs; or its significant role in the administration of agency programs, finances, property, or otherresources.
SOURCE: OMB Circular A-130, App. III

Malicious Applets – Small application programs that are automatically downloaded and executed and that perform an unauthorized function on an information system.
SOURCE: CNSSI-4009

Malicious Code – Software or firmware intended to perform an unauthorized process that will have adverse impact on the confidentiality, integrity, or availability of an information system. A virus, worm, Trojan horse, or other code-based entity that infects a host. Spyware and some forms of adware are also examples of malicious code.
SOURCE: SP 800-53; CNSSI-4009
A virus, worm, Trojan horse, or other code-based malicious entity that successfully infects a host.
SOURCE: SP 800-61

Malicious Logic – Hardware, firmware, or software that is intentionally included or inserted in a system for a harmful purpose.
SOURCE: CNSSI-4009

Malware – A program that is inserted into a system, usually covertly, with the intent of compromising the confidentiality, integrity, or availability of the victim's data, applications, or operating system or of otherwiseannoying or disrupting the victim.
SOURCE: SP 800-83
See malicious code. See also malicious applets and malicious logic.
SOURCE: SP800-53;CNSSI-4009

Man-in-the-middle Attack – (MitM) An attack on the authentication protocol run in which the attacker positions himself in between the claimant and verifier so that he can intercept and alter data traveling between them.
SOURCE: SP 800-63
A form of active wiretapping attack in which the attacker intercepts and selectively modifies communicated data to masquerade as one or more of the entities involved in a communication association.
SOURCE: CNSSI-4009

Management Client (MGC) – A configuration of a client node that enables a KMI external operational manager to manage KMI products and services by either 1) accessing a PRSN, or 2) exercising locally provided capabilities.

| | |
|---|---|
| | An MGC consists of a client platform and an advanced key processor(AKP).<br>SOURCE: CNSSI-4009 |
| Management Controls – | The security controls (i.e., safeguards or countermeasures) for an information system that focus on the management of risk and the management of information system security.<br>SOURCE: SP 800-37; SP 800-53; SP 800-53A; FIPS 200<br>Actions taken to manage the development, maintenance, and use of the system, including system-specific policies, procedures and rules of behavior, individual roles and responsibilities, individual accountability, and personnel security decisions.<br>SOURCE: CNSSI-4009 |
| Management Security Controls – | The security controls (i.e., safeguards or countermeasures) for an information system that focus on the management of risk and the management of information systems security.<br>SOURCE: CNSSI-4009 |
| Mandatory Access Control (MAC) – | A means of restricting access to system resources based on the sensitivity (as represented by a label) of the information contained in the system resource and the formal authorization (i.e., clearance) of users to access information of such sensitivity.<br>SOURCE: SP 800-44 |
| Mandatory Access Control – | Access controls (which) are driven by the results of a comparison between the user's trust level or clearance and the sensitivity designation of the information.<br>SOURCE: FIPS 191<br>A means of restricting access to objects based on the sensitivity (as represented by a security label) of the information contained in the objects and the formal authorization (i.e., clearance, formal access approvals, and need-to-know) of subjects to access information of such sensitivity.<br>SOURCE: CNSSI-4009 |
| Mandatory Modification – | Change to a COMSEC end-item that NSA requires to be completed and reported by a specified date. See optional modification.<br>SOURCE: CNSSI-4009 |
| Manipulative Communications Deception – | Alteration or simulation of friendly telecommunications for the purpose of deception. See communications deception and imitative communications deception.<br>SOURCE: CNSSI-4009 |
| Manual Cryptosystem – | Cryptosystem in which the cryptographic processes are performed without the use of crypto-equipment or auto-manual devices.<br>SOURCE: CNSSI-4009 |
| Manual Key Transport – | A nonelectronic means of transporting cryptographic keys by physically moving a device, document, or person containing or possessing the key or a key component.<br>SOURCE: SP 800-57 |

| | |
|---|---|
| Manual Key Transport – | A nonelectronic means of transporting cryptographic keys.<br>SOURCE: FIPS 140-2 |
| Manual Remote Rekeying – | Procedure by which a distant crypto-equipment is rekeyed electronically, with specific actions required by the receiving terminal operator. Synonymous with cooperative remote rekeying. See also automatic remote keying.<br>SOURCE: CNSSI-4009 |
| Marking – | See Security Marking. |
| Masquerading – | When an unauthorized agent claims the identity of another agent, it issaid to be masquerading.<br>SOURCE: SP 800-19<br>A type of threat action whereby an unauthorized entity gains access to a system or performs a malicious act by illegitimately posing as an authorized entity.<br>SOURCE: CNSSI-4009 |
| Master Cryptographic Ignition Key – | Key device with electronic logic and circuits providing the capability for adding more operational CIKs to a keyset.<br>SOURCE: CNSSI-4009 |
| Match/matching – | The process of comparing biometric information against a previously stored template(s) and scoring the level of similarity.<br>SOURCE: FIPS 201; CNSSI-4009 |
| Maximum Tolerable Downtime – | The amount of time mission/business processes can be disrupted without causing significant harm to the organization's mission.<br>SOURCE: SP 800-34 |
| Mechanisms – | An assessment object that includes specific protection-related items (e.g., hardware, software, or firmware) employed within or at the boundary of an information system.<br>SOURCE: SP 800-53A |
| Media – | Physical devices or writing surfaces including but not limited to magnetic tapes, optical disks, magnetic disks, Large Scale Integration(LSI) memory chips, and printouts (but not including display media) onto which information is recorded, stored, or printed within an information system.<br>SOURCE: FIPS 200; SP 800-53; CNSSI-4009 |
| Media Sanitization – | A general term referring to the actions taken to render data written onmedia unrecoverable by both ordinary and extraordinary means.<br>SOURCE: SP 800-88<br>The actions taken to render data written on media unrecoverable by both ordinary and extraordinary means.<br>SOURCE: CNSSI-4009 |
| Memorandum of Understanding/Agreement – (MOU/A) | A document established between two or more parties to define their respective responsibilities in accomplishing a particular goal or mission. In this guide, an MOU/A defines the responsibilities of two or more organizations in establishing, operating, and securing a system interconnection.<br>SOURCE: SP 800-47 |

A document established between two or more parties to define their respective responsibilities in accomplishing a particular goal or mission, e.g., establishing, operating, and securing a system interconnection.
SOURCE: CNSSI-4009

Memory Scavenging – The collection of residual information from data storage.
SOURCE: CNSSI-4009

Message Authentication Code – (MAC) A cryptographic checksum on data that uses a symmetric key to detect both accidental and intentional modifications of the data.
SOURCE: SP 800-63; FIPS 201

A cryptographic checksum that results from passing data through a message authentication algorithm.
SOURCE: FIPS 198

1. See Checksum.
2. A specific ANSI standard for a checksum.
SOURCE: CNSSI-4009

Message Digest – A cryptographic checksum, typically generated for a file that can be used to detect changes to the file; Secure Hash Algorithm-1 (SHA-1) is an example of a message digest algorithm.
SOURCE: SP 800-61

The result of applying a cryptographic hash function to a message.
SOURCE: SP 800-107

A digital signature that uniquely identifies data and has the property that changing a single bit in the data will cause a completely differentmessage digest to be generated.
SOURCE: SP 800-92

A cryptographic checksum, typically generated for a file that can be used to detect changes to the file. Synonymous with hash value/result.
SOURCE: CNSSI-4009

Message Externals – Information outside of the message text, such as the header, trailer, etc.
SOURCE: CNSSI-4009

Message Indicator – Sequence of bits transmitted over a communications system for synchronizing cryptographic equipment.
SOURCE: CNSSI-4009

Metrics – Tools designed to facilitate decisionmaking and improve performance and accountability through collection, analysis, and reporting of relevant performance-related data.
SOURCE: SP 800-55

MIME – See Multipurpose Internet Mail Extensions.

Mimicking – See Spoofing.

Min-Entropy – A measure of the difficulty that an attacker has to guess the most commonly chosen password used in a system.
SOURCE: SP 800-63

| | |
|---|---|
| Minimalist Cryptography – | Cryptography that can be implemented on devices with very limited memory and computing capabilities, such as RFID tags.<br>SOURCE: SP 800-98 |
| Minor Application – | An application, other than a major application, that requires attention to security due to the risk and magnitude of harm resulting from the loss, misuse, or unauthorized access to or modification of the information in the application. Minor applications are typically included as part of a general support system.<br>SOURCE: SP 800-18 |
| Misnamed Files – | A technique used to disguise a file's content by changing the file's name to something innocuous or altering its extension to a different type of file, forcing the examiner to identify the files by file signatureversus file extension.<br>SOURCE: SP 800-72; CNSSI-4009 |
| Mission Assurance Category – (MAC) | A Department of Defense Information Assurance Certification and Accreditation Process (DIACAP) term primarily used to determine the requirements for availability and integrity.<br>SOURCE: CNSSI-4009 |
| Mission Critical – | Any telecommunications or information system that is defined as a national security system (Federal Information Security Management Act of 2002 - FISMA) or processes any information the loss, misuse, disclosure, or unauthorized access to or modification of, would have a debilitating impact on the mission of an agency.<br>SOURCE: SP 800-60 |
| Mobile Code – | Software programs or parts of programs obtained from remote information systems, transmitted across a network, and executed on alocal information system without explicit installation or execution by the recipient.<br>SOURCE: SP 800-53; SP 800-18<br>A program (e.g., script, macro, or other portable instruction) that can be shipped unchanged to a heterogeneous collection of platforms and executed with identical semantics.<br>SOURCE: SP 800-28<br>Software programs or parts of programs obtained from remote information systems, transmitted across a network, and executed on alocal information system without explicit installation or execution by the recipient.<br>Note: Some examples of software technologies that provide the mechanisms for the production and use of mobile code include Java, JavaScript, ActiveX, VBScript, etc.<br>SOURCE: CNSSI-4009 |
| Mobile Code Technologies – | Software technologies that provide the mechanisms for the production and use of mobile code (e.g., Java, JavaScript, ActiveX, VBScript).<br>SOURCE: SP 800-53; SP 800-18 |

Mobile Device – Portable cartridge/disk-based, removable storage media (e.g., floppy disks, compact disks, USB flash drives, external hard drives, and other flash memory cards/drives that contain nonvolatile memory).
Portable computing and communications device with information storage capability (e.g., notebook/laptop computers, personal digital assistants, cellular telephones, digital cameras, and audio recording devices).
SOURCE: SP 800-53

Mobile Software Agent – Programs that are goal-directed and capable of suspending their execution on one platform and moving to another platform where they resume execution.
SOURCE: SP 800-19

Mode of Operation – An algorithm for the cryptographic transformation of data that features a symmetric key block cipher algorithm.
SOURCE: SP 800-38C
Description of the conditions under which an information system operates based on the sensitivity of information processed and the clearance levels, formal access approvals, and need-to-know of its users. Four modes of operation are authorized for processing or transmitting information: dedicated mode, system high mode, compartmented/partitioned mode, and multilevel mode.
SOURCE: CNSSI-4009

Moderate Impact – The loss of confidentiality, integrity, or availability that could be expected to have a serious adverse effect on organizational operations, organizational assets, individuals, other organizations, or the national security interests of the United States; (i.e., 1) causes a significant degradation in mission capability to an extent and durationthat the organization is able to perform its primary functions, but the effectiveness of the functions is significantly reduced; 2) results in significant damage to organizational assets; 3) results in significant financial loss; or 4) results in significant harm to individuals that doesnot involve loss of life or serious life threatening injuries).
SOURCE: CNSSI-4009

Moderate-Impact System – An information system in which at least one security objective (i.e., confidentiality, integrity, or availability) is assigned a FIPS 199 potential impact value of moderate and no security objective is assigned a FIPS 199 potential impact value of high.
SOURCE: SP 800-53; SP 800-60; SP 800-37; FIPS 200
An information system in which at least one security objective (i.e., confidentiality, integrity, or availability) is assigned a potential impact value of moderate and no security objective is assigned a potential impact value of high.
SOURCE: CNSSI-4009

| | |
|---|---|
| Multi-Hop Problem – | The security risks resulting from a mobile software agent visiting several platforms.<br>SOURCE: SP 800-19 |
| Multi-Releasable – | A characteristic of an information domain where access control mechanisms enforce policy-based release of information to authorized users within the information domain.<br>SOURCE: CNSSI-4009 |
| Multifactor Authentication – | Authentication using two or more factors to achieve authentication. Factors include: (i) something you know (e.g. password/PIN); (ii) something you have (e.g., cryptographic identification device, token); or (iii) something you are (e.g., biometric). See Authenticator.<br>SOURCE: SP 800-53 |
| Multilevel Device – | Equipment trusted to properly maintain and separate data of different security domains.<br>SOURCE: CNSSI-4009 |
| Multilevel Mode – | Mode of operation wherein all the following statements are satisfied concerning the users who have direct or indirect access to the system,its peripherals, remote terminals, or remote hosts: 1) some users do not have a valid security clearance for all the information processed in the information system; 2) all users have the proper security clearance and appropriate formal access approval for that informationto which they have access; and 3) all users have a valid need-to-knowonly for information to which they have access.<br>SOURCE: CNSSI-4009 |
| Multilevel Security (MLS) – | Concept of processing information with different classifications and categories that simultaneously permits access by users with different security clearances and denies access to users who lack authorization.<br>SOURCE: CNSSI-4009 |
| Multiple Component Incident – | A single incident that encompasses two or more incidents.<br>SOURCE: SP 800-61 |
| Multiple Security Levels (MSL) – | Capability of an information system that is trusted to contain, and maintain separation between, resources (particularly stored data) of different security domains.<br>SOURCE: CNSSI-4009 |
| Mutual Authentication – | Occurs when parties at both ends of a communication activity authenticate each other.<br>SOURCE: SP 800-32 |
| | The process of both entities involved in a transaction verifying each other.<br>SOURCE: CNSSI-4009 |

| | |
|---|---|
| Mutual Suspicion – | Condition in which two information systems need to rely upon each other to perform a service, yet neither trusts the other to properly protect shared data.<br>SOURCE: CNSSI-4009 |
| Naming Authority – | An organizational entity responsible for assigning distinguished names (DNs) and for assuring that each DN is meaningful and uniquewithin its domain.<br>SOURCE: SP 800-32 |
| National Information Assurance Partnership (NIAP) – | A U.S. government initiative established to promote the use of evaluated information systems products and champion the development and use of national and international standards for information technology security. NIAP was originally established as a collaboration between the National Institute of Standards and Technology (NIST) and the National Security Agency (NSA) in fulfilling their respective responsibilities under P.L. 100-235 (Computer Security Act of 1987). NIST officially withdrew from thepartnership in 2007 but NSA continues to manage and operate the program. The key operational component of NIAP is the Common Criteria Evaluation and Validation Scheme (CCEVS) which is the only U.S. government-sponsored and endorsed program for conducting internationally recognized security evaluations of commercial off-the-shelf (COTS) Information Assurance (IA) and IA-enabled information technology products. NIAP employs the CCEVS to provide government oversight or “validation” to U.S. CC evaluations to ensure correct conformance to the International Common Criteria for IT Security Evaluation (ISO/IEC 15408).<br>SOURCE: CNSSI-4009 |
| National Information Infrastructure – | Nationwide interconnection of communications networks, computers,databases, and consumer electronics that make vast amounts of information available to users. It includes both public and private networks, the Internet, the public switched network, and cable, wireless, and satellite communications.<br>SOURCE: CNSSI-4009 |
| National Security Emergency Preparedness Telecommuni-cations Services – | Telecommunications services that are used to maintain a state of readiness or to respond to and manage any event or crisis (local, national, or international) that causes or could cause injury or harm tothe population, damage to or loss of property, or degrade or threaten the national security or emergency preparedness posture of the United States.<br>SOURCE: SP 800-53; CNSSI-4009; 47 C.F.R., Part 64, App A |
| National Security Information – | Information that has been determined pursuant to Executive Order 12958 as amended by Executive Order 13292, or any predecessor order, or by the Atomic Energy Act of 1954, as amended, to require |

protection against unauthorized disclosure and is marked to indicate its classified status.
SOURCE: SP 800-53A; SP 800-60; FIPS 200

National Security Information (NSI) – See classified national security information.
SOURCE: CNSSI-4009

National Security System – Any information system (including any telecommunications system) used or operated by an agency or by a contractor of an agency, or other organization on behalf of an agency—(i) the function, operation, or use of which involves intelligence activities; involves cryptologic activities related to national security; involves command and control of military forces; involves equipment that is an integral part of a weapon or weapons system; or is critical to the direct fulfillment of military or intelligence missions (excluding a system that is to be used for routing administrative and business applications,for example, payroll, finance, logistics, and personnel management applications); or (ii) is protected at all times by procedures established for information that have been specifically authorized under criteria established by an Executive Order or an Act of Congress to be kept classified in the interest of national defense or foreign policy. [44 U.S.C., SEC. 3542]
SOURCE: FIPS 200; SP 800-37; SP 800-53; SP 800-53A; SP 800-60

Any information system (including any telecommunications system) used or operated by an agency or by a contractor of any agency, or other organization on behalf of an agency, the function, operation, or use of which: I. involves intelligence activities; II. involves cryptologic activities related to national security; III. Involves command and control of military forces; IV. involves equipment that is an integral part of a weapon or weapon system; or V. subject to subparagraph (B), is critical to the direct fulfillment of military or intelligence missions; or is protected at all times by procedures established for information that have been specifically authorized under criteria established by an Executive Order or an Act of Congress to be kept classified in the interest of national defense or foreign policy.
Subparagraph (B). Does not include a system that is to be used for routine administrative and business applications (including payroll, finance, logistics, and personnel management applications). (Title 44U.S. Code Section 3542, Federal Information Security Management Act of 2002.)
SOURCE: CNSSI-4009

National Vulnerability Database – (NVD) The U.S. government repository of standards-based vulnerability management data. This data enables automation of vulnerability management, security measurement, and compliance (e.g., FISMA).
SOURCE: http://nvd.nist.gov/

| | |
|---|---|
| Need To Know Determination – | Decision made by an authorized holder of official information that a prospective recipient requires access to specific official information to carry out official duties.<br>SOURCE: CNSSI-4009 |
| Need-To-Know – | A method of isolating information resources based on a user's need to have access to that resource in order to perform their job but no more. The terms 'need-to know" and "least privilege" express the same idea. Need-to-know is generally applied to people, while least privilege is generally applied to processes.<br>SOURCE: CNSSI-4009 |
| Needs Assessment (IT Security Awareness and Training) – | A process that can be used to determine an organization's awareness and training needs. The results of a needs assessment can provide justification to convince management to allocate adequate resources to meet the identified awareness and training needs.<br>SOURCE: SP 800-50 |
| Net-centric Architecture – | A complex system of systems composed of subsystems and services that are part of a continuously evolving, complex community of people, devices, information and services interconnected by a network that enhances information sharing and collaboration. Subsystems and services may or may not be developed or owned by the same entity, and, in general, will not be continually present during the full life cycle of the system of systems. Examples of this architecture include service-oriented architectures and cloud computing architectures.<br>SOURCE: SP 800-37 |
| Network – | Information system(s) implemented with a collection of interconnected components. Such components may include routers, hubs, cabling, telecommunications controllers, key distribution centers, and technical control devices.<br>SOURCE: SP800-53;CNSSI-4009 |
| Network Access – | Access to an organizational information system by a user (or a process acting on behalf of a user) communicating through a network(e.g., local area network, wide area network, Internet).<br>SOURCE: SP800-53;CNSSI-4009 |
| Network Access Control (NAC) – | A feature provided by some firewalls that allows access based on a user's credentials and the results of health checks performed on the telework client device.<br>SOURCE: SP 800-41 |
| Network Address Translation (NAT) – | A routing technology used by many firewalls to hide internal system addresses from an external network through use of an addressing schema.<br>SOURCE: SP 800-41 |
| Network Front-End – | Device implementing protocols that allow attachment of a computer system to a network.<br>SOURCE: CNSSI-4009 |

| | |
|---|---|
| Network Reference Monitor – | See Reference Monitor. |
| Network Resilience – | A computing infrastructure that provides continuous business operation (i.e., highly resistant to disruption and able to operate in a degraded mode if damaged), rapid recovery if failure does occur, andthe ability to scale to meet rapid or unpredictable demands.<br>SOURCE: CNSSI-4009 |
| Network Security – | See Information Assurance. |
| Network Security Officer – | SeeInformation Systems Security Officer. |
| Network Sniffing – | A passive technique that monitors network communication, decodes protocols, and examines headers and payloads for information of interest. It is both a review technique and a target identification and analysis technique.<br>SOURCE: SP 800-115 |
| Network Sponsor – | Individual or organization responsible for stating the security policy enforced by the network, designing the network security architecture to properly enforce that policy, and ensuring that the network is implemented in such a way that the policy is enforced.<br>SOURCE: CNSSI-4009 |
| Network System – | System implemented with a collection of interconnected components.A network system is based on a coherent security architecture and design.<br>SOURCE: CNSSI-4009 |
| Network Weaving – | Penetration technique in which different communication networks arelinked to access an information system to avoid detection and trace-back.<br>SOURCE: CNSSI-4009 |
| No-Lone Zone (NLZ) – | Area, room, or space that, when staffed, must be occupied by two or more appropriately cleared individuals who remain within sight of each other. See two-person integrity.<br>SOURCE: CNSSI-4009 |
| Non-Local Maintenance – | Maintenance activities conducted by individuals communicating through a network; either an external network (e.g., the Internet) or an internal network.<br>SOURCE: SP 800-53 |
| Non-Organizational User – | A user who is not an organizational user (including public users).<br>SOURCE: SP 800-53 |
| Non-repudiation – | Assurance that the sender of information is provided with proof of delivery and the recipient is provided with proof of the sender's identity, so neither can later deny having processed the information.<br>SOURCE: CNSSI-4009; SP 800-60<br>Protection against an individual falsely denying having performed a |

particular action. Provides the capability to determine whether a given individual took a particular action such as creating information,sending a message, approving information, and receiving a message.
SOURCE: SP 800-53; SP 800-18

Non-Repudiation – Is the security service by which the entities involved in a communication cannot deny having participated. Specifically, the sending entity cannot deny having sent a message (non-repudiation with proof of origin), and the receiving entity cannot deny having received a message (non-repudiation with proof of delivery).
SOURCE: FIPS 191
A service that is used to provide assurance of the integrity and origin of data in such a way that the integrity and origin can be verified and validated by a third party as having originated from a specific entity in possession of the private key (i.e., the signatory).
SOURCE: FIPS 186

Nonce – A value used in security protocols that is never repeated with the same key. For example, challenges used in challenge-response authentication protocols generally must not be repeated until authentication keys are changed, or there is a possibility of a replay attack. Using a nonce as a challenge is a different requirement than a random challenge, because a nonce is not necessarily unpredictable.
SOURCE: SP 800-63
A random or non-repeating value that is included in data exchanged by a protocol, usually for the purpose of guaranteeing the transmittal of live data rather than replayed data, thus detecting and protecting against replay attacks.
SOURCE: CNSSI-4009

NSA-Approved Cryptography – Cryptography that consists of: (i) an approved algorithm; (ii) an implementation that has been approved for the protection of classified information in a particular environment; and (iii) a supporting key management infrastructure.
SOURCE: SP 800-53

Null – Dummy letter, letter symbol, or code group inserted into an encrypted message to delay or prevent its decryption or to complete encrypted groups for transmission or transmission security purposes.
SOURCE: CNSSI-4009

Object – A passive entity that contains or receives information.
SOURCE: SP 800-27
Passive information system-related entity (e.g., devices, files, records, tables, processes, programs, domains) containing or receiving information. Access to an object implies access to the information it contains.
SOURCE: CNSSI-4009

Passive information system-related entity (e.g., devices, files, records, tables, processes, programs, domains) containing or receiving information. Access to an object (by a subject) implies access to the information it contains. See Subject.
SOURCE: SP 800-53

Object Identifier – A specialized formatted number that is registered with an internationally recognized standards organization. The unique alphanumeric/numeric identifier registered under the ISO registrationstandard to reference a specific object or object class. In the federal government PKI, they are used to uniquely identify each of the four policies and cryptographic algorithms supported.
SOURCE: SP 800-32

Object Reuse – Reassignment and reuse of a storage medium containing one or more objects after ensuring no residual data remains on the storage medium.
SOURCE: CNSSI-4009

Off-Card – Refers to data that is not stored within the PIV card or computation that is not done by the Integrated Circuit Chip (ICC) of the PIV card.
SOURCE: FIPS 201

Off-line Attack – An attack where the attacker obtains some data (typically by eavesdropping on an authentication protocol run, or by penetrating a system and stealing security files) that he/she is able to analyze in a system of his/her own choosing.
SOURCE: SP 800-63

Off-line Cryptosystem – Cryptographic system in which encryption and decryption are performed independently of the transmission and reception functions.
SOURCE: CNSSI-4009

Official Information – All information in the custody and control of a U.S. government department or agency that was acquired by U.S. government employees as a part of their official duties or because of their official status and has not been cleared for public release.
SOURCE: CNSSI-4009

On-Card – Refers to data that is stored within the PIV card or computation that is done by the ICC of the PIV card.
SOURCE: FIPS 201

Online Attack – An attack against an authentication protocol where the attacker either assumes the role of a claimant with a genuine verifier or actively alters the authentication channel. The goal of the attack may be to gain authenticated access or learn authentication secrets.
SOURCE: SP 800-63

Online Certificate Status Protocol (OCSP) – An online protocol used to determine the status of a public key certificate.
SOURCE: SP 800-63; FIPS 201

| | |
|---|---|
| Online Cryptosystem – | Cryptographic system in which encryption and decryption are performed in association with the transmitting and receiving functions.<br>SOURCE: CNSSI-4009 |
| One-part Code – | Code in which plain text elements and their accompanying code groups are arranged in alphabetical, numerical, or other systematic order, so one listing serves for both encoding and decoding. One-partcodes are normally small codes used to pass small volumes of low-sensitivity information.<br>SOURCE: CNSSI-4009 |
| One-time Cryptosystem – | Cryptosystem employing key used only once.<br>SOURCE: CNSSI-4009 |
| One-time Pad – | Manual one-time cryptosystem produced in pad form.<br>SOURCE: CNSSI-4009 |
| One-time Tape – | Punched paper tape used to provide key streams on a one-time basis in certain machine cryptosystems.<br>SOURCE: CNSSI-4009 |
| One-Way Hash Algorithm – | Hash algorithms which map arbitrarily long inputs into a fixed-size output such that it is very difficult (computationally infeasible) to find two different hash inputs that produce the same output. Such algorithms are an essential part of the process of producing fixed-size digital signatures that can both authenticate the signer and provide fordata integrity checking (detection of input modification after signature).<br>SOURCE: SP 800-49; CNSSI-4009 |
| Open Storage – | Any storage of classified national security information outside of approved containers. This includes classified information that is resident on information systems media and outside of an approved storage container, regardless of whether or not that media is in use (i.e., unattended operations).<br>SOURCE: CNSSI-4009 |
| Operating System (OS) Fingerprinting – | Analyzing characteristics of packets sent by a target, such as packet headers or listening ports, to identify the operating system in use on the target.<br>SOURCE: SP 800-115 |
| Operational Controls – | The security controls (i.e., safeguards or countermeasures) for an information system that primarily are implemented and executed by people (as opposed to systems).<br>SOURCE: SP 800-53; SP 800-37; FIPS 200<br>The security controls (i.e., safeguards or countermeasures) for an information system that are primarily implemented and executed by people (as opposed to systems).<br>SOURCE: CNSSI-4009; SP 800-53A |
| Operational Key – | Key intended for use over-the-air for protection of operational information or for the production or secure electrical transmission |

| | |
|---|---|
| | ofkey streams.<br>SOURCE: CNSSI-4009 |
| Operational Vulnerability Information – | Information that describes the presence of an information vulnerability within a specific operational setting or network.<br>SOURCE: CNSSI-4009 |
| Operational Waiver – | Authority for continued use of unmodified COMSEC end-items pending the completion of a mandatory modification.<br>SOURCE: CNSSI-4009 |
| Operations Code – | Code composed largely of words and phrases suitable for general communications use.<br>SOURCE: CNSSI-4009 |
| Operations Security (OPSEC) – | Systematic and proven process by which potential adversaries can be denied information about capabilities and intentions by identifying, controlling, and protecting generally unclassified evidence of the planning and execution of sensitive activities. The process involves five steps: identification of critical information, analysis of threats, analysis of vulnerabilities, assessment of risks, and application of appropriate countermeasures.<br>SOURCE: CNSSI-4009 |
| Optional Modification – | NSA-approved modification not required for universal implementation by all holders of a COMSEC end-item. This class of modification requires all of the engineering/doctrinal control of mandatory modification but is usually not related to security, safety, TEMPEST, or reliability. See mandatory modification.<br>SOURCE: CNSSI-4009 |
| Organization – | A federal agency, or, as appropriate, any of its operational elements.<br>SOURCE: FIPS 200<br>An entity of any size, complexity, or positioning within an organizational structure (e.g., a federal agency, or, as appropriate, anyof its operational elements).<br>SOURCE: SP 800-53; SP 800-53A; SP 800-37 |
| Organizational Maintenance – | Limited maintenance performed by a user organization.<br>SOURCE: CNSSI-4009 |
| Organizational Registration Authority (ORA) – | Entity within the PKI that authenticates the identity and the organizational affiliation of the users.<br>SOURCE: CNSSI-4009 |
| Organizational User – | An organizational employee or an individual the organization deems to have equivalent status of an employee (e.g., contractor, guest researcher, individual detailed from another organization, individual from allied nation).<br>SOURCE: SP 800-53 |
| Outside Threat – | An unauthorized entity from outside the domain perimeter that has the potential to harm an Information System through destruction, disclosure, modification of data, and/or denial of service.<br>SOURCE: SP 800-32 |

| | |
|---|---|
| Outside(r) Threat – | An unauthorized entity outside the security domain that has the potential to harm an information system through destruction, disclosure, modification of data, and/or denial of service.<br>SOURCE: CNSSI-4009 |
| Over-The-Air Key Distribution – | Providing electronic key via over-the-air rekeying, over-the-air key transfer, or cooperative key generation.<br>SOURCE: CNSSI-4009 |
| Over-The-Air Key Transfer – | Electronically distributing key without changing traffic encryption key used on the secured communications path over which the transferis accomplished.<br>SOURCE: CNSSI-4009 |
| Over-The-Air Rekeying (OTAR) – | Changing traffic encryption key or transmission security key in remote cryptographic equipment by sending new key directly to the remote cryptographic equipment over the communications path it secures.<br>SOURCE: CNSSI-4009 |
| Overt Channel – | Communications path within a computer system or network designed for the authorized transfer of data. See covert channel.<br>SOURCE: CNSSI-4009 |
| Overt Testing – | Security testing performed with the knowledge and consent of the organization's IT staff.<br>SOURCE: SP 800-115 |
| Overwrite Procedure – | A software process that replaces data previously stored on storage media with a predetermined set of meaningless data or random patterns.<br>SOURCE: CNSSI-4009 |
| Packet Filter – | A routing device that provides access control functionality for host addresses and communication sessions.<br>SOURCE: SP 800-41 |
| Packet Sniffer – | Software that observes and records network traffic.<br>SOURCE: SP 800-61; CNSSI-4009 |
| Parity – | Bit(s) used to determine whether a block of data has been altered.<br>SOURCE: CNSSI-4009 |
| Partitioned Security Mode – | Information systems security mode of operation wherein all personnel have the clearance, but not necessarily formal access approval and need-to-know, for all information handled by an information system.<br>SOURCE: CNSSI-4009 |
| Passive Attack – | An attack against an authentication protocol where the attacker intercepts data traveling along the network between the claimant and verifier, but does not alter the data (i.e., eavesdropping).<br>SOURCE: SP 800-63<br>An attack that does not alter systems or data.<br>SOURCE: CNSSI-4009 |

| | |
|---|---|
| Passive Security Testing – | Security testing that does not involve any direct interaction with the targets, such as sending packets to a target.<br>SOURCE: SP 800-115 |
| Passive Wiretapping – | The monitoring or recording of data while it is being transmitted overa communications link, without altering or affecting the data.<br>SOURCE: CNSSI-4009 |
| Password – | A secret that a claimant memorizes and uses to authenticate his or heridentity. Passwords are typically character strings.<br>SOURCE: SP 800-63 |
| Password – | A protected character string used to authenticate the identity of a computer system user or to authorize access to system resources.<br>SOURCE: FIPS 181 |
| Password – | A string of characters (letters, numbers, and other symbols) used to authenticate an identity or to verify access authorization.<br>SOURCE: FIPS 140-2<br>A protected/private string of letters, numbers, and/or special characters used to authenticate an identity or to authorize access to data.<br>SOURCE: CNSSI-4009 |
| Password Cracking – | The process of recovering secret passwords stored in a computer system or transmitted over a network.<br>SOURCE: SP 800-115 |
| Password Protected – | The ability to protect a file using a password access control, protecting the data contents from being viewed with the appropriate viewer unless the proper password is entered.<br>SOURCE: SP 800-72<br>The ability to protect the contents of a file or device from being accessed until the correct password is entered.<br>SOURCE: SP 800-124 |
| Patch – | An update to an operating system, application, or other software issued specifically to correct particular problems with the software.<br>SOURCE: SP 800-123 |
| Patch Management – | The systematic notification, identification, deployment, installation, and verification of operating system and application software code revisions. These revisions are known as patches, hot fixes, and service packs.<br>SOURCE: CNSSI-4009 |
| Path Histories – | Maintaining an authenticatable record of the prior platforms visited by a mobile software agent, so that a newly visited platform can determine whether to process the agent and what resource constraints to apply.<br>SOURCE: SP 800-19 |
| Payload – | The input data to the CCM generation-encryption process that is both authenticated and encrypted.<br>SOURCE: SP 800-38C |

**Peer Entity Authentication –** The process of verifying that a peer entity in an association is as claimed.
SOURCE: CNSSI-4009

**Penetration –** See Intrusion.

**Penetration Testing –** A test methodology in which assessors, using all available documentation (e.g., system design, source code, manuals) and working under specific constraints, attempt to circumvent the securityfeatures of an information system.
SOURCE: SP 800-53A
A test methodology in which assessors, typically working under specific constraints, attempt to circumvent or defeat the security features of an information system.
SOURCE: SP800-53;CNSSI-4009
Security testing in which evaluators mimic real-world attacks in an attempt to identify ways to circumvent the security features of an application, system, or network. Penetration testing often involves issuing real attacks on real systems and data, using the same tools andtechniques used by actual attackers. Most penetration tests involve looking for combinations of vulnerabilities on a single system or multiple systems that can be used to gain more access than could be achieved through a single vulnerability.
SOURCE: SP 800-115

**Per-Call Key –** Unique traffic encryption key generated automatically by certain secure telecommunications systems to secure single voice or data transmissions. See cooperative key generation.
SOURCE: CNSSI-4009

**Performance Reference Model – (PRM)** Framework for performance measurement providing common output measurements throughout the federal government. It allows agencies to better manage the business of government at a strategic level by providing a means for using an agency's EA to measure the success of information systems investments and their impact on strategic outcomes.
SOURCE: CNSSI-4009

**Perimeter –** (C&A) Encompasses all those components of the system that are to be accredited by the DAA, and excludes separately accredited systems to which the system is connected.
(Authorization) Encompasses all those components of the system or network for which a Body of Evidence is provided in support of a formal approval to operate.
SOURCE: CNSSI-4009

**Periods Processing –** The processing of various levels of classified and unclassified information at distinctly different times. Under the concept of periods processing, the system must be purged of all information from one processing period before transitioning to the next.
SOURCE: CNSSI-4009

| | |
|---|---|
| Perishable Data – | Information whose value can decrease substantially during a specified time. A significant decrease in value occurs when the operational circumstances change to the extent that the information is no longer useful.<br>SOURCE: CNSSI-4009 |
| Permuter – | Device used in cryptographic equipment to change the order in whichthe contents of a shift register are used in various nonlinear combining circuits.<br>SOURCE: CNSSI-4009 |
| Personal Firewall – | A utility on a computer that monitors network activity and blocks communications that are unauthorized.<br>SOURCE: SP 800-69 |
| Personal Identification Number – (PIN) | A password consisting only of decimal digits.<br>SOURCE: SP 800-63<br><br>A secret that a claimant memorizes and uses to authenticate his or heridentity. PINs are generally only decimal digits.<br>SOURCE: FIPS 201<br>An alphanumeric code or password used to authenticate an identity.<br>SOURCE: FIPS 140-2<br>A short numeric code used to confirm identity.<br>SOURCE: CNSSI-4009 |
| Personal Identity Verification – (PIV) | The process of creating and using a governmentwide secure and reliable form of identification for federal employees and contractors, in support of HSPD 12, *Policy for a Common Identification Standardfor Federal Employees and Contractors.*<br>SOURCE: CNSSI-4009 |
| Personal Identity Verification Accreditation – | The official management decision to authorize operation of a PIV Card Issuer after determining that the Issuer's reliability has satisfactorily been established through appropriate assessment and certification processes.<br>SOURCE: CNSSI-4009 |
| Personal Identity Verification Authorizing Official – | An individual who can act on behalf of an agency to authorize the issuance of a credential to an applicant.<br>SOURCE: CNSSI-4009 |
| Personal Identity Verification Card – (PIV Card) | Physical artifact (e.g., identity card, "smart" card) issued to an individual that contains stored identity credentials (e.g., photograph, cryptographic keys, digitized fingerprint representation, etc.) such that a claimed identity of the cardholder may be verified against the stored credentials by another person (human-readable and verifiable) or an automated process (computer-readable and verifiable).<br>SOURCE: FIPS 201; CNSSI-4009 |
| Personal Identity Verification | An authorized identity card creator that procures FIPS-approved blank identity cards, initializes them with appropriate software and |

| | |
|---|---|
| Issuer – | data elements for the requested identity verification and access control application, personalizes the cards with the identity credentials of the authorized subjects, and delivers the personalized card to the authorized subjects along with appropriate instructions forprotection and use.<br>SOURCE: FIPS 201 |
| Personal Identity Verification Registrar – | An entity that establishes and vouches for the identity of an applicant to a PIV Issuer. The PIV RA authenticates the applicant's identity bychecking identity source documents and identity proofing, and that ensures a proper background check has been completed, before the credential is issued.<br>SOURCE: FIPS 201 |
| Personal Identity Verification Sponsor – | An individual who can act on behalf of a department or agency to request a PIV Card for an applicant.<br>SOURCE: FIPS 201 |
| Personally Identifiable Information – (PII) | Information which can be used to distinguish or trace an individual's identity, such as their name, social security number, biometric records, etc., alone, or when combined with other personal or identifying information which is linked or linkable to a specific individual, such as date and place of birth, mother's maiden name, etc.<br>SOURCE: CNSSI-4009<br>Any information about an individual maintained by an agency, including (1) any information that can be used to distinguish or trace an individual‘s identity, such as name, social security number, date and place of birth, mother‘s maiden name, or biometric records; and (2) any other information that is linked or linkable to an individual, such as medical, educational, financial, and employment information.<br>SOURCE: SP 800-122 |
| Personnel Registration Manager – | The management role that is responsible for registering human users, i.e., users that are people.<br>SOURCE: CNSSI-4009 |
| Phishing – | Tricking individuals into disclosing sensitive personal information through deceptive computer-based means.<br>SOURCE: SP 800-83<br>Deceiving individuals into disclosing sensitive personal information through deceptive computer-based means.<br>SOURCE: CNSSI-4009<br>A digital form of social engineering that uses authentic-looking—but bogus—emails to request information from users or direct them to a fake Web site that requests information.<br>SOURCE: SP 800-115 |
| Physically Isolated Network – | A network that is not connected to entities or systems outside a physically controlled space.<br>SOURCE: SP 800-32 |

| | |
|---|---|
| PII Confidentiality Impact Level – | The PII confidentiality impact level—*low, moderate, or high*—indicates the potential harm that could result to the subject individuals and/or the organization if PII were inappropriately accessed, used, or disclosed.<br>SOURCE: SP 800-122 |
| Plaintext – | Data input to the Cipher or output from the Inverse Cipher.<br>SOURCE: FIPS 197 |
| Plaintext – | Intelligible data that has meaning and can be understood without the application of decryption.<br>SOURCE: SP 800-21<br>Unencrypted information.<br>SOURCE: CNSSI-4009 |
| Plaintext Key – | An unencrypted cryptographic key.<br>SOURCE: FIPS 140-2 |
| Plan of Action and Milestones – (POA&M) | A document that identifies tasks needing to be accomplished. It details resources required to accomplish the elements of the plan, anymilestones in meeting the tasks, and scheduled completion dates for the milestones.<br>SOURCE: SP 800-53; SP 800-53A; SP 800-37; SP 800-64; CNSSI-4009; OMB Memorandum 02-01 |
| Policy Approving Authority – (PAA) | First level of the PKI Certification Management Authority that approves the security policy of each PCA.<br>SOURCE: CNSSI-4009 |
| Policy-Based Access Control – (PBAC) | A form of access control that uses an authorization policy that is flexible in the types of evaluated parameters (e.g., identity, role, clearance, operational need, risk, heuristics).<br>SOURCE: CNSSI-4009 |
| Policy Certification Authority – (PCA) | Second level of the PKI Certification Management Authority that formulates the security policy under which it and its subordinate CAswill issue public key certificates.<br>SOURCE: CNSSI-4009 |
| Policy Management Authority – (PMA) | Body established to oversee the creation and update of Certificate Policies, review Certification Practice Statements, review the results of CA audits for policy compliance, evaluate non-domain policies for acceptance within the domain, and generally oversee and manage the PKI certificate policies. For the FBCA, the PMA is the Federal PKI Policy Authority.<br>SOURCE: SP 800-32 |
| Policy Mapping – | Recognizing that, when a CA in one domain certifies a CA in another domain, a particular certificate policy in the second domain may be considered by the authority of the first domain to be equivalent (but not necessarily identical in all respects) to a particular certificate policy in the first domain.<br>SOURCE: SP 800-15 |
| Port – | A physical entry or exit point of a cryptographic module that provides access to the module for physical signals, represented by |

logical information flows (physically separated ports do not share the same physical pin or wire).
SOURCE: FIPS 140-2

Port Scanning – Using a program to remotely determine which ports on a system are open (e.g., whether systems allow connections through those ports).
SOURCE: SP 800-61; CNSSI-4009

Portal – A high-level remote access architecture that is based on a server that offers teleworkers access to one or more applications through a singlecentralized interface.
SOURCE: SP 800-46

Portable Electronic Device (PED) – Any nonstationary electronic apparatus with singular or multiple capabilities of recording, storing, and/or transmitting data, voice, video, or photo images. This includes but is not limited to laptops, personal digital assistants, pocket personal computers, palmtops, MP3 players, cellular telephones, thumb drives, video cameras, and pagers.
SOURCE: CNSSI-4009

Positive Control Material – Generic term referring to a sealed authenticator system, permissive action link, coded switch system, positive enable system, or nuclear command and control documents, material, or devices.
SOURCE: CNSSI-4009

Potential Impact – The loss of confidentiality, integrity, or availability could be expectedto have:
1)a *limited* adverse effect (FIPS 199 low);
2)a *serious* adverse effect (FIPS 199 moderate); or
3)a *severe* or *catastrophic* adverse effect (FIPS 199 high) on organizational operations, organizational assets, or individuals.
SOURCE: SP 800-53; SP 800-60; SP 800-37; FIPS 199

Potential Impact – The loss of confidentiality, integrity, or availability could be expectedto have a limitedadverse effect; a seriousadverse effect, or a severe or catastrophic adverse effect on organizational operations, organizational assets, or individuals.
SOURCE: FIPS 200
The loss of confidentiality, integrity, or availability that could be expected to have a limited (low) adverse effect, a serious (moderate) adverse effect, or a severe or catastrophic (high) adverse effect on organizational operations, organizational assets, or individuals.
SOURCE: CNSSI-4009

Practice Statement – A formal statement of the practices followed by an authentication entity (e.g., RA, CSP, or verifier); typically the specific steps taken toregister and verify identities, issue credentials, and authenticate claimants.
SOURCE: SP 800-63

Precursor – A sign that an attacker may be preparing to cause an incident.
SOURCE: SP 800-61
A sign that an attacker may be preparing to cause an incident.

See indicator.
SOURCE: CNSSI-4009

Preproduction Model – Version of INFOSEC equipment employing standard parts and suitable for complete evaluation of form, design, and performance. Preproduction models are often referred to as beta models.
SOURCE: CNSSI-4009

Primary Services Node (PRSN) – A Key Management Infrastructure core node that provides the users' central point of access to KMI products, services, and information.
SOURCE: CNSSI-4009

Principal – An entity whose identity can be authenticated.
SOURCE: FIPS 196

Principal Accrediting Authority – (PAA) Senior official with authority and responsibility for all intelligence systems within an agency.
SOURCE: CNSSI-4009

Principal Certification Authority – (CA) The Principal Certification Authority is a CA designated by an agency to interoperate with the FBCA. An agency may designate multiple Principal CAs to interoperate with the FBCA.
SOURCE: SP 800-32

Print Suppression – Eliminating the display of characters in order to preserve their secrecy.
SOURCE: CNSSI-4009

Privacy – Restricting access to subscriber or Relying Party information in accordance with federal law and agency policy.
SOURCE: SP 800-32

Privacy Impact Assessment (PIA) – An analysis of how information is handled: 1) to ensure handling conforms to applicable legal, regulatory, and policy requirements regarding privacy; 2) to determine the risks and effects of collecting, maintaining, and disseminating information in identifiable form in anelectronic information system; and 3) to examine and evaluate protections and alternative processes for handling information to mitigate potential privacy risks.
SOURCE: SP 800-53; SP 800-18; SP 800-122; CNSSI-4009; OMB Memorandum 03-22

Privacy System – Commercial encryption system that affords telecommunications limited protection to deter a casual listener, but cannot withstand a technically competent cryptanalytic attack.
SOURCE: CNSSI-4009

Private Key – The secret part of an asymmetric key pair that is typically used to digitally sign or decrypt data.
SOURCE: SP 800-63

Private Key – A cryptographic key, used with a public key cryptographic algorithm,that is uniquely associated with an entity and is not made public. In an asymmetric (public) cryptosystem, the private key is associated with a public key. Depending on the algorithm, the private key may be used to—

1) Compute the corresponding public key,
2) Compute a digital signature that may be verified by the corresponding public key,
3) Decrypt data that was encrypted by the corresponding public key, or
4) Compute a piece of common shared data, together with other information.
SOURCE: SP 800-57

Private Key – A cryptographic key used with a public key cryptographic algorithm, which is uniquely associated with an entity, and not made public; it isused to generate a digital signature; this key is mathematically linked with a corresponding public key.
SOURCE: FIPS 196

Private Key – A cryptographic key, used with a public key cryptographic algorithm,that is uniquely associated with an entity and is not made public.
SOURCE: FIPS 140-2
In an asymmetric cryptography scheme, the private or secret key of a key pair which must be kept confidential and is used to decrypt messages encrypted with the public key or to digitally sign messages, which can then be validated with the public key.
SOURCE: CNSSI-4009

Privilege – A right granted to an individual, a program, or a process.
SOURCE: CNSSI-4009

Privilege Management – The definition and management of policies and processes that define the ways in which the user is provided access rights to enterprise systems. It governs the management of the data that constitutes the user's privileges and other attributes, including the storage, organization and access to information in directories.
SOURCE: NISTIR 7657

Privileged Account – An information system account with approved authorizations of a privileged user.
SOURCE: CNSSI-4009
An information system account with authorizations of a privileged user.
SOURCE: SP800-53

Privileged Accounts – Individuals who have access to set "access rights" for users on a given system. Sometimes referred to as system or network administrative accounts.
SOURCE: SP 800-12

Privileged Command – A human-initiated command executed on an information system involving the control, monitoring, or administration of the system including security functions and associated security-relevant information.
SOURCE: SP800-53;CNSSI-4009

| | |
|---|---|
| Privileged Process – | A computer process that is authorized (and, therefore, trusted) to perform security-relevant functions that ordinary processes are not authorized to perform.<br>SOURCE: CNSSI-4009 |
| Privileged User – | A user that is authorized (and, therefore, trusted) to perform security-relevant functions that ordinary users are not authorized to perform.<br>SOURCE: SP 800-53; CNSSI-4009 |
| Probability of Occurrence – | See Likelihood of Occurrence. |
| Probe – | A technique that attempts to access a system to learn something aboutthe system.<br>SOURCE: CNSSI-4009 |
| Product Source Node (PSN) – | The Key Management Infrastructure core node that provides central generation of cryptographic key material.<br>SOURCE: CNSSI-4009 |
| Production Model – | INFOSEC equipment in its final mechanical and electrical form.<br>SOURCE: CNSSI-4009 |
| Profiling – | Measuring the characteristics of expected activity so that changes to it can be more easily identified.<br>SOURCE: SP 800-61; CNSSI-4009 |
| Promiscuous Mode – | A configuration setting for a network interface card that causes it to accept all incoming packets that it sees, regardless of their intended destinations.<br>SOURCE: SP 800-94 |
| Proof of Possession Protocol – (PoP Protocol) | A protocol where a claimant proves to a verifier that he/she possessesand controls a token (e.g., a key or password).<br>SOURCE: SP 800-63 |
| Proprietary Information (PROPIN) – | Material and information relating to or associated with a company's products, business, or activities, including but not limited to financial information; data or statements; trade secrets; product research and development; existing and future product designs and performance specifications; marketing plans or techniques; schematics; client lists;computer programs; processes; and know-how that has been clearly identified and properly marked by the company as proprietary information, trade secrets, or company confidential information. The information must have been developed by the company and not be available to the government or to the public without restriction from another source.<br>SOURCE: CNSSI-4009 |
| Protected Distribution System (PDS) – | Wire line or fiber optic system that includes adequate safeguards and/or countermeasures (e.g., acoustic, electric, electromagnetic, and physical) to permit its use for the transmission of unencrypted information through an area of lesser classification or control.<br>SOURCE: CNSSI-4009 |

| | |
|---|---|
| Protection Philosophy – | Informal description of the overall design of an information system delineating each of the protection mechanisms employed. Combination of formal and informal techniques, appropriate to the evaluation class, used to show the mechanisms are adequate to enforce the security policy.<br>SOURCE: CNSSI-4009 |
| Protection Profile – | Common Criteria specification that represents an implementation-independent set of security requirements for a category of Target of Evaluations (TOE) that meets specific consumer needs.<br>SOURCE: CNSSI-4009 |
| Protective Distribution System – | Wire line or fiber optic system that includes adequate safeguards and/or countermeasures (e.g., acoustic, electric, electromagnetic, and physical) to permit its use for the transmission of unencrypted information.<br>SOURCE: SP 800-53 |
| Protective Packaging – | Packaging techniques for COMSEC material that discourage penetration, reveal a penetration has occurred or was attempted, or inhibit viewing or copying of keying material prior to the time it is exposed for use.<br>SOURCE: CNSSI-4009 |
| Protective Technologies – | Special tamper-evident features and materials employed for the purpose of detecting tampering and deterring attempts to compromise, modify, penetrate, extract, or substitute information processing equipment and keying material.<br>SOURCE: CNSSI-4009 |
| Protocol – | Set of rules and formats, semantic and syntactic, permitting information systems to exchange information.<br>SOURCE: CNSSI-4009 |
| Protocol Data Unit – | A unit of data specified in a protocol and consisting of protocol information and, possibly, user data.<br>SOURCE: FIPS 188 |
| Protocol Entity – | Entity that follows a set of rules and formats (semantic and syntactic)that determines the communication behavior of other entities.<br>SOURCE: FIPS 188 |
| Protocol Run – | An instance of the exchange of messages between a claimant and a verifier in a defined authentication protocol that results in the authentication (or authentication failure) of the claimant.<br>SOURCE: SP 800-63 |
| Proxy – | A proxy is an application that "breaks" the connection between clientand server. The proxy accepts certain types of traffic entering or leaving a network and processes it and forwards it. This effectively closes the straight path between the internal and external networks making it more difficult for an attacker to obtain internal addresses and other details of the organization's internal network. Proxy servers are available for common Internet services; for |

example, a Hyper Text Transfer Protocol (HTTP) proxy used for Web access, and a Simple Mail Transfer Protocol (SMTP) proxy used for email.
SOURCE: SP 800-44

An application that "breaks" the connection between client and server. The proxy accepts certain types of traffic entering or leaving a network and processes it and forwards it.
Note: This effectively closes the straight path between the internal and external networks, making it more difficult for an attacker to obtain internal addresses and other details of the organization's internal network. Proxy servers are available for common Internet services; for example, a Hyper Text Transfer Protocol (HTTP) proxy used for Web access, and a Simple Mail Transfer Protocol (SMTP) proxy used for email.
SOURCE: CNSSI-4009

Proxy Agent – A software application running on a firewall or on a dedicated proxy server that is capable of filtering a protocol and routing it between theinterfaces of the device.
SOURCE: CNSSI-4009

Proxy Server – A server that services the requests of its clients by forwarding those requests to other servers.
SOURCE: CNSSI-4009

Pseudorandom number generator – (PRNG) An algorithm that produces a sequence of bits that are uniquely determined from an initial value called a seed. The output of the PRNG "appears" to be random, i.e., the output is statistically indistinguishable from random values. A cryptographic PRNG has the additional property that the output is unpredictable, given that the seed is not known.
SOURCE: SP 800-57; CNSSI-4009

Pseudonym – A subscriber name that has been chosen by the subscriber that is not verified as meaningful by identity proofing.
SOURCE: SP 800-63

1. A subscriber name that has been chosen by the subscriber that is not verified as meaningful by identity proofing.
2. An assigned identity that is used to protect an individual's true identity.
SOURCE: CNSSI-4009

Public Domain Software – Software not protected by copyright laws of any nation that may be freely used without permission of, or payment to, the creator, and thatcarries no warranties from, or liabilities to the creator.
SOURCE: CNSSI-4009

Public Key – The public part of an asymmetric key pair that is typically used to verify signatures or encrypt data.
SOURCE: FIPS 201; SP 800-63

Public Key – A cryptographic key that is used with a public key cryptographic algorithm. The public key is uniquely associated with an entity and

may be made public. In an asymmetric (public) cryptosystem, the public key is associated with a private key. The public key may be known by anyone and, depending on the algorithm, may be used to—
1) Verify a digital signature that is signed by the corresponding private key,
2) Encrypt data that can be decrypted by the corresponding private key, or
3) Compute a piece of shared data.
SOURCE: SP 800-57

Public Key – A cryptographic key used with a public key cryptographic algorithm, uniquely associated with an entity, and which may be made public; it is used to verify a digital signature; this key is mathematically linked with a corresponding private key.
SOURCE: FIPS 196

Public Key – A cryptographic key used with a public key cryptographic algorithm that is uniquely associated with an entity and that may be made public.
SOURCE: FIPS 140-2
A cryptographic key that may be widely published and is used to enable the operation of an asymmetric cryptography scheme. This key is mathematically linked with a corresponding private key. Typically, a public key can be used to encrypt, but not decrypt, or to validate a signature, but not to sign.
SOURCE: CNSSI-4009

Public Key Certificate – A digital document issued and digitally signed by the private key of aCertification Authority that binds the name of a subscriber to a publickey. The certificate indicates that the subscriber identified in the certificate has sole control and access to the private key.
SOURCE: SP 800-63

Public Key Certificate – A set of data that unambiguously identifies an entity, contains the entity's public key, and is digitally signed by a trusted third party (certification authority).
SOURCE: FIPS 196

Public Key Certificate – A set of data that uniquely identifies an entity, contains the entity's public key, and is digitally signed by a trusted party, thereby binding the public key to the entity.
SOURCE: FIPS 140-2
See Also Certificate.

Public Key (Asymmetric) Cryptographic Algorithm – A cryptographic algorithm that uses two related keys, a public key and a private key. The two keys have the property that deriving the private key from the public key is computationally infeasible.
SOURCE: FIPS 140-2

Public Key Cryptography – Encryption system that uses a public-private key pair for encryption and/or digital signature.
SOURCE: CNSSI-4009

Public Key Enabling (PKE) – The incorporation of the use of certificates for security services such as authentication, confidentiality, data integrity, and non-repudiation.
SOURCE: CNSSI-4009

Public Key Infrastructure (PKI) – A set of policies, processes, server platforms, software, and workstations used for the purpose of administering certificates and public-private key pairs, including the ability to issue, maintain, and revoke public key certificates.
SOURCE: SP 800-32

Public Key Infrastructure – An architecture which is used to bind public keys to entities, enable other entities to verify public key bindings, revoke such bindings, andprovide other services critical to managing public keys.
SOURCE: FIPS 196

A Framework that is established to issue, maintain, and revoke publickey certificates.
SOURCE: FIPS 186

A support service to the PIV system that provides the cryptographic keys needed to perform digital signature-based identity verification and to protect communications and storage of sensitive verification system data within identity cards and the verification system.
SOURCE: FIPS 201

The framework and services that provide for the generation, production, distribution, control, accounting, and destruction of public key certificates. Components include the personnel, policies, processes, server platforms, software, and workstations used for the purpose of administering certificates and public-private key pairs, including the ability to issue, maintain, recover, and revoke public key certificates.
SOURCE: CNSSI-4009

Public Seed – A starting value for a pseudorandom number generator. The value produced by the random number generator may be made public. The public seed is often called a "salt."
SOURCE: CNSSI-4009

Purge – Rendering sanitized data unrecoverable by laboratory attack methods.
SOURCE: SP 800-88; CNSSI-4009

Quadrant – Short name referring to technology that provides tamper-resistant protection to cryptographic equipment.
SOURCE: CNSSI-4009

Quality of Service – The measurable end-to-end performance properties of a network service, which can be guaranteed in advance by a Service-Level Agreement between a user and a service provider, so as to satisfy specific customer application requirements. Note: These properties may include throughput (bandwidth), transit delay (latency), error rates, priority, security, packet loss, packet jitter, etc.
SOURCE: CNSSI-4009

Quarantine – Store files containing malware in isolation for future disinfection or examination.
SOURCE: SP 800-69

Radio Frequency Identification – (RFID) A form of automatic identification and data capture (AIDC) that uses electric or magnetic fields at radio frequencies to transmit information.
SOURCE: SP 800-98

Random Number Generator – (RNG) A process used to generate an unpredictable series of numbers. Each individual value is called random if each of the values in the total population of values has an equal probability of being selected.
SOURCE: SP 800-57; CNSSI-4009

Random Number Generator – (RNG) Random Number Generators (RNGs) used for cryptographic applications typically produce a sequence of zero and one bits that may be combined into sub-sequences or blocks of random numbers. There are two basic classes: deterministic and nondeterministic. A deterministic RNG consists of an algorithm that produces a sequence of bits from an initial value called a seed. A nondeterministic RNG produces output that is dependent on some unpredictable physical source that is outside human control.
SOURCE: FIPS 140-2

Randomizer – Analog or digital source of unpredictable, unbiased, and usually independent bits. Randomizers can be used for several different functions, including key generation or to provide a starting state for akey generator.
SOURCE: CNSSI-4009

RBAC – See Role-Based Access Control.

Read – Fundamental operation in an information system that results only in the flow of information from an object to a subject.
SOURCE: CNSSI-4009

Read Access – Permission to read information in an information system.
SOURCE: CNSSI-4009

Real-Time Reaction – Immediate response to a penetration attempt that is detected and diagnosed in time to prevent access.
SOURCE: CNSSI-4009

Recipient Usage Period – The period of time during the cryptoperiod of a symmetric key when protected information is processed.
SOURCE: SP 800-57

Reciprocity – Mutual agreement among participating enterprises to accept each other's security assessments in order to reuse information system resources and/or to accept each other's assessed security posture in order to share information.
SOURCE: CNSSI-4009

Mutual agreement among participating organizations to accept each other's security assessments in order to reuse information system

| | |
|---|---|
| | resources and/or to accept each other's assessed security posture in order to share information.<br>SOURCE: SP 800-37; SP 800-53; SP 800-53A |
| Records – | The recordings (automated and/or manual) of evidence of activities performed or results achieved (e.g., forms, reports, test results), which serve as a basis for verifying that the organization and the information system are performing as intended. Also used to refer tounits of related data fields (i.e., groups of data fields that can be accessed by a program and that contain the complete set of information on particular items).<br>SOURCE: SP 800-53; SP 800-53A; CNSSI-4009<br>All books, papers, maps, photographs, machine-readable materials, orother documentary materials, regardless of physical form or characteristics, made or received by an agency of the United States government under federal law or in connection with the transaction of public business and preserved or appropriate for preservation by that agency or its legitimate successor as evidence of the organization, functions, policies, decisions, procedures, operations, orother activities of the government or because of the informational value of the data in them. [44 U.S.C. SEC. 3301]<br>SOURCE: FIPS 200 |
| Records Management – | The process for tagging information for records-keeping requirements as mandated in the Federal Records Act and the National Archival and Records Requirements.<br>SOURCE: CNSSI-4009 |
| Recovery Point Objective – | The point in time to which data must be recovered after an outage.<br>SOURCE: SP 800-34 |
| Recovery Time Objective – | The overall length of time an information system's components can be in the recovery phase before negatively impacting the organization's mission or mission/business functions.<br>SOURCE: SP 800-34 |
| Recovery Procedures – | Actions necessary to restore data files of an information system and computational capability after a system failure.<br>SOURCE: CNSSI-4009 |
| RED – | In cryptographic systems, refers to information or messages that contain sensitive or classified information that is not encrypted. See also BLACK.<br>SOURCE: CNSSI-4009 |
| Red Signal – | Any electronic emission (e.g., plain text, key, key stream, subkey stream, initial fill, or control signal) that would divulge national security information if recovered.<br>SOURCE: CNSSI-4009 |
| Red Team – | A group of people authorized and organized to emulate a potential adversary's attack or exploitation capabilities against an enterprise's security posture. The Red Team's objective is to improve enterprise Information Assurance by demonstrating the impacts of successful |

| | |
|---|---|
| | attacks and by demonstrating what works for the defenders (i.e., the Blue Team) in an operational environment.<br>SOURCE: CNSSI-4009 |
| Red Team Exercise – | An exercise, reflecting real-world conditions, that is conducted as a simulated adversarial attempt to compromise organizational missionsand/or business processes to provide a comprehensive assessment of the security capability of the information system and organization.<br>SOURCE: SP 800-53 |
| Red/Black Concept – | Separation of electrical and electronic circuits, components, equipment, and systems that handle unencrypted information (Red), in electrical form, from those that handle encrypted information (Black) in the same form.<br>SOURCE: CNSSI-4009 |
| Reference Monitor – | The security engineering term for IT functionality that—<br>1)controls all access,<br>2)cannot be bypassed,<br>3)is tamper-resistant, and<br>4)provides confidence that the other three items are true.<br><br>SOURCE: SP 800-33<br>Concept of an abstract machine that enforces Target of Evaluation (TOE) access control policies.<br>SOURCE: CNSSI-4009 |
| Registration – | The process through which a party applies to become a subscriber of a Credentials Service Provider (CSP) and a Registration Authority validates the identity of that party on behalf of the CSP.<br>SOURCE: SP 800-63; CNSSI-4009 |
| Registration Authority (RA) – | A trusted entity that establishes and vouches for the identity of a subscriber to a CSP. The RA may be an integral part of a CSP, or it may be independent of a CSP, but it has a relationship to the CSP(s).<br>SOURCE: SP 800-63; CNSSI-4009 |
| Registration Authority – (RA) | Organization responsible for assignment of unique identifiers to registered objects.<br>SOURCE: FIPS 188 |
| Rekey – | To change the value of a cryptographic key that is being used in a cryptographic system/application.<br>SOURCE: CNSSI-4009 |
| Rekey (a certificate) – | To change the value of a cryptographic key that is being used in a cryptographic system application; this normally entails issuing a newcertificate on the new public key.<br>SOURCE: SP 800-32 |
| Release Prefix – | Prefix appended to the short title of U.S.-produced keying material toindicate its foreign releasability. "A" designates material that is releasable to specific allied nations, and "U.S." designates material |

intended exclusively for U. S. use.
SOURCE: CNSSI-4009

Relying Party – An entity that relies upon the subscriber's credentials, typically to process a transaction or grant access to information or a system.
SOURCE: SP 800-63; CNSSI-4009

Remanence – Residual information remaining on storage media after clearing. See magnetic remanence and clearing.
SOURCE: CNSSI-4009

Remediation – The act of correcting a vulnerability or eliminating a threat. Three possible types of remediation are installing a patch, adjusting configuration settings, or uninstalling a software application.
SOURCE: SP 800-40
The act of mitigating a vulnerability or a threat.
SOURCE: CNSSI-4009

Remediation Plan – A plan to perform the remediation of one or more threats or vulnerabilities facing an organization's systems. The plan typically includes options to remove threats and vulnerabilities and priorities for performing the remediation.
SOURCE: SP 800-40

Remote Access – Access to an organizational information system by a user (or an information system acting on behalf of a user) communicating through an external network (e.g., the Internet).
SOURCE: SP 800-53
Access by users (or information systems) communicating external to an information system security perimeter.
SOURCE: SP 800-18
The ability for an organization's users to access its nonpublic computing resources from external locations other than the organization's facilities.
SOURCE: SP 800-46
Access to an organization's nonpublic information system by an authorized user (or an information system) communicating through an external, non-organization-controlled network (e.g., the Internet).
SOURCE: CNSSI-4009

Remote Diagnostics/Maintenance – Maintenance activities conducted by authorized individuals communicating through an external network (e.g., the Internet).
SOURCE: CNSSI-4009

Remote Maintenance – Maintenance activities conducted by individuals communicating external to an information system security perimeter.
SOURCE: SP 800-18
Maintenance activities conducted by individuals communicating through an external network (e.g., the Internet).
SOURCE: SP 800-53

**Remote Rekeying** – Procedure by which a distant crypto-equipment is rekeyed electrically. See automatic remote rekeying and manual remote rekeying.
SOURCE: CNSSI-4009

**Removable Media** – Portable electronic storage media such as magnetic, optical, and solid-state devices, which can be inserted into and removed from a computing device, and that is used to store text, video, audio, and image information. Such devices have no independent processing capabilities. Examples include hard disks, floppy disks, zip drives, compact disks (CDs), thumb drives, pen drives, and similar USB storage devices.
SOURCE: CNSSI-4009

Portable electronic storage media such as magnetic, optical, and Solid-state devices, which can be inserted into and removed from a computing device, and that is used to store text, video, audio, and image information. Examples include hard disks, floppy disks, zip drives, compact disks, thumb drives, pen drives, and similar USB storage devices.
SOURCE: SP 800-53

**Renew (a certificate)** – The act or process of extending the validity of the data binding asserted by a public key certificate by issuing a new certificate.
SOURCE: SP 800-32

**Repair Action** – NSA-approved change to a COMSEC end-item that does not affect the original characteristics of the end-item and is provided for optional application by holders. Repair actions are limited to minor electrical and/or mechanical improvements to enhance operation, maintenance, or reliability. They do not require an identification label, marking, or control but must be fully documented by changes to the maintenance manual.
SOURCE: CNSSI-4009

**Replay Attacks** – An attack that involves the capture of transmitted authentication or access control information and its subsequent retransmission with the intent of producing an unauthorized effect or gaining unauthorized access.
SOURCE: CNSSI-4009

**Repository** – A database containing information and data relating to certificates as specified in a CP; may also be referred to as a directory.
SOURCE: SP 800-32

**Reserve Keying Material** – Key held to satisfy unplanned needs. See contingency key.
SOURCE: CNSSI-4009

**Residual Risk** – The remaining potential risk after all IT security measures are applied. There is a residual risk associated with each threat.
SOURCE: SP 800-33

Portion of risk remaining after security measures have been applied.
SOURCE: CNSSI-4009

Residue – Data left in storage after information-processing operations are complete, but before degaussing or overwriting has taken place.
SOURCE: CNSSI-4009

Resilience – The ability to quickly adapt and recover from any known or unknownchanges to the environment through holistic implementation of risk management, contingency, and continuity planning.
SOURCE: SP 800-34

Resource Encapsulation – Method by which the reference monitor mediates accesses to an information system resource. Resource is protected and not directly accessible by a subject. Satisfies requirement for accurate auditing of resource usage.
SOURCE: CNSSI-4009

Responder – The entity that responds to the initiator of the authentication exchange.
SOURCE: FIPS 196

Responsible Individual – A trustworthy person designated by a sponsoring organization to authenticate individual applicants seeking certificates on the basis of their affiliation with the sponsor.
SOURCE: SP 800-32

Responsibility to Provide – An information distribution approach whereby relevant essential information is made readily available and discoverable to the broadest possible pool of potential users.
SOURCE: CNSSI-4009

Restricted Data – All data concerning (i) design, manufacture, or utilization of atomic weapons; (ii) the production of special nuclear material; or (iii) the use of special nuclear material in the production of energy, but shall not include data declassified or removed from the Restricted Data category pursuant to Section 142 [of the Atomic Energy Act of 1954].
SOURCE: SP800-53;Atomic Energy Act of 1954

Revoke a Certificate – To prematurely end the operational period of a certificate effective at a specific date and time.
SOURCE: SP 800-32

RFID – See Radio Frequency Identification.

Rijndael – Cryptographic algorithm specified in the Advanced Encryption Standard (AES).
SOURCE: FIPS 197

Risk – The level of impact on organizational operations (including mission, functions, image, or reputation), organizational assets, or individuals resulting from the operation of an information system given the potential impact of a threat and the likelihood of that threat occurring.
SOURCE: FIPS 200

The level of impact on organizational operations (including mission, functions, image, or reputation), organizational assets, individuals,

| | |
|---|---|
| | other organizations, or the Nation resulting from the operation of an information system given the potential impact of a threat and the likelihood of that threat occurring.<br>SOURCE: SP 800-60<br>A measure of the extent to which an entity is threatened by a potential circumstance or event, and typically a function of: (i) the adverse impacts that would arise if the circumstance or event occurs; and (ii) the likelihood of occurrence.<br>Note: Information system-related security risks are those risks that arise from the loss of confidentiality, integrity, or availability of information or information systems and consider the adverse impactsto organizational operations (including mission, functions, image, or reputation), organizational assets, individuals, other organizations, and the Nation.<br>SOURCE: SP800-53<br>A measure of the extent to which an entity is threatened by a potential circumstance or event, and typically a function of: (1) the adverse impacts that would arise if the circumstance or event occurs; and (2) the likelihood of occurrence.<br>Note: Information system-related security risks are those risks that arise from the loss of confidentiality, integrity, or availability of information or information systems and reflect the potential adverse impacts to organizational operations (including mission, functions, image, or reputation), organizational assets, individuals, other organizations, and the Nation.<br>SOURCE: CNSSI-4009<br>A measure of the extent to which an entity is threatened by a potential circumstance or event, and typically a function of: (i) the adverse impacts that would arise if the circumstance or event occurs; and (ii) the likelihood of occurrence.<br>[Note: Information system-related security risks are those risks that arise from the loss of confidentiality, integrity, or availability of information or information systems and reflect the potential adverse impacts to organizational operations (including mission, functions, image, or reputation), organizational assets, individuals, other organizations, and the Nation. Adverse impacts to the Nation include, for example, compromises to information systems that support critical infrastructure applications or are paramount to government continuity of operations as defined by the Department of Homeland Security.]<br>SOURCE: SP 800-37; SP 800-53A<br>The probability that one or more adverse events will occur.<br>SOURCE: SP 800-61 |
| Risk-Adaptable Access Control – (RAdAC) | A form of access control that uses an authorization policy that takes into account operational need, risk, and heuristics.<br>SOURCE: CNSSI-4009 |

**Risk Analysis –** The process of identifying the risks to system security and determining the likelihood of occurrence, the resulting impact, and the additional safeguards that mitigate this impact. Part of risk management and synonymous with risk assessment.
SOURCE: SP 800-27
Examination of information to identify the risk to an information system. See risk assessment.
SOURCE: CNSSI-4009

**Risk Assessment –** The process of identifying risks to organizational operations (including mission, functions, image, or reputation), organizational assets, individuals, other organizations, and the Nation, arising through the operation of an information system.
Part of risk management, incorporates threat and vulnerability analyses and considers mitigations provided by security controls planned or in place. Synonymous with risk analysis.
SOURCE: SP 800-53; SP 800-53A; SP 800-37
The process of identifying, prioritizing, and estimating risks. This includes determining the extent to which adverse circumstances or events could impact an enterprise. Uses the results of threat and vulnerability assessments to identify risk to organizational operations and evaluates those risks in terms of likelihood of occurrence and impacts if they occur. The product of a risk assessment is a list of estimated potential impacts and unmitigated vulnerabilities. Risk assessment is part of risk management and is conducted throughout the Risk Management Framework (RMF).
SOURCE: CNSSI-4009

**Risk Executive – (or Risk Executive Function)** An individual or group within an organization that helps to ensure that: (i) security risk-related considerations for individual informationsystems, to include the authorization decisions for those systems, are viewed from an organization-wide perspective with regard to the overall strategic goals and objectives of the organization in carrying out its missions and business functions; and (ii) managing risk from individual information systems is consistent across the organization, reflects organizational risk tolerance, and is considered along with other organizational risks affecting mission/business success.
SOURCE: CNSSI-4009; SP 800-53A; SP 800-37

**Risk Management –** The process of managing risks to organizational operations (including mission, functions, image, reputation), organizational assets, individuals, other organizations, and the Nation, resulting from the operation of an information system, and includes: (i) the conduct of a risk assessment; (ii) the implementation of a risk mitigation strategy; and (iii) employment of techniques and procedures for the continuous monitoring of the security state of the information system.
SOURCE: SP 800-53; SP 800-53A; SP 800-37

| | |
|---|---|
| Risk Management – | The process of managing risks to organizational operations (including mission, functions, image, or reputation), organizational assets, or individuals resulting from the operation of an information system, and includes:<br>1) the conduct of a risk assessment;<br>2) the implementation of a risk mitigation strategy; and<br>3) employment of techniques and procedures for the continuous monitoring of the security state of the information system.<br>SOURCE: FIPS 200 |
| Risk Management – | The process of managing risks to agency operations (including mission, functions, image, or reputation), agency assets, or individuals resulting from the operation of an information system. It includes risk assessment; cost-benefit analysis; the selection, implementation, and assessment of security controls; and the formal authorization to operate the system. The process considers effectiveness, efficiency, and constraints due to laws, directives, policies, or regulations.<br>SOURCE: SP 800-82; SP 800-34<br>The process of managing risks to organizational operations (including mission, functions, image, or reputation), organizational assets, individuals, other organizations, or the nation resulting from the operation or use of an information system, and includes: (1) the conduct of a risk assessment; (2) the implementation of a risk mitigation strategy; (3) employment of techniques and procedures forthe continuous monitoring of the security state of the information system; and (4) documenting the overall risk management program.<br>SOURCE: CNSSI-4009 |
| Risk Management Framework – | A structured approach used to oversee and manage risk for an enterprise.<br>SOURCE: CNSSI-4009 |
| Risk Mitigation – | Risk mitigation involves prioritizing, evaluating, and implementing the appropriate risk-reducing controls recommended from the risk assessment process.<br>SOURCE: SP 800-30<br>Prioritizing, evaluating, and implementing the appropriate risk-reducing controls/countermeasures recommended from the risk management process.<br>SOURCE: CNSSI-4009 |
| Risk Tolerance – | The level of risk an entity is willing to assume in order to achieve a potential desired result.<br>SOURCE: SP 800-32<br>The defined impacts to an enterprise's information systems that an entity is willing to accept.<br>SOURCE: CNSSI-4009 |

Robust Security Network (RSN) – A wireless security network that only allows the creation of Robust Security Network Associations (RSNAs).
SOURCE: SP 800-48

Robust Security Network Association (RSNA) – A logical connection between communicating IEEE 802.11 entities established through the IEEE 802.11i key management scheme, also known as the four-way handshake.
SOURCE: SP 800-48

Robustness – The ability of an Information Assurance entity to operate correctly and reliably across a wide range of operational conditions, and to failgracefully outside of that operational range.
SOURCE: CNSSI-4009

Rogue Device – An unauthorized node on a network.
SOURCE: SP 800-115

Role – A group attribute that ties membership to function. When an entity assumes a role, the entity is given certain rights that belong to that role. When the entity leaves the role, those rights are removed. The rights given are consistent with the functionality that the entity needsto perform the expected tasks.
SOURCE: CNSSI-4009

Role-Based Access Control – (RBAC) A model for controlling access to resources where permitted actions on resources are identified with roles rather than with individual subject identities.
SOURCE: SP 800-95

Access control based on user roles (i.e., a collection of access authorizations a user receives based on an explicit or implicit assumption of a given role). Role permissions may be inherited through a role hierarchy and typically reflect the permissions needed to perform defined functions within an organization. A given role may apply to a single individual or to several individuals.
SOURCE: SP 800-53; CNSSI-4009

Root Certification Authority – In a hierarchical Public Key Infrastructure, the Certification Authority whose public key serves as the most trusted datum (i.e., thebeginning of trust paths) for a security domain.
SOURCE: SP 800-32; CNSSI-4009

Rootkit – A set of tools used by an attacker after gaining root-level access to a host to conceal the attacker's activities on the host and permit the attacker to maintain root-level access to the host through covert means.
SOURCE: SP 800-61; CNSSI-4009

Round Key – Round keys are values derived from the Cipher Key using the Key Expansion routine; they are applied to the State in the Cipher and Inverse Cipher.
SOURCE: FIPS 197

Rule-Based Security Policy – A security policy based on global rules imposed for all subjects. These rules usually rely on a comparison of the sensitivity of the objects being accessed and the possession of corresponding

attributes by the subjects requesting access.
SOURCE: SP 800-33
A security policy based on global rules imposed for all subjects. These rules usually rely on a comparison of the sensitivity of the objects being accessed and the possession of corresponding attributes by the subjects requesting access. Also known as discretionary access control (DAC).
SOURCE: CNSSI-4009

**Rules of Engagement (ROE) –** Detailed guidelines and constraints regarding the execution of information security testing. The ROE is established before the start of a security test, and gives the test team authority to conduct defined activities without the need for additional permissions.
SOURCE: SP 800-115

**Ruleset –** A table of instructions used by a controlled interface to determine what data is allowable and how the data is handled between interconnected systems.
SOURCE: SP800-115;CNSSI-4009
A set of directives that govern the access control functionality of a firewall. The firewall uses these directives to determine how packets should be routed between its interfaces.
SOURCE: SP 800-41

**S-box –** Nonlinear substitution table used in several byte substitution transformations and in the Key Expansion routine to perform a one-for-one substitution of a byte value.
SOURCE: FIPS 197

**S/MIME –** A set of specifications for securing electronic mail. Secure/ Multipurpose Internet Mail Extensions (S/MIME) is based upon the widely used MIME standard and describes a protocol for adding cryptographic security services through MIME encapsulation of digitally signed and encrypted objects. The basic security services offered by S/MIME are authentication, non-repudiation of origin, message integrity, and message privacy. Optional security services include signed receipts, security labels, secure mailing lists, and an extended method of identifying the signer's certificate(s).
SOURCE: SP 800-49

**Safeguards –** Protective measures prescribed to meet the security requirements (i.e., confidentiality, integrity, and availability) specified for an information system. Safeguards may include security features, management constraints, personnel security, and security of physical structures, areas, and devices. Synonymous with security controls andcountermeasures.
SOURCE: SP 800-53; SP 800-37; FIPS 200; CNSSI-4009

**Safeguarding Statement –** Statement affixed to a computer output or printout that states the highest classification being processed at the time the product was produced and requires control of the product, at that level, until determination of the true classification by an authorized individual.

Synonymous with banner.
SOURCE: CNSSI-4009

Salt – A non-secret value that is used in a cryptographic process, usually to ensure that the results of computations for one instance cannot be reused by an attacker.
SOURCE: SP 800-63; CNSSI-4009

Sandboxing – A method of isolating application modules into distinct fault domainsenforced by software. The technique allows untrusted programs written in an unsafe language, such as C, to be executed safely withinthe single virtual address space of an application. Untrusted machine interpretable code modules are transformed so that all memory accesses are confined to code and data segments within their fault domain. Access to system resources can also be controlled through a unique identifier associated with each domain.
SOURCE: SP 800-19

A restricted, controlled execution environment that prevents potentially malicious software, such as mobile code, from accessing any system resources except those for which the software is authorized.
SOURCE: CNSSI-4009

Sanitization – Process to remove information from media such that information recovery is not possible. It includes removing all labels, markings, and activity logs.
SOURCE: FIPS 200

A general term referring to the actions taken to render data written onmedia unrecoverable by both ordinary and, for some forms of sanitization, extraordinary means.
SOURCE: SP 800-53; CNSSI-4009

SCADA – See Supervisory Control and Data Acquisition.

Scanning – Sending packets or requests to another system to gain information to be used in a subsequent attack.
SOURCE: SP 800-61; CNSSI-4009

Scavenging – Searching through object residue to acquire data.
SOURCE: CNSSI-4009

Scoping Guidance – A part of tailoring guidance providing organizations with specific policy/regulatory-related, technology-related, system component allocation-related, operational/environmental-related, physical infrastructure-related, public access-related, scalability-related, common control-related, and security objective-related considerations on the applicability and implementation of individual security controls in the security control baseline.
SOURCE: SP 800-53

Scoping Guidance – Specific factors related to technology, infrastructure, public access, scalability, common security controls, and risk that can be

| | |
|---|---|
| | considered by organizations in the applicability and implementation of individual security controls in the security control baseline.<br>SOURCE: FIPS 200; CNSSI-4009 |
| Secret Key – | A cryptographic key that is used with a secret key (symmetric) cryptographic algorithm, that is uniquely associated with one or more entities and is not made public. The use of the term "secret" in this context does not imply a classification level, but rather implies the need to protect the key from disclosure.<br>SOURCE: SP 800-57<br>A cryptographic key that is used with a symmetric cryptographic algorithm that is uniquely associated with one or more entities and is not made public. The use of the term "secret" in this context does notimply a classification level, but rather implies the need to protect the key from disclosure.<br>SOURCE: CNSSI-4009 |
| Secret Key – | A cryptographic key that must be protected from unauthorized disclosure to protect data encrypted with the key. The use of the term"secret" in this context does not imply a classification level; rather, the term implies the need to protect the key from disclosure or substitution.<br>SOURCE: FIPS 201 |
| Secret Key – | A cryptographic key that is uniquely associated with one or more entities. The use of the term "secret" in this context does not imply a classification level, but rather implies the need to protect the key from disclosure or substitution.<br>SOURCE: FIPS 198 |
| Secret Key – | A cryptographic key, used with a secret key cryptographic algorithm, that is uniquely associated with one or more entities and should not be made public.<br>SOURCE: FIPS 140-2 |
| Secret Key (symmetric) Cryptographic Algorithm – | A cryptographic algorithm that uses a single secret key for both encryption and decryption.<br>SOURCE: FIPS 140-2<br><br>A cryptographic algorithm that uses a single key (i.e., a secret key) for both encryption and decryption.<br>SOURCE: CNSSI-4009 |
| Secret Seed – | A secret value used to initialize a pseudorandom number generator.<br>SOURCE: CNSSI-4009 |
| Secure/Multipurpose Internet Mail Extensions (S/MIME) – | A set of specifications for securing electronic mail. S/MIME is based upon the widely used MIME standard [MIME] and describes a protocol for adding cryptographic security services through MIME encapsulation of digitally signed and encrypted objects. The basic security services offered by S/MIME are authentication, non-repudiation of origin, message integrity, and message privacy. Optional security services include signed receipts, security labels, |

secure mailing lists, and an extended method of identifying the signer's certificate(s).
SOURCE: SP 800-49; CNSSI-4009

**Secure Communication Protocol –** A communication protocol that provides the appropriate confidentiality, authentication, and content integrity protection.
SOURCE: SP 800-57; CNSSI-4009

**Secure Communications –** Telecommunications deriving security through use of NSA-approvedproducts and/or Protected Distribution Systems.
SOURCE: CNSSI-4009

**Secure DNS (SECDNS) –** Configuring and operating DNS servers so that the security goals of data integrity and source authentication are achieved and maintained.
SOURCE: SP 800-81

**Secure Erase –** An overwrite technology using firmware-based process to overwrite a hard drive. Is a drive command defined in the ANSI ATA and SCSI disk drive interface specifications, which runs inside drive hardware. It completes in about 1/8 the time of 5220 block erasure.
SOURCE: SP 800-88

**Secure Hash Algorithm (SHA) –** A hash algorithm with the property that is computationally infeasible 1) to find a message that corresponds to a given message digest, or 2)to find two different messages that produce the same message digest.
SOURCE: CNSSI-4009

**Secure Hash Standard –** This Standard specifies four secure hash algorithms – SHA-1, SHA-256, SHA-384, and SHA-512 – for computing a condensed representation of electronic data (message). When a message of any length <264bits (for SHA-1 and SHA-256) or < 2128bits (for SHA-384 and SHA-512) is input to an algorithm, the result is an output called a message digest. The message digests range in length from 160 to 512 bits, depending on the algorithm. Secure hash algorithmsare typically used with other cryptographic algorithms, such as the digital signature algorithms and keyed-hash message authentication codes, or in the generation of random numbers (bits).
SOURCE: FIPS 180-2

Specification for a secure hash algorithm that can generate a condensed message representation called a message digest.
SOURCE: CNSSI-4009

**Secure Socket Layer (SSL) –** A protocol used for protecting private information during transmission via the Internet.
Note: SSL works by using a public key to encrypt data that's transferred over the SSL connection. Most Web browsers support SSL, and many Web sites use the protocol to obtain confidential userinformation, such as credit card numbers. By convention, URLs thatrequire an SSL connection start with "https:" instead of "http:."
SOURCE: CNSSI-4009

| | |
|---|---|
| Secure State – | Condition in which no subject can access any object in an unauthorized manner.<br>SOURCE: CNSSI-4009 |
| Secure Subsystem – | Subsystem containing its own implementation of the reference monitor concept for those resources it controls. Secure subsystem must depend on other controls and the base operating system for the control of subjects and the more primitive system objects.<br>SOURCE: CNSSI-4009 |
| Security – | A condition that results from the establishment and maintenance of protective measures that enable an enterprise to perform its mission or critical functions despite risks posed by threats to its use of information systems. Protective measures may involve a combination of deterrence, avoidance, prevention, detection, recovery, and correction that should form part of the enterprise's riskmanagement approach.<br>SOURCE: CNSSI-4009 |
| Security Assertion Markup Language (SAML) – | A specification for encoding security assertions in the Extensible Markup Language (XML).<br>SOURCE: SP 800-63<br>A framework for exchanging authentication and authorization information. Security typically involves checking the credentials presented by a party for authentication and authorization. SAML standardizes the representation of these credentials in an XML formatcalled "assertions," enhancing the interoperability between disparate applications.<br>SOURCE: SP 800-95<br>A protocol consisting of XML-based request and response message formats for exchanging security information, expressed in the form ofassertions about subjects, between online business partners.<br>SOURCE: CNSSI-4009 |
| Security Association – | A relationship established between two or more entities to enable them to protect data they exchange.<br>SOURCE: CNSSI-4009 |
| Security Attribute – | A security-related quality of an object. Security attributes may be represented as hierarchical levels, bits in a bit map, or numbers. Compartments, caveats, and release markings are examples of security attributes.<br>SOURCE: FIPS 188<br>An abstraction representing the basic properties or characteristics of an entity with respect to safeguarding information; typically associated with internal data structures (e.g., records, buffers, files) within the information system which are used to enable the implementation of access control and flow control policies; reflect special dissemination, handling, or distribution instructions; or support other aspects of the information security policy.<br>SOURCE: SP800-53;CNSSI-4009 |

| | |
|---|---|
| Security Authorization – | See Authorization. |
| Security Authorization – (To Operate) | See Authorization (to operate).<br>SOURCE: CNSSI-4009 |
| Security Authorization Boundary – | See Authorization Boundary. |
| Security Banner – | A banner at the top or bottom of a computer screen that states the overall classification of the system in large, bold type. Also can referto the opening screen that informs users of the security implications of accessing a computer resource.<br>SOURCE: CNSSI-4009 |
| Security Categorization – | The process of determining the security category for information or an information system. See Security Category.<br>SOURCE: SP 800-53<br>The process of determining the security category for information or an information system. Security categorization methodologies are described in CNSS Instruction 1253 for national security systems and in FIPS 199 for other than national security systems.<br>SOURCE: SP 800-37; SP 800-53A |
| Security Category – | The characterization of information or an information system based on an assessment of the potential impact that a loss of confidentiality,integrity, or availability of such information or information system would have on organizational operations, organizational assets, or individuals.<br>SOURCE: FIPS 200; FIPS 199; SP 800-18<br>The characterization of information or an information system based on an assessment of the potential impact that a loss of confidentiality,integrity, or availability of such information or information system would have on organizational operations, organizational assets, individuals, other organizations, and the Nation.<br>SOURCE: SP800-53;CNSSI-4009; SP 800-60 |
| Security Concept of Operations – (Security CONOP) | A security-focused description of an information system, its operational policies, classes of users, interactions between the systemand its users, and the system's contribution to the operational mission.<br>SOURCE: CNSSI-4009 |
| Security Content Automation Protocol (SCAP) – | A method for using specific standardized testing methods to enable automated vulnerability management, measurement, and policy compliance evaluation against a standardized set of security requirements.<br>SOURCE: CNSSI-4009 |
| Security Control Assessment – | The testing and/or evaluation of the management, operational, and technical security controls in an information system to determine |

the extent to which the controls are implemented correctly, operating as intended, and producing the desired outcome with respect to meeting the security requirements for the system.
SOURCE: SP 800-37; SP 800-53; SP 800-53A
The testing and/or evaluation of the management, operational, and technical security controls to determine the extent to which the controls are implemented correctly, operating as intended, and producing the desired outcome with respect to meeting the security requirements for the system and/or enterprise.
SOURCE: CNSSI-4009

Security Control Assessor – The individual, group, or organization responsible for conducting a security control assessment.
SOURCE: SP 800-37; SP 800-53A

Security Control Baseline – The set of minimum security controls defined for a low-impact, moderate-impact, or high-impact information system.
SOURCE: SP 800-53; FIPS 200
One of the sets of minimum security controls defined for federal information systems in NIST Special Publication 800-53 and CNSS Instruction 1253.
SOURCE: SP 800-53A

Security Control Enhancements – Statements of security capability to 1) build in additional, but related,functionality to a basic control; and/or 2) increase the strength of a basic control.
SOURCE: CNSSI-4009; SP 800-53A
Statements of security capability to: (i) build in additional, but related, functionality to a security control; and/or (ii) increase the strength of the control.
SOURCE: SP 800-53; SP 800-18

Security Control Inheritance – A situation in which an information system or application receives protection from security controls (or portions of security controls) that are developed, implemented, assessed, authorized, and monitored by entities other than those responsible for the system or application; entities either internal or external to the organization where the system or application resides. See Common Control.
SOURCE: SP 800-37; SP 800-53; SP 800-53A; CNSSI-4009

Security Controls – The management, operational, and technical controls (i.e., safeguardsor countermeasures) prescribed for an information system to protect the confidentiality, integrity, and availability of the system and its information.
SOURCE: SP 800-53; SP 800-37; SP 800-53A; SP 800-60; FIPS 200; FIPS 199; CNSSI-4009

Security Controls Baseline – The set of minimum security controls defined for a low-impact, moderate-impact, or high-impact information system.
SOURCE: CNSSI-4009

| | |
|---|---|
| Security Domain – | A set of subjects, their information objects, and a common security policy.<br>SOURCE: SP 800-27 |
| Security Domain – | A collection of entities to which applies a single security policy executed by a single authority.<br>SOURCE: FIPS 188<br>A domain that implements a security policy and is administered by a single authority.<br>SOURCE: SP800-37;SP800-53;CNSSI-4009 |
| Security Engineering – | An interdisciplinary approach and means to enable the realization of secure systems. It focuses on defining customer needs, security protection requirements, and required functionality early in the systems development life cycle, documenting requirements, and then proceeding with design, synthesis, and system validation while considering the complete problem.<br>SOURCE: CNSSI-4009 |
| Security Fault Analysis (SFA) – | An assessment, usually performed on information system hardware, to determine the security properties of a device when hardware fault is encountered.<br>SOURCE: CNSSI-4009 |
| Security Features Users Guide – (SFUG) | Guide or manual explaining how the security mechanisms in a specific system work.<br>SOURCE: CNSSI-4009 |
| Security Filter – | A secure subsystem of an information system that enforces security policy on the data passing through it.<br>SOURCE: CNSSI-4009 |
| Security Functions – | The hardware, software, and/or firmware of the information system responsible for enforcing the system security policy and supporting the isolation of code and data on which the protection is based.<br>SOURCE: SP 800-53 |
| Security Goals – | The five security goals are confidentiality, availability, integrity, accountability, and assurance.<br>SOURCE: SP 800-27 |
| Security Impact Analysis – | The analysis conducted by an organizational official to determine the extent to which changes to the information system have affected the security state of the system.<br>SOURCE: SP 800-53; SP 800-53A; SP 800-37; CNSSI-4009 |
| Security Incident – | See Incident. |
| Security Inspection – | Examination of an information system to determine compliance with security policy, procedures, and practices.<br>SOURCE: CNSSI-4009 |
| Security Kernel – | Hardware, firmware, and software elements of a trusted computing base implementing the reference monitor concept. Security kernel must mediate all accesses, be protected from modification, and be verifiable as correct.<br>SOURCE: CNSSI-4009 |

Security Label – The means used to associate a set of security attributes with a specificinformation object as part of the data structure for that object.
SOURCE: SP 800-53

Security Label – A marking bound to a resource (which may be a data unit) that namesor designates the security attributes of that resource.
SOURCE: FIPS 188

Information that represents or designates the value of one or more security relevant-attributes (e.g., classification) of a system resource.
SOURCE: CNSSI-4009

Security Level – A hierarchical indicator of the degree of sensitivity to a certain threat.It implies, according to the security policy being enforced, a specific level of protection.
SOURCE: FIPS 188

Security Marking – Human-readable information affixed to information system components, removable media, or output indicating the distribution limitations, handling caveats, and applicable security markings.
SOURCE: SP 800-53

Security Markings – Human-readable indicators applied to a document, storage media, orhardware component to designate security classification, categorization, and/or handling restrictions applicable to the information contained therein. For intelligence information, these could include compartment and sub-compartment indicators and handling restrictions.
SOURCE: CNSSI-4009

Security Mechanism – A device designed to provide one or more security services usually rated in terms of strength of service and assurance of the design.
SOURCE: CNSSI-4009

Security Net Control Station – Management system overseeing and controlling implementation of network security policy.
SOURCE: CNSSI-4009

Security Objective – Confidentiality, integrity, or availability.
SOURCE: SP 800-53; SP 800-53A; SP 800-60; SP 800-37; FIPS 200; FIPS 199

Security Perimeter – See Authorization Boundary.

A physical or logical boundary that is defined for a system, domain, or enclave, within which a particular security policy or security architecture is applied.
SOURCE: CNSSI-4009

Security Plan – Formal document that provides an overview of the security requirements for an information system or an information security program and describes the security controls in place or planned for meeting those requirements.

See 'System Security Plan'or 'Information Security Program Plan.'
SOURCE: SP 800-53; SP 800-53A; SP 800-37; SP 800-18

Security Policy – The statement of required protection of the information objects.
SOURCE: SP 800-27

Security Policy – A set of criteria for the provision of security services. It defines and constrains the activities of a data processing facility in order to maintain a condition of security for systems and data.
SOURCE: FIPS 188
A set of criteria for the provision of security services.
SOURCE: SP800-37;SP800-53;CNSSI-4009

Security Posture – The security status of an enterprise's networks, information, and systems based on IA resources (e.g., people, hardware, software, policies) and capabilities in place to manage the defense of the enterprise and to react as the situation changes.
SOURCE: CNSSI-4009

Security Program Plan – Formal document that provides an overview of the security requirements for an organization-wide information security programand describes the program management security controls and common security controls in place or planned for meeting those requirements.
SOURCE: CNSSI-4009

Security Range – Highest and lowest security levels that are permitted in or on an information system, system component, subsystem, or network.
SOURCE: CNSSI-4009

Security-Relevant Change – Any change to a system's configuration, environment, information content, functionality, or users which has the potential to change the risk imposed upon its continued operations.
SOURCE: CNSSI-4009

Security-Relevant Event – An occurrence (e.g., an auditable event or flag) considered to have potential security implications to the system or its environment that may require further action (noting, investigating, or reacting).
SOURCE: CNSSI-4009

Security-Relevant Information – Any information within the information system that can potentially impact the operation of security functions in a manner that could result in failure to enforce the system security policy or maintain isolation of code and data.
SOURCE: SP 800-53

Security Requirements – Requirements – Requirements levied on an information system that are derived from applicable laws, Executive Orders, directives, policies, standards, instructions, regulations, or procedures, or organizational mission/business case needs to ensure the confidentiality, integrity, and availability of the information being processed, stored, or transmitted.
SOURCE: FIPS 200; SP 800-53; SP 800-53A; SP 800-37; CNSSI-4009

| | |
|---|---|
| Security Requirements Baseline – | Description of the minimum requirements necessary for an information system to maintain an acceptable level of risk.<br>SOURCE: CNSSI-4009 |
| Security Requirements TraceabilityMatrix (SRTM) – | Matrix that captures all security requirements linked to potential risksand addresses all applicable C&A requirements. It is, therefore, a correlation statement of a system's security features and compliance methods for each security requirement.<br>SOURCE: CNSSI-4009 |
| Security Safeguards – | Protective measures and controls prescribed to meet the security requirements specified for an information system. Safeguards may include security features, management constraints, personnel security, and security of physical structures, areas, and devices.<br>SOURCE: CNSSI-4009 |
| Security Service – | A capability that supports one, or many, of the security goals. Examples of security services are key management, access control, and authentication.<br>SOURCE: SP 800-27<br>A capability that supports one, or more, of the security requirements (Confidentiality, Integrity, Availability). Examples of security services are key management, access control, and authentication.<br>SOURCE: CNSSI-4009 |
| Security Specification – | Detailed description of the safeguards required to protect an information system.<br>SOURCE: CNSSI-4009 |
| Security Strength – | A measure of the computational complexity associated with recovering certain secret and/or security-critical information concerning a given cryptographic algorithm from known data (e.g. plaintext/ciphertext pairs for a given encryption algorithm).<br>SOURCE: SP 800-108<br>A number associated with the amount of work (that is, the number of operations) that is required to break a cryptographic algorithm or system. Sometimes referred to as a security level.<br>SOURCE: FIPS 186 |
| Security Tag – | Information unit containing a representation of certain security-related information (e.g., a restrictive attribute bit map).<br>SOURCE: FIPS 188 |
| Security Target – | Common Criteria specification that represents a set of security requirements to be used as the basis of an evaluation of an identified Target of Evaluation (TOE).<br>SOURCE: CNSSI-4009 |
| Security Test & Evaluation – (ST&E) | Examination and analysis of the safeguards required to protect an information system, as they have been applied in an operational environment, to determine the security posture of that system.<br>SOURCE: CNSSI-4009 |

| | |
|---|---|
| Security Testing – | Process to determine that an information system protects data and maintains functionality as intended.<br>SOURCE: CNSSI-4009 |
| Seed Key – | Initial key used to start an updating or key generation process.<br>SOURCE: CNSSI-4009 |
| Senior Agency Information Security Officer (SAISO) – | Official responsible for carrying out the Chief Information Officer responsibilities under the Federal Information Security Management Act (FISMA) and serving as the Chief Information Officer's primaryliaison to the agency's authorizing officials, information system owners, and information system security officers.<br>SP 800-53 Note: Organizations subordinate to federal agencies may use the term Senior Information Security Officer or Chief Information Security Officer to denote individuals filling positions with similar responsibilities toSenior Agency Information Security Officers.<br>SOURCE: SP 800-53; SP 800-53A; SP 800-37; SP 800-60; FIPS 200; CNSSI-4009; 44 U.S.C., Sec. 3544 |
| Senior Information Security Officer – | See Senior Agency Information Security Officer. |
| Sensitive Compartmented Information (SCI) – | Classified information concerning or derived from intelligence sources, methods, or analytical processes, which is required to be handled within formal access control systems established by the Director of National Intelligence.<br>SOURCE: SP800-53;CNSSI-4009 |
| Sensitive Compartmented Information Facility (SCIF) – | Accredited area, room, or group of rooms, buildings, or installation where SCI may be stored, used, discussed, and/or processed.<br>SOURCE: CNSSI-4009 |
| Sensitive Information – | Information, the loss, misuse, or unauthorized access to or modification of, that could adversely affect the national interest or theconduct of federal programs, or the privacy to which individuals are entitled under 5 U.S.C. Section 552a (the Privacy Act), but that has not been specifically authorized under criteria established by an Executive Order or an Act of Congress to be kept classified in the interest of national defense or foreign policy.<br>SOURCE: SP 800-53<br>Information, the loss, misuse, or unauthorized access to or modification of, that could adversely affect the national interest or theconduct of federal programs, or the privacy to which individuals are entitled under 5 U.S.C. Section 552a (the Privacy Act), but that has not been specifically authorized under criteria established by an Executive Order or an Act of Congress to be kept classified in the interest of national defense or foreign policy. (Systems that are not national security systems, but contain sensitive information, are to be protected in accordance with the requirements of the Computer |

| | |
|---|---|
| | Security Act of 1987 [P.L.100-235].)<br>SOURCE: CNSSI-4009 |
| Sensitivity – | A measure of the importance assigned to information by its owner, for the purpose of denoting its need for protection.<br>SOURCE: SP 800-60; CNSSI-4009 |
| Sensitivity Label – | Information representing elements of the security label(s) of a subject and an object. Sensitivity labels are used by the trusted computing base (TCB) as the basis for mandatory access control decisions. See security label.<br>SOURCE: CNSSI-4009 |
| Service-Level Agreement – | Defines the specific responsibilities of the service provider and sets the customer expectations.<br>SOURCE: CNSSI-4009 |
| Shared Secret – | A secret used in authentication that is known to the claimant and the verifier.<br>SOURCE: SP 800-63 |
| Shielded Enclosure – | Room or container designed to attenuate electromagnetic radiation, acoustic signals, or emanations.<br>SOURCE: CNSSI-4009 |
| Short Title – | Identifying combination of letters and numbers assigned to certain COMSEC materials to facilitate handling, accounting, and controlling.<br>SOURCE: CNSSI-4009 |
| Signature – | A recognizable, distinguishing pattern associated with an attack, suchas a binary string in a virus or a particular set of keystrokes used to gain unauthorized access to a system.<br>SOURCE: SP 800-61<br>A recognizable, distinguishing pattern. See also attack signature or digital signature.<br>SOURCE: CNSSI-4009 |
| Signature Certificate – | A public key certificate that contains a public key intended for verifying digital signatures rather than encrypting data or performing any other cryptographic functions.<br>SOURCE: SP 800-32; CNSSI-4009 |
| Signature Generation – | Uses a digital signature algorithm and a private key to generate a digital signature on data.<br>SOURCE: SP 800-57<br>The process of using a digital signature algorithm and a private key to generate a digital signature on data.<br>SOURCE: FIPS 186 |
| Signature Validation – | The (mathematical) verification of the digital signature and obtaining<br>the appropriate assurances (e.g., public key validity, private key possession, etc.).<br>SOURCE: FIPS 186 |

**Signature Verification** – Uses a digital signature algorithm and a public key to verify a digital signature.
SOURCE: SP 800-57
The process of using a digital signature algorithm and a public key to verify a digital signature on data.
SOURCE: SP 800-89; FIPS 186

**Signed Data** – Data on which a digital signature is generated.
SOURCE: FIPS 196

**Single Point Keying** – Means of distributing key to multiple, local crypto equipment or devices from a single fill point.
SOURCE: CNSSI-4009

**Single-Hop Problem** – The security risks resulting from a mobile software agent moving from its home platform to another platform.
SOURCE: SP 800-19

**Situational Awareness** – Within a volume of time and space, the perception of an enterprise'ssecurity posture and its threat environment; the comprehension/meaning of both taken together (risk); and the projection of their status into the near future.
SOURCE: CNSSI-4009

**Skimming** – The unauthorized use of a reader to read tags without the authorization or knowledge of the tag's owner or the individual in possession of the tag.
SOURCE: SP 800-98

**Smart Card** – A credit card-sized card with embedded integrated circuits that can store, process, and communicate information.
SOURCE: CNSSI-4009

**Sniffer** – See Packet Sniffer or Passive Wiretapping.

**Social Engineering** – An attempt to trick someone into revealing information (e.g., a password) that can be used to attack systems or networks.
SOURCE: SP 800-61
A general term for attackers trying to trick people into revealing sensitive information or performing certain actions, such as downloading and executing files that appear to be benign but are actually malicious.
SOURCE: SP 800-114
The process of attempting to trick someone into revealing information (e.g., a password).
SOURCE: SP 800-115
An attempt to trick someone into revealing information (e.g., a password) that can be used to attack an enterprise.
SOURCE: CNSSI-4009

**Software** – Computer programs and associated data that may be dynamically written or modified during execution.
SOURCE: CNSSI-4009

**Software Assurance –** Level of confidence that software is free from vulnerabilities, either intentionally designed into the software or accidentally inserted at anytime during its life cycle, and that the software functions in the intended manner.
SOURCE: CNSSI-4009

**Software System Test and Evaluation Process –** Process that plans, develops, and documents the qualitative/quantitative demonstration of the fulfillment of all baseline functional performance, operational, and interface requirements.
SOURCE: CNSSI-4009

**Software-Based Fault Isolation –** A method of isolating application modules into distinct fault domainsenforced by software. The technique allows untrusted programs written in an unsafe language, such as C, to be executed safely withinthe single virtual address space of an application. Untrusted machine interpretable code modules are transformed so that all memory accesses are confined to code and data segments within their fault domain. Access to system resources can also be controlled through a unique identifier associated with each domain.
SOURCE: SP 800-19

**Spam –** The abuse of electronic messaging systems to indiscriminately send unsolicited bulk messages.
SOURCE: SP 800-53
Unsolicited bulk commercial email messages.
SOURCE: SP 800-45
Electronic junk mail or the abuse of electronic messaging systems to indiscriminately send unsolicited bulk messages.
SOURCE: CNSSI-4009

**Spam Filtering Software –** A program that analyzes emails to look for characteristics of spam, and typically places messages that appear to be spam in a separate email folder.
SOURCE: SP 800-69

**Special Access Program (SAP) –** A program established for a specific class of classified information that imposes safeguarding and access requirements that exceed those normally required for information at the same classification level.
SOURCE: SP800-53;CNSSI-4009

**Special Access Program Facility – (SAPF)** Facility formally accredited by an appropriate agency in accordance with DCID 6/9 in which SAP information may be processed.
SOURCE: CNSSI-4009

**Special Character –** Any non-alphanumeric character that can be rendered on a standard American-English keyboard. Use of a specific special character may be application-dependent.
The list of special characters follows:
` ~ ! @ # $ % ^ & * ( ) _ + | } { " : ? > < [ ] \ ; ' , . / - =
SOURCE: CNSSI-4009

Specification – An assessment object that includes document-based artifacts (e.g., policies, procedures, plans, system security requirements, functional specifications, and architectural designs) associated with an information system.
SOURCE: SP 800-53A

Spillage – Security incident that results in the transfer of classified or CUI information onto an information system not accredited (i.e., authorized) for the appropriate security level.
SOURCE: CNSSI-4009

Split Knowledge – A procedure by which a cryptographic key is split into n multiple key components, individually providing no knowledge of the original key, which can be subsequently combined to recreate the original cryptographic key
SOURCE: SP 800-57

Split Knowledge – A process by which a cryptographic key is split into multiple key components, individually sharing no knowledge of the original key, that can be subsequently input into, or output from, a cryptographic module by separate entities and combined to recreate the original cryptographic key.
SOURCE: FIPS 140-2

1. Separation of data or information into two or more parts, each part constantly kept under control of separate authorized individuals or teams so that no one individual or team will know the whole data.
2. A process by which a cryptographic key is split into multiple key components, individually sharing no knowledge of the original key, which can be subsequently input into, or output from, a cryptographicmodule by separate entities and combined to recreate the original cryptographic key.
SOURCE: CNSSI-4009

Spoofing – "IP spoofing" refers to sending a network packet that appears to come from a source other than its actual source.
SOURCE: SP 800-48

Spoofing – Involves—
1)the ability to receive a message by masquerading as the legitimatereceiving destination, or
2)masquerading as the sending machine and sending a message to a destination.
SOURCE: FIPS 191

1. Faking the sending address of a transmission to gain illegal entry into a secure system. Impersonating, masquerading, piggybacking, and mimicking are forms of spoofing.
2. The deliberate inducement of a user or resource to take incorrect action.
SOURCE: CNSSI-4009

Spread Spectrum – Telecommunications techniques in which a signal is transmitted in a bandwidth considerably greater than the frequency content of the

| | |
|---|---|
| | original information. Frequency hopping, direct sequence spreading, time scrambling, and combinations of these techniques are forms of spread spectrum.<br>SOURCE: CNSSI-4009 |
| Spyware – | Software that is secretly or surreptitiously installed into an information system to gather information on individuals or organizations without their knowledge; a type of malicious code.<br>SOURCE: SP 800-53; CNSSI-4009 |
| SSL – | See Secure Sockets Layer. |
| Standard – | A published statement on a topic specifying characteristics, usually measurable, that must be satisfied or achieved in order to comply with the standard.<br>SOURCE: FIPS 201 |
| Start-Up KEK | Key-encryption-key held in common by a group of potential communicating entities and used to establish ad hoc tactical networks.<br>SOURCE: CNSSI-4009 |
| State – | Intermediate Cipher result that can be pictured as a rectangular array of bytes.<br>SOURCE: FIPS 197 |
| Static Key – | A key that is intended for use for a relatively long period of time and is typically intended for use in many instances of a cryptographic keyestablish scheme<br>SOURCE: SP 800-57 |
| Steganography – | The art and science of communicating in a way that hides the existence of the communication. For example, a child pornography image can be hidden inside another graphic image file, audio file, orother file format.<br>SOURCE: SP 800-72; SP 800-101<br>The art, science, and practice of communicating in a way that hides the existence of the communication.<br>SOURCE: CNSSI-4009 |
| Storage Object – | Object supporting both read and write accesses to an information system.<br>SOURCE: CNSSI-4009 |
| Strength of Mechanism (SoM) – | A scale for measuring the relative strength of a security mechanism.<br>SOURCE: CNSSI-4009 |
| Striped Core – | A network architecture in which user data traversing a core IP network is decrypted, filtered and re-encrypted one or more times.<br>Note: The decryption, filtering, and re-encryption are performed within a "Red gateway"; consequently, the core is "striped" becausethe data path is alternately Black, Red, and Black.<br>SOURCE: CNSSI-4009 |
| Strong Authentication – | The requirement to use multiple factors for authentication and advanced technology, such as dynamic passwords or digital |

certificates, to verify an entity's identity.
SOURCE: CNSSI-4009

**Subassembly –** Major subdivision of an assembly consisting of a package of parts, elements, and circuits that perform a specific function.
SOURCE: CNSSI-4009

**Subject –** The person whose identity is bound to a particular credential.
SOURCE: SP 800-63

Generally an individual, process, or device causing information to flow among objects or changes to the system state.
See Object.
SOURCE: SP 800-53

An active entity (generally an individual, process, or device) that causes information to flow among objects or changes the system state. See also object.
SOURCE: CNSSI-4009

**Subject Security Level –** Sensitivity label(s) of the objects to which the subject has both read and write access. Security level of a subject must always be dominated by the clearance level of the user associated with the subject.
SOURCE: CNSSI-4009

**Subordinate Certification Authority –** In a hierarchical PKI, a Certification Authority whose certificate signature key is certified by another CA, and whose activities are constrained by that other CA.
SOURCE: SP 800-32; CNSSI-4009

**Subscriber –** A party who receives a credential or token from a CSP (Credentials Service Provider) and becomes a claimant in an authentication protocol.
SOURCE: SP 800-63; CNSSI-4009

**Subsystem –** A major subdivision or component of an information system consisting of information, information technology, and personnel thatperform one or more specific functions.
SOURCE: SP 800-53; SP 800-53A; SP 800-37

**Suite A –** A specific set of classified cryptographic algorithms used for the protection of some categories of restricted mission-critical information.
SOURCE: CNSSI-4009

**Suite B –** A specific set of cryptographic algorithms suitable for protecting national security systems and information throughout the U.S. government and to support interoperability with allies and coalition partners.
SOURCE: CNSSI-4009, as modified

**Superencryption –** Process of encrypting encrypted information. Occurs when a message, encrypted off-line, is transmitted over a secured, online circuit, or when information encrypted by the originator is

| | |
|---|---|
| | multiplexed onto a communications trunk, which is then bulk encrypted.<br>SOURCE: CNSSI-4009 |
| Superior Certification Authority – | In a hierarchical PKI, a Certification Authority who has certified the certificate signature key of another CA, and who constrains the activities of that CA.<br>SOURCE: SP 800-32; CNSSI-4009 |
| Supersession – | Scheduled or unscheduled replacement of COMSEC material with a different edition.<br>SOURCE: CNSSI-4009 |
| Supervisory Control and Data Acquisition (SCADA) – | A generic name for a computerized system that is capable of gathering and processing data and applying operational controls over long distances. Typical uses include power transmission and distribution and pipeline systems. SCADA was designed for the unique communication challenges (delays, data integrity, etc.) posed by the various media that must be used, such as phone lines, microwave, and satellite. Usually shared rather than dedicated.<br>SOURCE: SP 800-82<br>Networks or systems generally used for industrial controls or to manage infrastructure such as pipelines and power systems.<br>SOURCE: CNSSI-4009 |
| Supplementation (Assessment Procedures) – | The process of adding assessment procedures or assessment details to assessment procedures in order to adequately meet the organization's risk management needs.<br>SOURCE: SP 800-53A |
| Supplementation (Security Controls) – | The process of adding security controls or control enhancements to a security control baseline from NIST Special Publication 800-53 or CNSS Instruction 1253 in order to adequately meet the organization'srisk management needs.<br>SOURCE: SP 800-53A |
| Supply Chain – | A system of organizations, people, activities, information, and resources, possibly international in scope, that provides products or services to consumers.<br>SOURCE: SP800-53;CNSSI-4009 |
| Supply Chain Attack – | Attacks that allow the adversary to utilize implants or other vulnerabilities inserted prior to installation in order to infiltrate data, or manipulate information technology hardware, software, operating systems, peripherals (information technology products) or services at any point during the life cycle.<br>SOURCE: CNSSI-4009 |
| Suppression Measure – | Action, procedure, modification, or device that reduces the level of, or inhibits the generation of, compromising emanations in an information system.<br>SOURCE: CNSSI-4009 |
| Surrogate Access – | See Discretionary Access Control. |

| | |
|---|---|
| Syllabary – | List of individual letters, combination of letters, or syllables, with their equivalent code groups, used for spelling out words or proper names not present in the vocabulary of a code. A syllabary may also be a spelling table.<br>SOURCE: CNSSI-4009 |
| Symmetric Encryption Algorithm – | Encryption algorithms using the same secret key for encryption and decryption.<br>SOURCE: SP 800-49; CNSSI-4009 |
| Symmetric Key – | A cryptographic key that is used to perform both the cryptographic operation and its inverse, for example to encrypt and decrypt, or create a message authentication code and to verify the code.<br>SOURCE: SP 800-63; CNSSI-4009 |
| Symmetric Key – | A single cryptographic key that is used with a secret (symmetric) key algorithm.<br>SOURCE: SP 800-21 [2ndEd] |
| Synchronous Crypto-Operation – | Encryption algorithms using the same secret key for encryption and decryption.<br>SOURCE: CNSSI-4009 |
| System – | See Information System.<br>Any organized assembly of resources and procedures united and regulated by interaction or interdependence to accomplish a set of specific functions. See also information system.<br>SOURCE: CNSSI-4009 |
| System Administrator – | A person who manages the technical aspects of a system.<br>SOURCE: SP 800-40<br>Individual responsible for the installation and maintenance of an information system, providing effective information system utilization, adequate security parameters, and sound implementation of established Information Assurance policy and procedures.<br>SOURCE: CNSSI-4009 |
| System Assets – | Any software, hardware, data, administrative, physical, communications, or personnel resource within an information system.<br>SOURCE: CNSSI-4009 |
| System Development Life Cycle – (SDLC) | The scope of activities associated with a system, encompassing the system's initiation, development and acquisition, implementation, operation and maintenance, and ultimately its disposal that instigates another system initiation.<br>SOURCE: SP 800-34; CNSSI-4009 |
| System Development Methodologies – | Methodologies developed through software engineering to manage the complexity of system development. Development methodologies include software engineering aids and high-level design analysis tools.<br>SOURCE: CNSSI-4009 |
| System High – | Highest security level supported by an information system.<br>SOURCE: CNSSI-4009 |

| | |
|---|---|
| System High Mode – | Information systems security mode of operation wherein each user, with direct or indirect access to the information system, its peripherals, remote terminals, or remote hosts, has all of the following: a. valid security clearance for all information within an information system; b. formal access approval and signed nondisclosure agreements for all the information stored and/or processed (including all compartments, subcompartments and/or special access programs); and c. valid need-to-know for some of the information contained within the information system.<br>SOURCE: CNSSI-4009 |
| System Indicator – | Symbol or group of symbols in an off-line encrypted message identifying the specific cryptosystem or key used in the encryption.<br>SOURCE: CNSSI-4009 |
| System Integrity – | The quality that a system has when it performs its intended function in an unimpaired manner, free from unauthorized manipulation of thesystem, whether intentional or accidental.<br>SOURCE: SP 800-27<br>Attribute of an information system when it performs its intended function in an unimpaired manner, free from deliberate or inadvertentunauthorized manipulation of the system.<br>SOURCE: CNSSI-4009 |
| System Interconnection – | The direct connection of two or more IT systems for the purpose of sharing data and other information resources.<br>SOURCE: SP 800-47; CNSSI-4009 |
| System Low – | Lowest security level supported by an information system.<br>SOURCE: CNSSI-4009 |
| System Of Records – | A group of any records under the control of any agency from which information is retrieved by the name of the individual or by some identifying number, symbol, or other identifying particular assigned to the individual.<br>SOURCE: SP 800-122 |
| System Owner – | Person or organization having responsibility for the development, procurement, integration, modification, operation and maintenance, and/or final disposition of an information system.<br>SOURCE: CNSSI-4009 |
| System Profile – | Detailed security description of the physical structure, equipment component, location, relationships, and general operating environment of an information system.<br>SOURCE: CNSSI-4009 |
| System Security – | See Information System Security. |
| System Security Plan – | Formal document that provides an overview of the security requirements for the information system and describes the security controls in place or planned for meeting those requirements.<br>SOURCE: SP 800-37; SP 800-53; SP 800-53A; SP 800-18; FIPS 200 |

The formal document prepared by the information system owner (or common security controls owner for inherited controls) that provides an overview of the security requirements for the system and describesthe security controls in place or planned for meeting those requirements. The plan can also contain as supporting appendices or as references, other key security-related documents such as a risk assessment, privacy impact assessment, system interconnection agreements, contingency plan, security configurations, configuration management plan, and incident response plan.
SOURCE: CNSSI-4009

System Software – The special software within the cryptographic boundary (e.g., operating system, compilers or utility programs) designed for a specific computer system or family of computer systems to facilitate the operation and maintenance of the computer system, associated programs, and data.
SOURCE: FIPS 140-2

System-Specific Security Control – A security control for an information system that has not been designated as a common security control or the portion of a hybrid control that is to be implemented within an information system.
SOURCE: SP 800-37; SP 800-53; SP 800-53A; CNSSI-4009

Systems Security Engineering – See Information Systems Security Engineering.

Systems Security Officer – See Information Systems Security Officer.

Tabletop Exercise – A discussion-based exercise where personnel with roles and responsibilities in a particular IT plan meet in a classroom setting or in breakout groups to validate the content of the plan by discussing their roles during an emergency and their responses to a particular emergency situation. A facilitator initiates the discussion by presenting a scenario and asking questions based on the scenario.
SOURCE: SP 800-84

Tactical Data – Information that requires protection from disclosure and modificationfor a limited duration as determined by the originator or information owner.
SOURCE: CNSSI-4009

Tactical Edge – The platforms, sites, and personnel (U. S. military, allied, coalition partners, first responders) operating at lethal risk in a battle space or crisis environment characterized by 1) a dependence on information systems and connectivity for survival and mission success, 2) high threats to the operational readiness of both information systems and connectivity, and 3) users are fully engaged, highly stressed, and dependent on the availability, integrity, and transparency of their information systems.
SOURCE: CNSSI-4009

| | |
|---|---|
| Tailored Security Control Baseline – | A set of security controls resulting from the application of tailoring guidance to the security control baseline. See Tailoring.<br>SOURCE: SP 800-37; SP 800-53; SP 800-53A |
| Tailoring – | The process by which a security control baseline is modified based on: (i) the application of scoping guidance; (ii) the specification of compensating security controls, if needed; and (iii) the specification of organization-defined parameters in the security controls via explicit assignment and selection statements.<br>SOURCE: SP 800-37; SP 800-53; SP 800-53A; CNSSI-4009 |
| Tailoring (Assessment Procedures) – | The process by which assessment procedures defined in Special Publication 800-53A are adjusted, or scoped, to match the characteristics of the information system under assessment, providingorganizations with the flexibility needed to meet specific organizational requirements and to avoid overly-constrained assessment approaches.<br>SOURCE: SP 800-53A |
| Tampering – | An intentional event resulting in modification of a system, its intended behavior, or data.<br>SOURCE: CNSSI-4009 |
| Target Of Evaluation (TOE) – | In accordance with Common Criteria, an information system, part ofa system or product, and all associated documentation, that is the subject of a security evaluation.<br>SOURCE: CNSSI-4009 |
| Technical Controls – | The security controls (i.e., safeguards or countermeasures) for an information system that are primarily implemented and executed by the information system through mechanisms contained in the hardware, software, or firmware components of the system.<br>SOURCE: SP 800-53; SP 800-53A; SP 800-37; FIPS 200 |
| Technical Non-repudiation – | The contribution of public key mechanisms to the provision of technical evidence supporting a non-repudiation security service.<br>SOURCE: SP 800-32 |
| Technical Reference Model(TRM) – | A component-driven, technical framework that categorizes the standards and technologies to support and enable the delivery of service components and capabilities.<br>SOURCE: CNSSI-4009 |
| Technical Security Controls – | Security controls (i.e., safeguards or countermeasures) for an information system that are primarily implemented and executed by the information system through mechanisms contained in the hardware, software, or firmware components of the system.<br>SOURCE: CNSSI-4009 |
| Technical Vulnerability Information – | Detailed description of a weakness to include the implementable steps (such as code) necessary to exploit that weakness.<br>SOURCE: CNSSI-4009 |
| Telecommunications – | Preparation, transmission, communication, or related processing of information (writing, images, sounds, or other data) by electrical, |

electromagnetic, electromechanical, electro-optical, or electronic means.
SOURCE: CNSSI-4009

Telework – The ability for an organization's employees and contractors to perform work from locations other than the organization's facilities.
SOURCE: SP 800-46

Tempest – A name referring to the investigation, study, and control of unintentional compromising emanations from telecommunications and automated information systems equipment.
SOURCE: FIPS 140-2

TEMPEST – A name referring to the investigation, study, and control of compromising emanations from telecommunications and automated information systems equipment.
SOURCE: CNSSI-4009

TEMPEST Test – Laboratory or on-site test to determine the nature of compromising emanations associated with an information system.
SOURCE: CNSSI-4009

TEMPEST Zone – Designated area within a facility where equipment with appropriate TEMPEST characteristics (TEMPEST zone assignment) may be operated.
SOURCE: CNSSI-4009

Test – A type of assessment method that is characterized by the process of exercising one or more assessment objects under specified conditionsto compare actual with expected behavior, the results of which are used to support the determination of security control effectiveness over time.
SOURCE: SP 800-53A

Test Key – Key intended for testing of COMSEC equipment or systems.
SOURCE: CNSSI-4009

Threat – Any circumstance or event with the potential to adversely impact organizational operations (including mission, functions, image, or reputation), organizational assets, individuals, other organizations, or the Nation through an information system via unauthorized access, destruction, disclosure, modification of information, and/or denial of service.
SOURCE: SP 800-53; SP 800-53A; SP 800-27; SP 800-60; SP 800-37; CNSSI-4009
The potential source of an adverse event.
SOURCE: SP 800-61

Threat – Any circumstance or event with the potential to adversely impact organizational operations (including mission, functions, image, or reputation), organizational assets, or individuals through an information system via unauthorized access, destruction, disclosure, modification of information, and/or denial of service. Also, the

| | |
|---|---|
| | potential for a threat-source to successfully exploit a particular information system vulnerability.<br>SOURCE: FIPS 200 |
| Threat Analysis – | The examination of threat sources against system vulnerabilities to determine the threats for a particular system in a particular operational environment.<br>SOURCE: SP 800-27<br>See Threat Assessment.<br>SOURCE: CNSSI-4009 |
| Threat Assessment – | Formal description and evaluation of threat to an information system.<br>SOURCE: SP 800-53; SP 800-18<br>Process of formally evaluating the degree of threat to an information system or enterprise and describing the nature of the threat.<br>SOURCE: CNSSI-4009; SP 800-53A |
| Threat Monitoring – | Analysis, assessment, and review of audit trails and other informationcollected for the purpose of searching out system events that may constitute violations of system security.<br>SOURCE: CNSSI-4009 |
| Threat Source – | The intent and method targeted at the intentional exploitation of a vulnerability or a situation and method that may accidentally trigger avulnerability. Synonymous with Threat Agent.<br>SOURCE: FIPS 200; SP 800-53; SP 800-53A; SP 800-37<br>The intent and method targeted at the intentional exploitation of a vulnerability or a situation and method that may accidentally exploit a vulnerability.<br>SOURCE: CNSSI-4009 |
| Time Bomb – | Resident computer program that triggers an unauthorized act at a predefined time.<br>SOURCE: CNSSI-4009 |
| Time-Compliance Date – | Date by which a mandatory modification to a COMSEC end-item must be incorporated if the item is to remain approved for operationaluse.<br>SOURCE: CNSSI-4009 |
| Time-Dependent Password – | Password that is valid only at a certain time of day or during a specified interval of time.<br>SOURCE: CNSSI-4009 |
| TOE Security Functions (TSF) – | Set consisting of all hardware, software, and firmware of the TOE that must be relied upon for the correct enforcement of the TOE Security Policy (TSP).<br>SOURCE: CNSSI-4009 |
| TOE Security Policy (TSP) – | Set of rules that regulate how assets are managed, protected, and distributed within the TOE.<br>SOURCE: CNSSI-4009 |

Token – Something that the claimant possesses and controls (typically a key or password) used to authenticate the claimant's identity.
SOURCE: SP 800-63
Something that the claimant possesses and controls (such as a key or password) that is used to authenticate a claim. See also cryptographic token.
SOURCE: CNSSI-4009

Total Risk – The potential for the occurrence of an adverse event if no mitigating action is taken (i.e., the potential for any applicable threat to exploit asystem vulnerability).
SOURCE: SP 800-16

Tracking Cookie – A cookie placed on a user's computer to track the user's activity on different Web sites, creating a detailed profile of the user's behavior.
SOURCE: SP 800-83

Tradecraft Identity – An identity used for the purpose of work-related interactions that may or may not be synonymous with an individual's true identity.
SOURCE: CNSSI-4009

Traditional INFOSEC Program – Program in which NSA acts as the central procurement agency for the development and, in some cases, the production of INFOSEC items. This includes the Authorized Vendor Program. Modificationsto the INFOSEC end-items used in products developed and/or produced under these programs must be approved by NSA.
SOURCE: CNSSI-4009

Traffic Analysis – A form of passive attack in which an intruder observes information about calls (although not necessarily the contents of the messages) and makes inferences, e.g., from the source and destination numbers, or frequency and length of the messages.
SOURCE: SP 800-24
The analysis of patterns in communications for the purpose of gaining intelligence about a system or its users. It does not require examination of the content of the communications, which may or may not be decipherable. For example, an adversary may be able to detect a signal from a reader that could enable it to infer that a particular activity is occurring (e.g., a shipment has arrived, someoneis entering a facility) without necessarily learning an identifier or associated data.
SOURCE: SP 800-98
Gaining knowledge of information by inference from observable characteristics of a data flow, even if the information is not directly available (e.g., when the data is encrypted). These characteristics include the identities and locations of the source(s) and destination(s)of the flow, and the flow's presence, amount, frequency, and durationof occurrence.
SOURCE: CNSSI-4009

| | |
|---|---|
| Traffic Encryption Key (TEK) – | Key used to encrypt plain text or to superencrypt previously encrypted text and/or to decrypt cipher text.<br>SOURCE: CNSSI-4009 |
| Traffic Padding – | Generation of mock communications or data units to disguise the amount of real data units being sent.<br>SOURCE: CNSSI-4009 |
| Traffic-Flow Security (TFS) – | Techniques to counter Traffic Analysis.<br>SOURCE: CNSSI-4009 |
| Training (Information Security) – | Training strives to produce relevant and needed (information) security skills and competencies.<br>SOURCE: SP 800-50 |
| Training Assessment – | An evaluation of the training efforts.<br>SOURCE: SP 800-16 |
| Training Effectiveness – | A measurement of what a given student has learned from a specific course or training event.<br>SOURCE: SP 800-16 |
| Training Effectiveness Evaluation – | Information collected to assist employees and their supervisors in assessing individual students' subsequent on-the-job performance, to provide trend data to assist trainers in improving both learning and teaching, and to be used in return-on-investment statistics to enable responsible officials to allocate limited resources in a thoughtful, strategic manner among the spectrum of IT security awareness, security literacy, training, and education options for optimal results among the workforce as a whole.<br>SOURCE: SP 800-16 |
| Tranquility – | Property whereby the security level of an object cannot change while the object is being processed by an information system.<br>SOURCE: CNSSI-4009 |
| Transmission – | The state that exists when information is being electronically sent from one location to one or more other locations.<br>SOURCE: CNSSI-4009 |
| Transmission Security – (TRANSEC) | Measures (security controls) applied to transmissions in order to prevent interception, disruption of reception, communications deception, and/or derivation of intelligence by analysis of transmission characteristics such as signal parameters or message externals.<br>Note: TRANSEC is that field of COMSEC which deals with the security of communication transmissions, rather than that of the information being communicated.<br>SOURCE: CNSSI-4009 |
| Trap Door – | 1. A means of reading cryptographically protected information by the use of private knowledge of weaknesses in the cryptographic algorithm used to protect the data. |

2. In cryptography, one-to-one function that is easy to compute in onedirection, yet believed to be difficult to invert without special information.
SOURCE: CNSSI-4009

Transport Layer Security (TLS) – An authentication and security protocol widely implemented in browsers and Web servers.
SOURCE: SP 800-63

Triple DES – An implementation of the Data Encryption Standard (DES) algorithm that uses three passes of the DES algorithm instead of one as used in ordinary DES applications. Triple DES provides much stronger encryption than ordinary DES but it is less secure than AES.
SOURCE: CNSSI-4009

Trojan Horse – A non-self-replicating program that seems to have a useful purpose, but in reality has a different, malicious purpose.
SOURCE: SP 800-61

A computer program that appears to have a useful function, but also has a hidden and potentially malicious function that evades security mechanisms, sometimes by exploiting legitimate authorizations of a system entity that invokes the program.
SOURCE: CNSSI-4009

Trust Anchor – A public key and the name of a certification authority that is used to validate the first certificate in a sequence of certificates. The trust anchor public key is used to verify the signature on a certificate issued by a trust anchor certification authority. The security of the validation process depends upon the authenticity and integrity of the trust anchor. Trust anchors are often distributed as self-signed certificates.
SOURCE: SP 800-57

An established point of trust (usually based on the authority of some person, office, or organization) from which an entity begins the validation of an authorized process or authorized (signed) package. A "trust anchor" is sometimes defined as just a public key used for different purposes (e.g., validating a Certification Authority, validating a signed software package or key, validating the process [or person] loading the signed software or key).
SOURCE: CNSSI-4009

Trust List – The collection of trusted certificates used by Relying Parties to authenticate other certificates.
SOURCE: SP 800-32; CNSSI-4009

Trusted Agent – Entity authorized to act as a representative of an agency in confirming Subscriber identification during the registration process. Trusted Agents do not have automated interfaces with Certification Authorities.
SOURCE: SP 800-32; CNSSI-4009

| | |
|---|---|
| Trusted Certificate – | A certificate that is trusted by the Relying Party on the basis of secureand authenticated delivery. The public keys included in trusted certificates are used to start certification paths. Also known as a "trust anchor."<br>SOURCE: SP 800-32; CNSSI-4009 |
| Trusted Channel – | A channel where the endpoints are known and data integrity is protected in transit. Depending on the communications protocol used, data privacy may be protected in transit. Examples include SSL, IPSEC, and secure physical connection.<br>SOURCE: CNSSI-4009 |
| Trusted Computer System – | A system that employs sufficient hardware and software assurance measures to allow its use for processing simultaneously a range of sensitive or classified information.<br>SOURCE: CNSSI-4009 |
| Trusted Computing Base (TCB) – | Totality of protection mechanisms within a computer system, including hardware, firmware, and software, the combination responsible for enforcing a security policy.<br>SOURCE: CNSSI-4009 |
| Trusted Distribution – | Method for distributing trusted computing base (TCB) hardware, software, and firmware components that protects the TCB from modification during distribution.<br>SOURCE: CNSSI-4009 |
| Trusted Foundry – | Facility that produces integrated circuits with a higher level of integrity assurance.<br>SOURCE: CNSSI-4009 |
| Trusted Identification Forwarding – | Identification method used in information system networks wherebythe sending host can verify an authorized user on its system is attempting a connection to another host. The sending host transmitsthe required user authentication information to the receiving host.<br>SOURCE: CNSSI-4009 |
| Trusted Path – | A mechanism by which a user (through an input device) can communicate directly with the security functions of the information system with the necessary confidence to support the system security policy. This mechanism can only be activated by the user or the security functions of the information system and cannot be imitated by untrusted software.<br>SOURCE: SP 800-53;CNSSI-4009 |
| Trusted Path – | A means by which an operator and a target of evaluation security function can communicate with the necessary confidence to support the target of evaluation security policy.<br>SOURCE: FIPS 140-2 |
| Trusted Platform Module (TPM)Chip – | A tamper-resistant integrated circuit built into some computer motherboards that can perform cryptographic operations (including |

| | |
|---|---|
| | key generation) and protect small amounts of sensitive information, such as passwords and cryptographic keys.<br>SOURCE: SP 800-111 |
| Trusted Process – | Process that has been tested and verified to operate only as intended.<br>SOURCE: CNSSI-4009 |
| Trusted Recovery – | Ability to ensure recovery without compromise after a system failure.<br>SOURCE: CNSSI-4009 |
| Trusted Software – | Software portion of a trusted computing base (TCB).<br>SOURCE: CNSSI-4009 |
| Trusted Timestamp – | A digitally signed assertion by a trusted authority that a specific digital object existed at a particular time.<br>SOURCE: SP 800-32; CNSSI-4009 |
| Trustworthiness – | The attribute of a person or organization that provides confidence to others of the qualifications, capabilities, and reliability of that entity to perform specific tasks and fulfill assigned responsibilities.<br>SOURCE: SP 800-79<br>The attribute of a person or enterprise that provides confidence to others of the qualifications, capabilities, and reliability of that entity to perform specific tasks and fulfill assigned responsibilities.<br>SOURCE: CNSSI-4009<br>Security decisions with respect to extended investigations to determine and confirm qualifications, and suitability to perform specific tasks and responsibilities.<br>SOURCE: FIPS 201 |
| Trustworthy System – | Computer hardware, software and procedures that—<br>1)are reasonably secure from intrusion and misuse;<br>2)provide a reasonable level of availability, reliability, and correct operation;<br>3)are reasonably suited to performing their intended functions; and<br>4)adhere to generally accepted security procedures.<br>SOURCE: SP 800-32 |
| TSEC – | Telecommunications Security.<br>SOURCE: CNSSI-4009 |
| TSEC Nomenclature – | System for identifying the type and purpose of certain items of COMSEC material.<br>SOURCE: CNSSI-4009 |
| Tunneled Password Protocol – | A protocol where a password is sent through a protected channel. For example, the TLS protocol is often used with a verifier's public key certificate to (1) authenticate the verifier to the claimant, (2) establish an encrypted session between the verifier and claimant, and (3) transmit the claimant's password to the verifier. The encrypted TLS session protects the claimant's password from eavesdroppers.<br>SOURCE: SP 800-63 |

Tunneling – Technology enabling one network to send its data via another network's connections. Tunneling works by encapsulating a network protocol within packets carried by the second network.
SOURCE: CNSSI-4009

Two-Part Code – Code consisting of an encoding section, in which the vocabulary items (with their associated code groups) are arranged in alphabetical or other systematic order, and a decoding section, in which the code groups (with their associated meanings) are arranged in a separate alphabetical or numeric order.
SOURCE: CNSSI-4009

Two-Person Control (TPC) – Continuous surveillance and control of positive control material at all times by a minimum of two authorized individuals, each capable of detecting incorrect and unauthorized procedures with respect to the task being performed and each familiar with established security and safety requirements.
SOURCE: CNSSI-4009

Two-Person Integrity (TPI) – System of storage and handling designed to prohibit individual accessby requiring the presence of at least two authorized individuals, each capable of detecting incorrect or unauthorized security procedures with respect to the task being performed. See no-lone zone.
SOURCE: CNSSI-4009

Type 1 Key – Generated and distributed under the auspices of NSA for use in a cryptographic device for the protection of national security information.
SOURCE: CNSSI-4009, as modified

Type 1 Product – Cryptographic equipment, assembly or component classified or certified by NSA for encrypting and decrypting national security information when appropriately keyed. Developed using established NSA business processes and containing NSA-approved algorithms. Used to protect systems requiring the most stringent protection mechanisms.
SOURCE: CNSSI-4009, as modified

Type 2 Key – Generated and distributed under the auspices of NSA for use in a cryptographic device for the protection of unclassified information.
SOURCE: CNSSI-4009, as modified

Type 2 Product – Cryptographic equipment, assembly, or component certified by NSA for encrypting or decrypting sensitive information when appropriately keyed. Developed using established NSA business processes and containing NSA-approved algorithms. Used to protect systems requiring protection mechanisms exceeding best commercial practices including systems used for the protection of unclassified information.
SOURCE: CNSSI-4009, as modified

| | |
|---|---|
| Type 3 Key – | Used in a cryptographic device for the protection of unclassified sensitive information, even if used in a Type 1 or Type 2 product.<br>SOURCE: CNSSI-4009 |
| Type 3 Product – | Unclassified cryptographic equipment, assembly, or component used,when appropriately keyed, for encrypting or decrypting unclassified sensitive U.S. government or commercial information, and to protect systems requiring protection mechanisms consistent with standard commercial practices. Developed using established commercial standards and containing NIST-approved cryptographic algorithms/modules or successfully evaluated by the National Information Assurance Partnership (NIAP).<br>SOURCE: CNSSI-4009 |
| Type 4 Key – | Used by a cryptographic device in support of its Type 4 functionality,i.e., any provision of key that lacks U.S. government endorsement or oversight.<br>SOURCE: CNSSI-4009 |
| Type 4 Product – | Unevaluated commercial cryptographic equipment, assemblies, or components that neither NSA nor NIST certify for any government usage. These products are typically delivered as part of commercial offerings and are commensurate with the vendor's commercial practices. These products may contain either vendor proprietary algorithms, algorithms registered by NIST, or algorithms registered by NIST and published in a FIPS.<br>SOURCE: CNSSI-4009 |
| Type Accreditation – | A form of accreditation that is used to authorize multiple instances of a major application or general support system for operation at approved locations with the same type of computing environment. In situations where a major application or general support system is installed at multiple locations, a type accreditation will satisfy C&A requirements only if the application or system consists of a common set of tested and approved hardware, software, and firmware.<br>SOURCE: CNSSI-4009 |
| Type Certification – | The certification acceptance of replica information systems based on the comprehensive evaluation of the technical and nontechnical security features of an information system and other safeguards, made as part of and in support of the formal approval process, to establish the extent to which a particular design and implementation meet a specified set of security requirements.<br>SOURCE: CNSSI-4009 |
| U.S. Person – | Federal law and Executive Order define a U.S. Person as: a citizen ofthe United States; an alien lawfully admitted for permanent residence; an unincorporated association with a substantial number of members who are citizens of the U.S. or are aliens lawfully admitted for permanent residence; and/or a corporation that is incorporated in the U.S.<br>SOURCE: CNSSI-4009 |

| | |
|---|---|
| U.S.-Controlled Facility – | Base or building to which access is physically controlled by U.S. individuals who are authorized U.S. government or U.S. government contractor employees.<br>SOURCE: CNSSI-4009 |
| U.S.-Controlled Space – | Room or floor within a facility that is not a U.S.-controlled facility, access to which is physically controlled by U.S. individuals who are authorized U.S. government or U.S. government contractor employees. Keys or combinations to locks controlling entrance to U.S.-controlled spaces must be under the exclusive control of U.S. individuals who are U.S. government or U.S. government contractor employees.<br>SOURCE: CNSSI-4009 |
| Unauthorized Access – | A person gains logical or physical access without permission to a network, system, application, data, or other IT resource.<br>SOURCE: SP 800-61 |
| Unauthorized Access – | Occurs when a user, legitimate or unauthorized, accesses a resource that the user is not permitted to use.<br>SOURCE: FIPS 191<br>Any access that violates the stated security policy.<br>SOURCE: CNSSI-4009 |
| Unauthorized Disclosure – | An event involving the exposure of information to entities not authorized access to the information.<br>SOURCE: SP 800-57; CNSSI-4009 |
| Unsigned data – | Data included in an authentication token, in addition to a digital signature.<br>SOURCE: FIPS 196 |
| Unclassified – | Information that has not been determined pursuant to E.O. 12958, as amended, or any predecessor order, to require protection against unauthorized disclosure and that is not designated as classified.<br>SOURCE: CNSSI-4009 |
| Untrusted Process – | Process that has not been evaluated or examined for correctness and adherence to the security policy. It may include incorrect or malicious code that attempts to circumvent the security mechanisms.<br>SOURCE: CNSSI-4009 |
| Update (a Certificate) – | The act or process by which data items bound in an existing public key certificate, especially authorizations granted to the subject, are changed by issuing a new certificate.<br>SOURCE: SP 800-32; CNSSI-4009 |
| Update (key) – | Automatic or manual cryptographic process that irreversibly modifiesthe state of a COMSEC key.<br>SOURCE: CNSSI-4009 |
| US-CERT – | A partnership between the Department of Homeland Security and the public and private sectors, established to protect the nation's |

Internet infrastructure. US-CERT coordinates defense against and responses to cyber attacks across the nation.
SOURCE: CNSSI-4009

User – Individual or (system) process authorized to access an information system.
SOURCE: FIPS 200
Individual, or (system) process acting on behalf of an individual, authorized to access an information system.
SOURCE: SP 800-53; SP 800-18; CNSSI-4009

User – An individual or a process (subject) acting on behalf of the individualthat accesses a cryptographic module in order to obtain cryptographicservices.
SOURCE: FIPS 140-2

User ID – Unique symbol or character string used by an information system to identify a specific user.
SOURCE: CNSSI-4009

User Initialization – A function in the life cycle of keying material; the process whereby a user initializes its cryptographic application (e.g., installing and initializing software and hardware).
SOURCE: SP 800-57

User Partnership Program (UPP) – Partnership between the NSA and a U.S. government agency to facilitate development of secure information system equipment incorporating NSA-approved cryptography. The result of this program is the authorization of the product or system to safeguard national security information in the user's specific application.
SOURCE: CNSSI-4009

User Registration – A function in the life cycle of keying material; a process whereby an entity becomes a member of a security domain.
SOURCE: SP 800-57

User Representative (COMSEC) – Individual authorized by an organization to order COMSEC keying material and interface with the keying system, provide information tokey users, and ensure the correct type of key is ordered.
SOURCE: CNSSI-4009

User Representative (Risk Management) – The person that defines the system's operational and functional requirements, and who is responsible for ensuring that user operational interests are met throughout the systems authorization process.
SOURCE: CNSSI-4009

Valid Data Element – A payload, an associated data string, or a nonce that satisfies the restrictions of the formatting function.
SOURCE: SP 800-38C

Validation – The process of demonstrating that the system under consideration meets in all respects the specification of that system.
SOURCE: FIPS 201
Confirmation (through the provision of strong, sound, objective evidence) that requirements for a specific intended use or

| | |
|---|---|
| | application have been fulfilled (e.g., a trustworthy credential has been presented, or data or information has been formatted in accordance with a defined set of rules, or a specific process has demonstrated that an entity under consideration meets, in all respects, its defined attributes or requirements).<br>SOURCE: CNSSI-4009 |
| Variant – | One of two or more code symbols having the same plain text equivalent.<br>SOURCE: CNSSI-4009 |
| Verification – | Confirmation, through the provision of objective evidence, that specified requirements have been fulfilled (e.g., an entity's requirements have been correctly defined, or an entity's attributes have been correctly presented; or a procedure or function performs asintended and leads to the expected outcome).<br>SOURCE: CNSSI-4009<br>See Also Identity Verification. |
| Verified Name – | A subscriber name that has been verified by identity proofing.<br>SOURCE: SP 800-63 |
| Verifier – | An entity that verifies the claimant's identity by verifying the claimant's possession of a token using an authentication protocol. To do this, the verifier may also need to validate credentials that link the token and identity and check their status.<br>SOURCE: SP 800-63 |
| Verifier – | An entity which is or represents the entity requiring an authenticated identity. A verifier includes the functions necessary for engaging in authentication exchanges.<br>SOURCE: FIPS 196 |
| Verifier Impersonation Attack – | An attack where the attacker impersonates the verifier in an authentication protocol, usually to learn a password.<br>SOURCE: SP 800-63 |
| Victim – | A machine that is attacked.<br>SOURCE: SP 800-61 |
| Virtual Machine (VM) – | Software that allows a single host to run one or more guest operatingsystems.<br>SOURCE: SP 800-115 |
| Virtual Private Network (VPN) – | A virtual network, built on top of existing physical networks, that provides a secure communications tunnel for data and other information transmitted between networks.<br>SOURCE: SP 800-46<br>Protected information system link utilizing tunneling, security controls (see Information Assurance), and endpoint address translation giving the impression of a dedicated line<br>SOURCE: CNSSI-4009 |
| Virus – | A self-replicating program that runs and spreads by modifying other programs or files.<br>SOURCE: SP 800-61 |

A computerthat can copy itself and infect a computer without permission or knowledge of the user. A virus might corrupt or delete data on a computer, use email programs to spread itself to other computers, or even erase everything on a hard disk.
SOURCE: CNSSI-4009

Virus Hoax – An urgent warning message about a nonexistent virus.
SOURCE: SP 800-61

Vulnerability – Weakness in an information system, system security procedures, internal controls, or implementation that could be exploited or triggered by a threat source.
SOURCE: SP 800-53; SP 800-53A; SP 800-37; SP 800-60; SP 800-115; FIPS 200

A weakness in a system, application, or network that is subject to exploitation or misuse.
SOURCE: SP 800-61

Weakness in an information system, system security procedures, internal controls, or implementation that could be exploited by a threat source.
SOURCE: CNSSI-4009

Vulnerability Analysis – See Vulnerability Assessment.

Vulnerability Assessment – Formal description and evaluation of the vulnerabilities in an information system.
SOURCE: SP 800-53; SP 800-37

Systematic examination of an information system or product to determine the adequacy of security measures, identify security deficiencies, provide data from which to predict the effectiveness of proposed security measures, and confirm the adequacy of such measures after implementation.
SOURCE: SP 800-53A; CNSSI-4009

Warm Site – An environmentally conditioned workspace that is partially equipped with information systems and telecommunications equipment to support relocated operations in the event of a significant disruption.
SOURCE: SP 800-34

Backup site which typically contains the data links and preconfigured equipment necessary to rapidly start operations, but does not contain live data. Thus commencing operations at a warm site will (at a minimum) require the restoration of current data.
SOURCE: CNSSI-4009

Web Bug – A tiny image, invisible to a user, placed on Web pages in such a way to enable third parties to track use of Web servers and collect information about the user, including IP address, host name, browser type and version, operating system name and version, and cookies.
SOURCE: SP 800-28

Malicious code, invisible to a user, placed on Web sites in such a waythat it allows third parties to track use of Web servers and collect information about the user, including IP address, host name, browser type and version, operating system name and version, and Web browser cookie.
SOURCE: CNSSI-4009

**Web Content Filtering Software** – A program that prevents access to undesirable Web sites, typically by comparing a requested Web site address to a list of known bad Web sites.
SOURCE: SP 800-69

**Web Risk Assessment** – Processes for ensuring Web sites are in compliance with applicable policies.
SOURCE: CNSSI-4009

**White Team** – 1. The group responsible for refereeing an engagement between a Red Team of mock attackers and a Blue Team of actual defenders of their enterprise's use of information systems. In an exercise, the White Team acts as the judges, enforces the rules of the exercise, observes the exercise, scores teams, resolves any problems that may arise, handles all requests for information or questions, and ensures that the competition runs fairly and does not cause operational problems for the defender's mission. The White Team helps to establish the rules of engagement, the metrics for assessing results and the procedures for providing operational security for the engagement. The White Team normally has responsibility for deriving lessons-learned, conducting the post engagement assessment, and promulgating results.
2. Can also refer to a small group of people who have prior knowledge of unannounced Red Team activities. The White Team acts as observers during the Red Team activity and ensures the scopeof testing does not exceed a predefined threshold.
SOURCE: CNSSI-4009

**Wi-Fi Protected Access-2 (WPA2)** – The approved Wi-Fi Alliance interoperable implementation of the IEEE 802.11i security standard. For federal government use, the implementation must use FIPS-approved encryption, such as AES.
SOURCE: CNSSI-4009

**Wiki** – Web applications or similar tools that allow identifiable users to add content (as in an Internet forum) and allow anyone to edit that content collectively.
SOURCE: CNSSI-4009

**Wired Equivalent Privacy (WEP)** – A security protocol, specified in the IEEE 802.11 standard, that is designed to provide a WLAN with a level of security and privacy comparable to what is usually expected of a wired LAN. WEP is no longer considered a viable encryption mechanism due to known weaknesses.
SOURCE: SP 800-48

| | |
|---|---|
| Wireless Access Point (WAP) – | A device that acts as a conduit to connect wireless communication devices together to allow them to communicate and create a wireless network.<br>SOURCE: CNSSI-4009 |
| Wireless Application Protocol – (WAP) | A standard that defines the way in which Internet communications and other advanced services are provided on wireless mobile devices.<br>SOURCE: CNSSI-4009 |
| Wireless Technology – | Technology that permits the transfer of information between separated points without physical connection.<br><br>Note: Currently wireless technologies use infrared, acoustic, radio frequency, and optical.<br>SOURCE: CNSSI-4009 |
| Work Factor – | Estimate of the effort or time needed by a potential perpetrator, with specified expertise and resources, to overcome a protective measure.<br>SOURCE: CNSSI-4009 |
| Workcraft Identity – | Synonymous with Tradecraft Identity.<br>SOURCE: CNSSI-4009 |
| Worm – | A self-replicating, self-propagating, self-contained program that uses networking mechanisms to spread itself. See malicious code.<br>SOURCE: SP 800-61; CNSSI-4009 |
| Write – | Fundamental operation in an information system that results only in the flow of information from a subject to an object. See access type.<br>SOURCE: CNSSI-4009 |
| Write Access – | Permission to write to an object in an information system.<br>SOURCE: CNSSI-4009 |
| Write-Blocker – | A device that allows investigators to examine media while preventingdata writes from occurring on the subject media.<br>SOURCE: SP 800-72 |
| X.509 Certificate – | The International Organization for Standardization/International Telecommunication Union – Standardization Department (ISO/ITU-T) X.509 standard defined two types of certificates – the X.509 public key certificate and the X.509 attribute certificate. Most commonly, an X.509 certificate refers to the X.509 public key certificate.<br>SOURCE: SP 800-57 |
| X.509 Public Key Certificate – | The public key for a user (or device) and a name for the user (or device), together with some other information, rendered unforgeableby the digital signature of the certification authority that issued the certificate, encoded in the format defined in the ISO/ITU-T X.509 standard.<br>SOURCE: SP 800-57; CNSSI-4009 adapted |
| Zero Fill – | To fill unused storage locations in an information system with the representation of the character denoting "0."<br>SOURCE: CNSSI-4009 |

| | |
|---|---|
| Zeroization – | A method of erasing electronically stored data, cryptographic keys, and CSPs by altering or deleting the contents of the data storage to prevent recovery of the data.<br>SOURCE: FIPS 140-2<br>A method of erasing electronically stored data, cryptographic keys, and Credentials Service Providers (CSPs) by altering or deleting the contents of the data storage to prevent recovery of the data.<br>SOURCE: CNSSI-4009 |
| Zeroize – | To remove or eliminate the key from a cryptographic equipment or fill device.<br>SOURCE: CNSSI-4009 |
| Zombie – | A program that is installed on a system to cause it to attack other systems.<br>SOURCE: SP 800-83 |
| Zone Of Control – | Three-dimensional space surrounding equipment that processes classified and/or sensitive information within which TEMPEST exploitation is not considered practical or where legal authority to identify and remove a potential TEMPEST exploitation exists.<br>SOURCE: CNSSI-4009 |

## NON-NIST REFERENCES

| | |
|---|---|
| 40 U.S.C., Sec. 11101 | U.S. Code, Title 40 – Public Buildings, Property, and Works, Subtitle III – Information Technology Management, Chapter 111 – General, Section 11101. Definitions. |
| 40 U.S.C., Sec. 11331 | U.S. Code, Title 40 – Public Buildings, Property, and Works, Subtitle III – Information Technology Management, Chapter 113 – Responsibility for Acquisitions of Information Technology, Subchapter III – Other Responsibilities, Section 11331. Responsibilities for federal information systems standards. |
| 41 U.S.C., Sec. 403 | Title 41 – Public Contracts, Chapter 7 – Office of Federal Procurement Policy, Section 403. Definitions. |
| 44 U.S.C., Sec. 3502 | U.S. Code, Title 44 – Public Printing and Documents, Chapter 35 – Coordination of Federal Information Policy, Subchapter I – Federal Information Policy, Section 3502. Definitions. |
| 44 U.S.C., Sec. 3541 | U.S. Code, Title 44 – Public Printing and Documents, Chapter 35 – Coordination of Federal Information Policy, Subchapter III – Information Security, Section 3541. Purposes. |

| | |
|---|---|
| 44 U.S.C., Sec. 3542 | U.S. Code, Title 44 – Public Printing and Documents, Chapter 35 – Coordination of Federal Information Policy, Subchapter III – Information Security, Section 3542. Definitions. |
| 44 U.S.C., Sec. 3544 | U.S. Code, Title 44 – Public Printing and Documents, Chapter 35 – Coordination of Federal Information Policy, Subchapter III – Information Security, Section 3544. Federal agency responsibilities. |
| 47 C.F.R., Part 64, App A | Code of Federal Regulations, Title 47 – Telecommunication, Chapter I– Federal Communications Commission, Subchapter B – CommonCarrier Services, Part 64 – Miscellaneous Rules Relating to Common Carriers, Appendix A to Part 64 – Telecommunications Service Priority (TSP) System for NationalSecurity Emergency Preparedness (NSEP). |
| Atomic Energy Act of 1954 | *Definition of Restricted Data (42 U.S.C., Section 2011).* |
| CNSSI-4009 | The Committee on National Security Systems Instruction No 4009 *"National Information Assurance Glossary."* |
| DCID 6/3 | Director of Central Intelligence Directive 6/3 "Protecting Sensitive Compartmented Information Within Information Systems." |
| DCID 6/9 | Director of Central Intelligence Directive 6/9 "Physical Security Standards for Sensitive Compartmented Information Facilities." |
| E.O. 13292 | Executive Office of the President, Executive Order 13292— Further Amendment to Executive Order 12958, as Amended, Classified National Security Information, March 25, 2003. |
| Federal Information Security Management Act (FISMA) | P.L. 107-347, December 2002. |
| OMB Circular A-130, App. III | U.S. Office of Management and Budget, Circular No. A-130 Revised,(Transmittal Memorandum No. 4), Appendix III, Security of Federal Automated information Resources. November 28, 2000. |
| OMB Memorandum 02-01 | U.S. Office of Management and Budget, Memorandum 02-01, Guidance for Preparing and Submitting Security Plans of Action and Milestones. October 17, 2001. |

| | |
|---|---|
| OMB Memorandum 03-22 | U.S. Office of Management and Budget, Memorandum 03-22, OMB Guidance for Implementing the Privacy Provisions of the E-Government Act of 2002. September 29, 2003. |
| Public Law 104-106 Sec. 5125(b) | S. 1124, Division E [Public Law 104-106], 104thU.S. Cong., Information Technology Management Reform Act, February 10, 1996. Section 5125(b). |

In: Information Security Terms
Editors: Daniel S. Cox and Eric R. Ellis
ISBN: 978-1-62100-787-6


*Chapter 2*

# SYSTEM AND NETWORK SECURITY ACRONYMS AND ABBREVIATIONS*

*United States Department of Commerce*

## REPORTS ON COMPUTER SYSTEMS TECHNOLOGY

The Information Technology Laboratory (ITL) at the National Institute of Standards and Technology (NIST) promotes the U.S. economy and public welfare by providing technical leadership for the nation's measurement and standards infrastructure. ITL develops tests, test methods, reference data, proof of concept implementations, and technical analysis to advance the development and productive use of information technology. ITL's responsibilities include the development of technical, physical, administrative, and management standards and guidelines for the cost-effective security and privacy of sensitive unclassified information in Federal computer systems. This Interagency Report discusses ITL's research, guidance, and outreach efforts in computer security and its collaborative activities with industry, government, and academic organizations.

## ACKNOWLEDGMENTS

The authors, Karen Scarfone of the National Institute of Standards and Technology (NIST) and Victoria Thompson of Booz Allen Hamilton, wish to thank their colleagues who reviewed drafts of this report, particularly Liz Lennon and Tim Grance of NIST. Thanks also go to individuals and organizations that submitted suggestions, particularly Tim Kramer, Mark Seecof, Janine Paris, the U.S. Department of Energy, and the U.S. Department of State. The authors also thank their colleagues who created acronym and abbreviation lists for their publications that were subsequently used as sources of information for this report.

* This is an edited, reformatted and augmented version of the National Institute of Standards and Technology publication, Report 7581, dated September 2009.

## TRADEMARK INFORMATION

All names are registered trademarks or trademarks of their respective companies.

## NOTE TO REVIEWERS

Reviewers are encouraged to submit additional acronyms and abbreviations related to system and network security, particularly for emerging technologies, for consideration as additions to this report. All suggestions and corrections should be sent to securityacronyms@nist.gov.

## 1. INTRODUCTION

This report contains a list of selected acronyms and abbreviations for system and network security terms with their generally accepted or preferred definitions. It is intended as a resource for federal agencies and other users of system and network security publications.

The capitalization, spelling, and definitions of acronyms and abbreviations frequently vary among publications. It is easy to understand why this happens. While some acronyms and abbreviations (e.g., WWW) have one universally recognized and understood definition within the domain of system and network security, others (e.g., IA, MAC) have multiple valid definitions depending upon the context in which they are used. Some acronyms bear little resemblance to their definitions, such as Modes of Operation Validation System for the Triple DES Algorithm (TMOVS). Others use unexpected capitalization or spelling (e.g., Electronic Business using eXtensible Markup Language [ebXML] and Organisation for Economic Co-operation and Development [OECD]). As a result, acronyms, abbreviations, and their definitions may be inaccurately or inconsistently defined by authors, perpetuating errors and confusing or misleading readers.

This report is meant to help reduce these errors and confusion by providing the generally accepted or preferred definitions of a list of frequently used acronyms and abbreviations. The list does not include *all* system and network security terms, nor is it a compendium of every acronym and abbreviation found in system and network security documents published by NIST. Readers should refer to each document's list of acronyms and abbreviations (typically found in an appendix) for definitions applicable to that particular document.

The following conventions have been used in the preparation of the list of acronyms and abbreviations in this report.

- Abbreviations and acronyms generally appear in all capital letters, although there are occasional exceptions—for example, meter (m) and decibels referenced to one milliwatt (dBm).
- Technical terms are not capitalized unless they are proper nouns. Names of people, places, and groups, and the titles of protocols, standards, and algorithms are considered proper nouns. For example, certification and accreditation (C&A) is not capitalized, but Advanced Encryption Standard (AES) is capitalized.

- Collective nouns are not capitalized (e.g., wide area network [WAN]).
- When two or more definitions of the same acronym or abbreviation are given, the acronym or abbreviation is italicized and repeated for each definition. Definitions are listed alphabetically.

## 2. Acronym and Abbreviation List

This section consists of a list of selected system and network security acronyms and abbreviations, along with their generally accepted definitions. When there are multiple definitions for a single term, the acronym or abbreviation is italicized and each definition is listed separately.

### Numeric

| | |
|---|---|
| 1xRTT | one times radio transmission technology |
| 3DES | Triple Data Encryption Standard |
| 3G | 3rd Generation |
| 3GPP | 3rd Generation Partnership Project |
| 3GPP2 | 3rd Generation Partnership Project 2 |

### A

| | |
|---|---|
| A | address resource record type |
| AA | ABAC attribute authority |
| AAA | authentication, authorization, and accounting |
| AAAK | authentication, authorization, and accounting key |
| AAD | additional authenticated data |
| AAR | after action report |
| AAS | adaptive antenna system |
| ABAC | attribute-based access control |
| ACE | access control entry |
| ACL | access control list |
| ACM | Association for Computing Machinery |
| ACO | authenticated cipher offset |
| *AD* | Active Directory |
| *AD* | authenticated data |
| ADS | alternate data stream |
| AES | Advanced Encryption Standard |
| AES-CBC | Advanced Encryption Standard-Cipher Block Chaining |
| AES-CTR | Advanced Encryption Standard-Counter Mode |
| AFH | adaptive frequency hopping |
| A-GPS | assisted global positioning system |

| | |
|---|---|
| AH | Authentication Header |
| AIDC | automatic identification and data capture |
| AIM | Association for Automatic Identification and Mobility |
| AIT | automatic identification technology |
| AJAX | Asynchronous JavaScript and XML |
| AK | authorization key |
| AKID | authorization key identifier |
| AKM | authentication and key management |
| ALG | application layer gateway |
| ANSI | American National Standards Institute |
| AP | access point |
| API | application programming interface |
| APWG | Anti-Phishing Working Group |
| ARIN | American Registry for Internet Numbers |
| ARP | Address Resolution Protocol |
| ARPA | Advanced Research Projects Agency |
| *AS* | authentication server |
| *AS* | authentication service |
| *AS* | autonomous system |
| ASC | Anti-Spyware Coalition |
| ASC X9 | Accredited Standards Committee X9 |
| ASCII | American Standard Code for Information Interchange |
| ASLR | address space layout randomization |
| ASN | autonomous system number |
| ASN.1 | Abstract Syntax Notation 1 |
| ASP | active server pages |
| ATA | Advanced Technology Attachment |
| ATIM | Announcement Traffic Indication Message |
| *ATM* | asynchronous transfer mode |
| *ATM* | automated teller machine |
| AV | antivirus |
| AVIEN | Anti-Virus Information Exchange Network |
| AVP | attribute-value pair |

## B

| | |
|---|---|
| B2B | business-to-business |
| *BCP* | best current practice |
| *BCP* | business continuity plan |
| BGP | Border Gateway Protocol |
| BGP-4 | Border Gateway Protocol 4 |
| *BIA* | Bump-in-the-API |
| *BIA* | business impact analysis |
| BioAPI | Biometric Application Programming Interface |
| BIOS | basic input/output system |

| | |
|---|---|
| BITS | Bump-in-the-Stack |
| BPML | Business Process Modeling Language |
| BPSS | Business Process Specification Schema |
| BRP | business recovery (resumption) plan |
| BS | base station |
| BSC | base station controller |
| BSI | British Standards Institution |
| BSIA | British Security Industry Association |
| BSP | best security practice |
| BSS | basic service set |
| BSSID | basic service set identifier |
| BTNS | better-than-nothing-security |
| BTS | base transceiver station |
| BU | binding update |
| BUA | binding update acknowledgement |

## C

| | |
|---|---|
| C&A | certification and accreditation |
| *CA* | certificate authority |
| *CA* | certification agent |
| *CA* | certification authority |
| CAC | common access card |
| CAIDA | Cooperative Association for Internet Data Analysis |
| CAPTCHA | Completely Automated Public Turing Test to Tell Computers and Humans Apart |
| CARO | Computer Antivirus Research Organization |
| CAVP | Cryptographic Algorithm Validation Program |
| CBC | Cipher Block Chaining |
| CBC-MAC | Cipher Block Chaining Message Authentication Code |
| CBEFF | Common Biometric Exchange File Format |
| CC | Common Criteria |
| CCETM | Common Configuration Enumeration |
| CCEVS | Common Criteria Evaluation and Validation Scheme |
| CCIPS | Computer Crime and Intellectual Property Section |
| CCK | complementary code keying |
| CCM | Counter Mode with CBC-MAC |
| CCMP | Counter Mode with CBC-MAC Protocol |
| CCRA | Common Criteria Recognition Arrangement |
| CCSS | Common Configuration Scoring System |
| ccTLD | country code top-level domain |
| *CD* | checking disabled |
| *CD* | compact disc |
| CDFS | compact disc file system |
| CDMA | code division multiple access |

| | |
|---|---|
| CD-R | compact disc-recordable |
| CD-ROM | compact disc-read only memory |
| CD-RW | compact disc-rewritable |
| CEO | chief executive officer |
| CERIAS | Center for Education and Research in Information Assurance and Security |
| CERT | computer emergency response team |
| CERT®/CC | CERT® Coordination Center |
| CF | CompactFlash® |
| CFAA | Computer Fraud and Abuse Act |
| CFB | Cipher Feedback |
| CFI | computer and financial investigations |
| CFR | Code of Federal Regulations |
| CFTT | computer forensics tool testing |
| CGA | cryptographically generated addresses |
| CGI | Common Gateway Interface |
| CHAP | Challenge-Handshake Authentication Protocol |
| CHUID | cardholder unique identifier |
| CIDR | Classless Inter-Domain Routing |
| CIFS | Common Internet File System |
| CIO | chief information officer |
| CIP | critical infrastructure protection |
| CIPC | Critical Infrastructure Protection Committee |
| CIPSEA | Confidential Information Protection and Statistical Efficiency Act |
| *CIRC* | computer incident response capability |
| *CIRC* | computer incident response center |
| CIRDB | CERIAS Incident Response Database |
| CIRT | computer incident response team |
| CIS | Center for Internet Security |
| CISO | chief information security officer |
| CLF | common log format |
| CLI | command line interface |
| CLR | common language runtime |
| cm | centimeter |
| CMA | Certificate Management Authority |
| CMAC | Cipher-based Method Authentication Code |
| CME | Common Malware Enumeration |
| CMOS | complementary metal oxide semiconductor |
| *CMS* | Centers for Medicare and Medicaid Services |
| *CMS* | Cryptographic Message Syntax |
| CMSS | Common Misuse Scoring System |
| CMVP | Cryptographic Module Validation Program |
| *CN* | common name |
| *CN* | correspondent node |
| CNSS | Committee on National Security Systems |
| CNSSI | Committee on National Security Systems Instruction |

| | |
|---|---|
| CoA | care-of address |
| codec | coder/decoder |
| COI | conflict of interest |
| COM | Component Object Model |
| COOP | continuity of operations |
| COPPA | Children's Online Privacy Protection Act |
| CORBA® | Common Object Request Broker Architecture |
| COTS | commercial off-the-shelf |
| *CP* | certificate policy |
| *CP* | contingency plan |
| CPE™ | Common Platform Enumeration |
| CPI | compression parameter index |
| CPNI | Centre for the Protection of National Infrastructure |
| CPS | certification practice statement |
| CPU | central processing unit |
| CRAM | challenge-response authentication mechanism |
| CRC | cyclic redundancy check |
| CRL | certificate revocation list |
| CS | client/server |
| CSIA | Cyber Security Industries Alliance |
| CSIRC | computer security incident response capability |
| CSIRT | computer security incident response team |
| *CSO* | chief security officer |
| *CSO* | computer security object |
| CSP | Credentials Service Provider |
| CSR | certificate signing request |
| CSRC | Computer Security Resource Center |
| CSRDA | Cyber Security Research and Development Act of 2002 |
| CSS | cascading style sheet |
| CSV | comma-separated values |
| CTO | chief technology officer |
| CTR | counter mode encryption |
| CVE | Common Vulnerabilities and Exposures |
| CVSS | Common Vulnerability Scoring System |
| CWE | Common Weakness Enumeration |

**D**

| | |
|---|---|
| DA | destination address |
| *DAA* | designated accrediting authority |
| *DAA* | designated approving authority |
| DAC | discretionary access control |
| DAD | duplicate address detection |
| DAML | DARPA Agent Markup Language |
| D-AMPS | Digital Advanced Mobile Phone Service |

| | |
|---|---|
| DAO | Data Access Object |
| DARPA | Defense Advanced Research Projects Agency |
| dBm | decibels referenced to one milliwatt |
| DBMS | database management system |
| DC | domain controller |
| DCE | Distributed Computing Environment |
| DCOM | Distributed Component Object Model |
| DCS | distributed control system |
| DDMS | Department of Defense Metadata Specification |
| DDoS | distributed denial of service |
| DEA | Data Encryption Algorithm |
| DEP | Data Execution Prevention |
| DES | Data Encryption Standard |
| *DFS* | Distributed File System |
| *DFS* | dynamic frequency selection |
| DH | Diffie-Hellman |
| DHAAD | Dynamic Home Agent Address Discovery |
| DHCP | Dynamic Host Configuration Protocol |
| DHCPv6 | Dynamic Host Configuration Protocol for Internet Protocol v6 |
| DHS | U.S. Department of Homeland Security |
| DIMS | Digital Identity Management Service |
| DISA | U.S. Defense Information Systems Agency |
| DLL | dynamic link library |
| DMA | direct memory access |
| DMZ | demilitarized zone |
| *DN* | distinguished name |
| *DN* | domain name |
| DNP | Distributed Network Protocol |
| DNS | domain name system |
| DNSBL | Domain Name System Blacklist |
| DNSSEC | Domain Name System Security Extensions |
| DOC | U.S. Department of Commerce |
| DoD | U.S. Department of Defense |
| DOE | U.S. Department of Energy |
| DOI | domain of interpretation |
| DOJ | U.S. Department of Justice |
| DOM | Document Object Model |
| DoS | denial of service |
| DPA | differential power analysis |
| DRA | data recovery agent |
| DRM | digital rights management |
| DRP | disaster recovery plan |
| *DS* | Delegation Signer |
| *DS* | distribution system |
| DS Field | differentiated services field |
| DSA | Digital Signature Algorithm |

| | |
|---|---|
| DSL | digital subscriber line |
| DSML | Directory Services Markup Language |
| DSN | delivery status notification |
| DSOD | dynamic separation of duty |
| DSS | Digital Signature Standard |
| DSTM | Dual Stack Transition Mechanism |
| DTC | Distributed Transaction Coordinator |
| DTD | Document Type Definition |
| DTR | derived test requirement |
| DUID | DHCP unique identifier |
| DVD | digital video disc |
| DVD-R | digital video disc - recordable |
| DVD-ROM | digital video disc - read only memory |
| DVD-RW | digital video disc - rewritable |

## E

| | |
|---|---|
| EAL | evaluation assurance level |
| EAP | Extensible Authentication Protocol |
| EAP-FAST | Extensible Authentication Protocol-Flexible Authentication via Secure Tunneling |
| EAPOL | Extensible Authentication Protocol Over LAN |
| EAPOL-KCK | Extensible Authentication Protocol Over LAN Key Confirmation Key |
| EAPOL-KEK | Extensible Authentication Protocol Over LAN Key Encryption Key |
| EAP-TLS | Extensible Authentication Protocol-Transport Layer Security |
| EAP-TTLS | Extensible Authentication Protocol-Tunneled Transport Layer Security |
| EBGP | Exterior Border Gateway Protocol |
| ebXML | Electronic Business using eXtensible Markup Language |
| EC2N | Elliptic Curve over G[2N] |
| ECB | Electronic Codebook (mode) |
| ECC | Elliptic Curve Cryptography |
| ECDH | Elliptic Curve Diffie-Hellman |
| ECDSA | Elliptic Curve Digital Signature Algorithm |
| ECM | Enterprise Configuration Manager |
| ECP | Encryption Control Protocol |
| ECPA | Electronic Communications Privacy Act |
| EDGE | Enhanced Data rates for GSM Evolution |
| EDI | electronic data interchange |
| EDR | enhanced data rate |
| EEPROM | electronically erasable programmable read-only memory |
| EFI | Extensible Firmware Interface |
| EFS | Encrypting File System |

| | |
|---|---|
| EGP | Exterior Gateway Protocol |
| EH | extension header |
| EICAR | European Institute for Computer Antivirus Research |
| EIGRP | Enhanced Interior Gateway Routing Protocol |
| EIK | EAP Integrity Key |
| email | electronic mail |
| *EMS* | energy management system |
| *EMS* | Enhanced Messaging Service |
| EMSK | Extended Master Session Key |
| EPAL | Enterprise Privacy Authorization Language |
| EPC | electronic product code |
| EPCIS | Electronic Product Code Information Services |
| EPHI | electronic protected health information |
| EPS | events per second |
| ERP | enterprise resource planning |
| ESMS | enterprise security management system |
| ESMTP | Extended Simple Mail Transfer Protocol |
| ESN | electronic serial number |
| ESP | Encapsulating Security Payload |
| ESS | Extended Service Set |
| ETSI | European Telecommunications Standards Institute |
| EU | European Union |
| EUI-64 | Extended Unique Identifier 64 bit |
| EV-DO | Evolution-Data Optimized |
| ext2fs | Second Extended Filesystem |
| ext3fs | Third Extended Filesystem |

**F**

| | |
|---|---|
| FAQ | frequently asked questions |
| FAR | Federal Acquisition Regulation |
| FASC-N | Federal Agency Smart Credential Number |
| FASP | Federal Agency Security Practices |
| FAT | file allocation table |
| FBCA | Federal Bridge Certification Authority |
| FBI | Federal Bureau of Investigation |
| FBI CJIS | Federal Bureau of Investigation Criminal Justice Information Services Division |
| FCC | Federal Communications Commission |
| FCC ID | Federal Communications Commission Identification number |
| FCL | final checklist list |
| FCPF | Federal PKI Common Policy Framework |
| FCRA | Fair Credit Reporting Act |
| FCS | frame check sequence |
| FDA | Food and Drug Administration |

| | |
|---|---|
| FDCC | Federal Desktop Core Configuration |
| FDCE | Federated Development and Certification Environment |
| FDE | full disk encryption |
| FDIC | Federal Deposit Insurance Corporation |
| FEA | Federal Enterprise Architecture |
| FEK | file encryption key |
| FFMIA | Federal Financial Management Improvement Act |
| FHSS | frequency hopping spread spectrum |
| FIB | forwarding information base |
| FICC | Federal Identity Credentialing Committee |
| FIPS | Federal Information Processing Standards |
| FIRSTTM | Forum of Incident Response and Security Teams |
| FISCAM | Federal Information System Controls Audit Manual |
| FISMA | Federal Information Security Management Act of 2002 |
| FISSEA | Federal Information Systems Security Educators' Association |
| FLETC | Federal Law Enforcement Training Center |
| FMR | false match rate |
| FMS | Fluhrer-Mantin-Shamir |
| FNMR | false non match rate |
| FOIA | Freedom of Information Act |
| FPC | Federal Preparedness Circular |
| FPKI | Federal Public Key Infrastructure |
| FPKIA | Federal Public Key Infrastructure Architecture |
| FPKIPA | Federal Public Key Infrastructure Policy Authority |
| FQDN | fully qualified domain name |
| FRR | false rejection rate |
| FSO | field security office |
| FTC | Federal Trade Commission |
| FTCA | Federal Trade Commission Act |
| FTP | File Transfer Protocol |
| FUS | Fast User Switching |
| FY | fiscal year |

## G

| | |
|---|---|
| GAO | U.S. Government Accountability Office |
| GB g | igabyte |
| GFAC | generalized framework for access control |
| GFIRST | Government Forum of Incident Response and Security Teams |
| GHz | gigahertz |
| GIG | Global Information Grid |
| GINA | graphical identification and authentication |
| GKEK | Group Key Encryption Key |

| | |
|---|---|
| GLB *or* GLBA | Gramm-Leach-Bliley Act |
| GMK | Group Master Key |
| GnuPG | GNU Privacy Guard |
| GOTS | government off-the-shelf |
| GPL | general public license |
| GPMC | Group Policy Management Console |
| GPO | Group Policy Object |
| GPRS | general packet radio service |
| GPS | global positioning system |
| GR | graceful restart |
| GRE | Generic Routing Encapsulation |
| GRS | General Records Schedule |
| GS1 | Global Standards One |
| GSA | U.S. General Services Administration |
| GSM | Global System for Mobile Communications |
| GTC | Generic Token Card |
| GTEK | group traffic encryption key |
| GTK | group temporal key |
| gTLD | generic top-level domain |
| GTSM | Generalized TTL Security Mechanism |
| GUI | graphical user interface |

## H

| | |
|---|---|
| *HA* | high availability |
| *HA* | home agent |
| HAG | high assurance guard |
| HCI | host controller interface |
| HERF | hazards of electromagnetic radiation to fuel |
| HERO | hazards of electromagnetic radiation to ordnance |
| HERP | hazards of electromagnetic radiation to personnel |
| HF | high frequency |
| HFS | Hierarchical File System |
| HHS | U.S. Department of Health and Human Services |
| HINFO | host information |
| HIP | Host Identity Protocol |
| HIPAA | Health Insurance Portability and Accountability Act |
| HIPERLAN | high-performance radio local area network |
| HKLM | HKEY_Local_Machine |
| HL7 | Health Level Seven |
| HMAC | keyed-hash message authentication code |
| HMI | human-machine interface |
| HPA | host protected area |
| HPFS | High-Performance File System |
| HR | human resources |

| | |
|---|---|
| HSARPA | Homeland Security Advanced Research Projects Agency |
| HSPD | Homeland Security Presidential Directive |
| HTCIA | High Technology Crime Investigation Association |
| HTCP | Hyper Text Caching Protocol |
| HTML | Hypertext Markup Language |
| HTTP | Hypertext Transfer Protocol |
| HTTPS | Secure Hypertext Transfer Protocol |
| Hz | hertz |

# I

| | |
|---|---|
| I&A | identification and authentication |
| I/O | input/output |
| I3P | Institute for Information Infrastructure Protection |
| IA | information assurance |
| IAB | Internet Architecture Board |
| IACIS® | International Association of Computer Investigative Specialists |
| IAIP | Information Analysis and Infrastructure Protection |
| IANA | Internet Assigned Numbers Authority |
| IAO | information assurance officer |
| IATF | Information Assurance Technical Framework |
| IBC | iterated block cipher |
| IBE | identity-based encryption |
| iBGP | Internal Border Gateway Protocol |
| IBMJSSE | IBM Java Secure Socket Extension |
| IBSS | independent basic service set |
| IC3 | Internet Crime Complaint Center |
| ICAMP | Incident Cost Analysis and Modeling Project |
| ICANN | Internet Corporation for Assigned Names and Numbers |
| ICCID | Integrated Circuit Card Identification |
| ICCP | Inter-control Center Communications Protocol |
| ICF | Internet Connection Firewall |
| ICMP | Internet Control Message Protocol |
| ICP | Internet Cache Protocol |
| *ICS* | industrial control system |
| *ICS* | Internet Connection Sharing |
| ICSA | International Computer Security Association |
| ICV | integrity check value |
| ID | identification |
| IDARTTM | Information Design Assurance Red Team |
| *IDE* | integrated development environment |
| *IDE* | Integrated Drive Electronics |
| IDEA | International Data Encryption Algorithm |
| iDEN | Integrated Digital Enhanced Network |
| ID-FF | Identity Federation Framework |

| | |
|---|---|
| IDMEF | Intrusion Detection Message Exchange Format |
| IDMS | identity management system |
| IDPS | intrusion detection and prevention system |
| IDS | intrusion detection system |
| ID-SIS | Identity Service Interface Specifications |
| ID-WSF | Identity Web Services Framework |
| ID-WSF DST | Identity Web Services Framework Data Services Template |
| IE | Internet Explorer |
| IEC | International Electrotechnical Commission |
| IED | intelligent electronic device |
| IEEE-SA | IEEE Standards Association |
| IESG | Internet Security Steering Group |
| IETF | Internet Engineering Task Force |
| IETF BCP | Internet Engineering Task Force Best Current Practice |
| IETF RFC | Internet Engineering Task Force Request for Comments |
| IGMP | Internet Group Management Protocol |
| IGP | interior gateway protocol |
| IID | interface identifier |
| IIF | information in identifiable form |
| IIHI | individually identifiable health information |
| IIS | Internet Information Services |
| IKE | Internet Key Exchange |
| IM | instant messaging |
| IMAP | Internet Message Access Protocol |
| IMEI | International Mobile Equipment Identity |
| IMSI | International Mobile Subscriber Identity |
| INCITS | InterNational Committee for Information Technology Standards |
| IP | Internet Protocol |
| IPA | initial privacy assessment |
| IPComp | Internet Protocol Payload Compression Protocol |
| IPng | Internet Protocol Next Generation |
| IPS | intrusion prevention system |
| IPsec | Internet Protocol Security |
| IPv4 | Internet Protocol version 4 |
| IPv6 | Internet Protocol version 6 |
| IPX | Internet Packet Exchange |
| *IR* | infrared |
| *IR* | interagency report |
| IRC | Internet Relay Chat |
| IrDA® | Infrared Data Association® |
| IRQ | interrupt request line |
| IRS | Internal Revenue Service |
| IRTF | Internet Research Task Force |
| IS | information system |
| *ISA* | interconnection security agreement |
| *ISA* | International Society of Automation |

| | |
|---|---|
| ISAC | information sharing and analysis center |
| ISAKMP | Internet Security Association and Key Management Protocol |
| ISAP | Information Security Automation Program |
| ISAPI | Internet Server Application Programming Interface |
| ISATAP | Intra-Site Automatic Tunnel Addressing Protocol |
| ISF | Information Security Forum |
| ISID | Industrial Security Incident Database |
| IS-IS | Intermediate System-to-Intermediate System |
| *ISM* | industrial, scientific, and medical |
| *ISM* | information security marking |
| ISMS | information security management system |
| ISO | International Organization for Standardization |
| ISP | Internet service provider |
| ISSEA | International Systems Security Engineering Association |
| ISSO | information systems security officer |
| ISSPM | information systems security program manager |
| IT | information technology |
| ITAA | Information Technology Association of America |
| ITF | Interrogator Talks First |
| ITL | Information Technology Laboratory |
| ITU | International Telecommunications Union |
| ITU-T | International Telecommunications Union-Telecommunication Standardization Sector |
| IUT | implementation under test |
| IV | initialization vector |

## J

| | |
|---|---|
| Java EE | Java Platform, Enterprise Edition |
| JAXR | Java API for XML Registries |
| JFFS2 | Journaling Flash File System, version 2 |
| JIT | just-in-time |
| JPEG | Joint Photographic Experts Group |
| JRE | Java Runtime Environment |
| JSM | Java Security Manager |
| JSP | Java Server Pages |
| JSSE | Java Secure Socket Extension |
| JTAG | Joint Test Action Group |
| JTC1 | Joint Technical Committee 1 (International Organization for Standardization [ISO]/International Electrotechnical Commission [IEC]) |
| JVM | Java Virtual Machine |

## K

| | |
|---|---|
| KB | kilobyte |
| Kbps | kilobit per second |
| KDC | key distribution center |
| KEK | key encryption key |
| KG | key generator |
| KGD | key generation and distribution |
| kHz | kilohertz |
| KINK | Kerberized Internet Negotiation of Keys |
| KSG | key stream generator |
| KSK | key signing key |

## L

| | |
|---|---|
| L2CAP | Logical Link Control and Adaptation Protocol |
| L2F | Layer 2 Forwarding |
| L2TP | Layer 2 Tunneling Protocol |
| L2VPN | Layer 2 Virtual Private Network |
| L3VPN | Layer 3 Virtual Private Network |
| LACNIC | Latin American and Caribbean IP Addresses Registry |
| LAN | local area network |
| LCD | liquid crystal display |
| LDA | local delivery agent |
| LDAP | Lightweight Directory Access Protocol |
| LED | light emitting diode |
| LF | low frequency |
| LFSR | linear feedback shift register |
| LIR | local Internet registry |
| LM | LAN Manager |
| LMP | Link Manager Protocol |
| LOC | location (DNS record) |
| LOS | line-of-sight |
| LRA | Local Registration Authority |
| LUA | limited user account |

## M

| | |
|---|---|
| m | meter |
| *MAC* | mandatory access control |
| *MAC* | media access control (layer) |
| *MAC* | Medium Access Control |
| *MAC* | message authentication code |
| MAF | multi-mode authentication framework |

| | |
|---|---|
| MAN | metropolitan area network |
| MAPS | Mail Abuse Prevention System |
| MB | megabyte |
| Mbps | megabits per second |
| MBR | master boot record |
| MBSA | Microsoft Baseline Security Analyzer |
| MD | message digest |
| ME | mobile equipment |
| MED | multi-exit discriminator |
| MEP | message exchange pattern |
| MES | manufacturing execution system |
| MHz | megahertz |
| MIB | management information base |
| *MIC* | mandatory integrity control |
| *MIC* | message integrity check |
| *MIC* | message integrity code |
| MIKEY | Multimedia Internet KEYing |
| MIME | Multipurpose Internet Mail Extensions |
| MIMO | multiple-input, multiple-output |
| MIN | mobile identification number |
| Mini SD | mini secure digital |
| MIP | Mobile Internet Protocol |
| MitM | man-in-the-middle (attack) |
| MLD | Multicast Listener Discovery |
| *MMC* | Microsoft Management Console |
| *MMC* | MultiMediaCard |
| MMCmobile | MultiMediaCard Mobile |
| MMS | Multimedia Messaging Service |
| MN | mobile node |
| MO | magneto-optical |
| MOA | memorandum of agreement |
| MOBIKE | IKEv2 Mobility and Multihoming Protocol |
| MODP | modular exponential |
| MOSS | MIME Object Security Services |
| MOU | memorandum of understanding |
| MOVS | Modes of Operation Validation System |
| MPA | Mobile Prefix Advertisement |
| MPLS | multiprotocol label switching |
| MPS | Mobile Prefix Solicitation |
| MQV | Menezes-Qu-Vanstone |
| MRI | magnetic resonance imaging |
| *MS* | Microsoft |
| *MS* | mobile subscriber |
| MSC | mobile switching center |
| MS-CHAP | Microsoft Challenge Handshake Authentication Protocol |
| MS-DOS | Microsoft Disk Operating System |

| | |
|---|---|
| MSDP | Multicast Source Discovery Protocol |
| MSEC | multicast security |
| MSEL | Master Scenario Events List |
| MSIL | Microsoft Intermediate Language |
| MSISDN | Mobile Subscriber Integrated Services Digital Network |
| MSK | master session key |
| MSKB | Microsoft Knowledge Base |
| MSSP | managed security services provider |
| MSWG | Metadata Standards Working Group |
| MTA | mail transfer agent |
| MTM | Mobile Trusted Module |
| *MTU* | master telemetry unit |
| *MTU* | master terminal unit |
| *MTU* | maximum transmission unit |
| MUA | mail user agent |
| mW | milliwatt |
| MX | mail exchanger |

**N**

| | |
|---|---|
| NA | Neighbor Advertisement |
| NAC | network access control |
| NACI | National Agency Check and Inquiries |
| NAP | Network Access Protection |
| NARA | National Archives and Records Administration |
| NAS | network access server |
| NAT | network address translation |
| NAT-PT | network address translation—protocol translation |
| NAT-T | network address translation traversal |
| NBA | network behavior analysis |
| NBAD | network behavior anomaly detection |
| NCES | NetCentric Enterprise Services |
| NCP | National Checklist Program |
| NCSD | National Cyber Security Division |
| NCSI | NIST National Center for Standards and Certification Information |
| ND | Neighbor Discovery |
| NDAC | nondiscretionary access control |
| NetBEUI | NetBIOS Extended User Interface |
| NetBIOS | Network Basic Input/Output System |
| NetBT | NetBIOS over TCP/IP |
| NFAT | network forensic analysis tool |
| NFC | near field communication |
| *NFS* | network file system |
| *NFS* | Network File Sharing |
| NH | next header |

| | |
|---|---|
| NIAC | National Infrastructure Advisory Council |
| NIAP | National Information Assurance Partnership |
| NIC | network interface card |
| NICC | National Infrastructure Coordinating Center |
| NIJ | National Institute of Justice |
| NIPC | National Infrastructure Protection Center |
| NIS | Network Information System |
| NISAC | National Infrastructure Simulation and Analysis Center |
| NISCC | National Infrastructure Security Co-ordination Centre |
| NIST | National Institute of Standards and Technology |
| NISTIR | National Institute of Standards and Technology Interagency Report |
| NLOS | non-line-of-sight |
| NPIVP | NIST Personal Identity Verification Program |
| NPPI | nonpublic personal information |
| *NS* | name server |
| *NS* | Neighbor Solicitation |
| NSA | National Security Agency |
| NSAPI | Netscape Server Application Programming Interface |
| NSEC | Next Secure |
| NSI | national security information |
| NSRL | National Software Reference Library |
| NSS | Network Security Services |
| NSTB | National SCADA Test Bed |
| NSTISSC | National Security Telecommunications and Information Systems Security Committee |
| NSTISSI | National Security Telecommunications and Information Systems Security Instruction |
| NTFS | New Technology File System |
| NTLM | NT LAN Manager |
| NTP | Network Time Protocol |
| NTTAA | National Technology Transfer and Advancement Act of 1995 |
| NUD | Neighbor Unreachability Detection |
| NVD | National Vulnerability Database |
| NVLAP | National Voluntary Laboratory Accreditation Program |
| NW3C | National White Collar Crime Center |
| NX | no execute |

## O

| | |
|---|---|
| OASISTM | Organization for the Advancement of Structured Information Standards |
| OCC | Office of the Comptroller of the Currency |
| OCIO | Office of the Chief Information Officer |
| OCSP | Online Certificate Status Protocol |
| ODBC | Open Database Connectivity |

| | |
|---|---|
| OECD | Organisation for Economic Co-operation and Development |
| OEM | original equipment manufacturer |
| OFB | output feedback (mode) |
| OFDM | orthogonal frequency-division multiplexing |
| OGSATM | Open Grid Services Architecture |
| OHA | Open Handset Alliance |
| OIG | Office of Inspector General |
| OLE | object linking and embedding |
| OMB | Office of Management and Budget |
| ONS | Object Naming Service |
| OOB | out-of-band |
| OPC | OLE for Process Control |
| OpenPGP | An Open Specification for Pretty Good Privacy |
| OPM | U.S. Office of Personnel Management |
| ORB | open relay blacklist |
| OS | operating system |
| OSHA | Occupational Safety and Health Administration |
| OSI | Open Systems Interconnection |
| OSPF | Open Shortest Path First |
| OSS | open source software |
| OSSTMM | Open Source Security Testing Methodology Manual |
| OSVDB | Open Source Vulnerability Database |
| OTP | one-time password |
| OU | organizational unit |
| OVAL | Open Vulnerability and Assessment Language |
| OWASP | Open Web Application Security Project |
| OWL-S | Web Ontology Language for Services |

## P

| | |
|---|---|
| P2P | peer-to-peer |
| *PAC* | Privilege Attribute Certificate |
| *PAC* | Protected Access Credential |
| PAD | peer authorization database |
| PAM | pluggable authentication module |
| PAN | personal area network |
| PAOS | Reverse HTTP Binding for SOAP |
| *PAP* | Password Authentication Protocol |
| *PAP* | policy access point |
| PAS | publicly available specification |
| PBA | pre-boot authentication |
| PBAC | policy-based access control |
| PBCC | Packet Binary Convolutional Code |
| PBE | pre-boot environment |
| PBX | private branch exchange |

| | |
|---|---|
| PC | personal computer |
| *PCI* | Payment Card Industry |
| *PCI* | personal identity verification card issuer |
| PCI DSS | Payment Card Industry Data Security Standard |
| PCMCIA | Personal Computer Memory Card International Association |
| PCN | process control network |
| PCP | IP Payload Compression Protocol |
| PCS | process control system |
| PCSF | Process Control System Forum |
| PCSRF | Process Control Security Requirements Forum |
| PDA | personal digital assistant |
| PDD | Presidential Decision Directive |
| PDF | Portable Document Format |
| PDP | policy decision point |
| PDS | protective distribution systems |
| PEAP | Protected Extensible Authentication Protocol |
| PED | portable electronic devices |
| PEM | Privacy Enhanced Mail |
| PEP | policy enforcement point |
| PFS | perfect forward secrecy |
| PGP | Pretty Good Privacy |
| PHI | protected health information |
| PHP | PHP: Hypertext Preprocessor |
| PHY | Physical (layer) |
| PIA | privacy impact assessment |
| PICSTM | Platform for Internet Content Selection |
| PII | personally identifiable information |
| PIM | personal information management |
| PIM-SM | Protocol Independent Multicast—Sparse Mode |
| PIN | personal identification number |
| PIP | policy information point |
| PIR | Public Interest Registry |
| PIV | personal identity verification |
| PKCS | Public Key Cryptography Standard |
| PKI | public key infrastructure |
| PKM | privacy key management |
| PKMv1 | Privacy Key Management Protocol version 1 |
| PKMv2 | Privacy Key Management Protocol version 2 |
| PL | public law |
| PLC | programmable logic controller |
| PMA | Policy Management Authority |
| PMK | pairwise master key |
| PMKSA | Pairwise Master Key Security Association |
| PMP | point-to-multipoint |
| PMTU | path maximum transmission unit |
| PN | packet number |

| | |
|---|---|
| PNG | Portable Network Graphics |
| POA&M | plan of action and milestones |
| *POC* | point of contact |
| *POC* | proof of concept |
| PoE | Power over Ethernet |
| POP | Post Office Protocol |
| POP3 | Post Office Protocol version 3 |
| PP | protection profile |
| PPP | Point-to-Point Protocol |
| PPTP | Point-to-Point Tunneling Protocol |
| PPVPN | provisioner-provided virtual private network |
| PRA | Paperwork Reduction Act |
| Pre-PAK | pre-primary authorization key |
| PRF | pseudorandom function |
| PRNG | pseudorandom number generator |
| PSK | pre-shared key |
| PSTN | public switched telephone network |
| PTA | privacy threshold assessment (or analysis) |
| PTK | pairwise transient key |
| PTV | perceived target value |
| PUB | publication |
| PUK | PIN unblocking key |
| PVG | patch and vulnerability group |

## Q

| | |
|---|---|
| QoP | quality of protection |
| QoS | quality of service |

## R

| | |
|---|---|
| R&D | research and development |
| R/W | read/write |
| *RA* | receiver address |
| *RA* | Registration Authority |
| *RA* | remote assistance |
| *RA* | Router Advertisement |
| RAdAC | risk adaptive access control |
| RADIUS | Remote Authentication Dial In User Service |
| RAID | redundant array of independent disks |
| RAM | random access memory |
| RAT | remote administration tool |
| RBAC | role-based access control |
| RC2 | Rivest Cipher 2 |

| | |
|---|---|
| RC4 | Rivest Cipher 4 |
| RCE | route cache entry |
| RCFL | Regional Computer Forensics Laboratory |
| RCP | Remote Copy Protocol |
| RDBMS | relational database management system |
| RDP | Remote Desktop Protocol |
| REL | rights expression language |
| REP | Robots Exclusion Protocol |
| REST | Representational State Transfer |
| RF | radio frequency |
| RFC | request for comments |
| RFD | route flap damping |
| RFID | radio frequency identification |
| RFP | request for proposal |
| RIB | routing information base |
| RIP | Routing Information Protocol |
| RIPE NCC | Réseaux IP Européens Network Coordination Centre |
| RIPng | Routing Information Protocol next generation |
| RIR | regional internet registries |
| RIS | Remote Installation Services |
| RMA | reliability, maintainability, and availability |
| RMON | Remote Monitoring |
| RNG | random number generator |
| ROE | rules of engagement |
| ROM | read-only memory |
| RP | responsible person (record) |
| RPC | remote procedure call |
| RPF | Reverse Path Forwarding |
| RPO | recovery point objective |
| RR | resource record |
| RRSIG | resource record signature |
| *RS* | relay station |
| *RS* | Router Solicitation |
| RSA | Rivest-Shamir-Adelman |
| RSBAC | rule set-based access control |
| RSN | Robust Security Network |
| RSNA | Robust Security Network Association |
| RSNIE | Robust Security Network Information Element |
| RSO | reduced sign-on |
| RSS | Really Simple Syndication |
| RSSI | received signal strength indication |
| RSVP | Resource ReSerVation Protocol |
| RTF | Rich Text Format |
| RTLS | real-time location system |
| RTO | recovery time objective |
| RTP | Real-Time Transport Protocol |

| | |
|---|---|
| RTU | remote terminal unit or remote telemetry unit |
| RuBAC | rule-based access control |
| R-UIM | Removable User Identity Module |

## S

| | |
|---|---|
| S/MIME | Secure/Multipurpose Internet Mail Extensions |
| *S4* | security association |
| *S4* s | ource address |
| SACL | system access control list |
| SAD | security association database |
| SAFER | Secure And Fast Encryption Routine |
| SAID | security association identifier |
| SAISO | senior agency information security officer |
| *SAM* | Security Account Manager |
| *SAM* | software asset management |
| SAMATE | Software Assurance Metrics and Tool Evaluation |
| SAMLTM | Security Assertion Markup LanguageTM |
| SAN | storage area network |
| S-BGP | Secure Border Gateway Protocol |
| SC | subcommittee |
| SCADA | supervisory control and data acquisition |
| SCAP | Security Content Automation Protocol |
| SCP | Secure Copy Protocol |
| SCSI | Small Computer System Interface |
| SCTP | Stream Control Transmission Protocol |
| SD | Secure Digital |
| SDIO | Secure Digital Input Output |
| SDK | software development kit |
| SDLC | System Development Life Cycle |
| SDO | standards development organization |
| *SDP* | Session Description Protocol |
| *SDP* | Service Discovery Protocol |
| SEI | Software Engineering Institute |
| SEM | security event management |
| SEND | Secure Neighbor Discovery |
| SEP | secure entry point |
| SFTP | Secure File Transfer Protocol |
| SHA | Secure Hash Algorithm |
| SHA-1 | Secure Hash Algorithm 1 |
| shim6 | Site Multihoming by IPv6 Intermediation |
| SHS | Secure Hash Standard |
| SIA | Security Industry Association |
| SID | security identifier |
| SIEM | security information and event management |

| | |
|---|---|
| SIG | special interest group |
| SIIT | Stateless IP/ICMP Translation Algorithm |
| *SIM* | security information management |
| *SIM* | subscriber identity module |
| SIP | Session Initiation Protocol |
| SIS | safety instrumented system |
| SKEME | Secure Key Exchange Mechanism |
| SLA | service level agreement |
| SMB | Server Message Block |
| SME | subject matter expert |
| S/MIME | Secure/Multipurpose Internet Mail Extensions |
| *SMS* | Short Message Service |
| *SMS* | Systems Management Server |
| SMT | scar, mark and tattoo |
| SMTP | Simple Mail Transfer Protocol |
| SNL | Sandia National Laboratories |
| SNMP | Simple Network Management Protocol |
| SNTP | Simple Network Time Protocol |
| *SOA* | service-oriented architecture |
| *SOA* | start of authority (resource record) |
| SoBGP | Secure Origin Border Gateway Protocol |
| SoD | separation of duties |
| SOHO | small office/home office |
| SOP | standard operating procedure |
| SOR | system of records |
| SORN | system of records notice |
| SOX | Sarbanes-Oxley Act of 2002 |
| *SP* | service pack |
| *SP* | special publication |
| SPD | security policy database |
| SPI | security parameters index |
| SPL | Structured Product Labeling |
| SPMLTM | Service Provisioning Markup LanguageTM |
| SPP-ICS | System Protection Profile for Industrial Control Systems |
| SQL | Structured Query Language |
| SR | service release |
| SRES | signed response |
| SRTP | Secure Real-Time Transport Protocol |
| SS | subscriber station |
| SSDP | Simple Service Discovery Protocol |
| SSE-CMM | Systems Security Engineering-Capability Maturity Model |
| SSH | Secure Shell |
| SSI | Server Side Includes |
| SSID | service set identifier |
| SSL | Secure Sockets Layer |
| SSLF | Specialized Security-Limited Functionality |

| | |
|---|---|
| SSN | social security number |
| SSO | single sign-on |
| SSoD | static separation of duty |
| SSP | secure simple pairing |
| SSPI | Security Support Provider Interface |
| ST | security target |
| STA | station |
| STIG | security technical implementation guide |
| STS | security token service |
| SUID | Set-User-ID |
| SWSA | Semantic Web Services Initiative Architecture |
| SZ | security zone |

## T

| | |
|---|---|
| *TA* | test assertion |
| *TA* | transmitter address |
| TACACS | Terminal Access Controller Access Control System |
| TAG | technical advisory group |
| TB | terabyte |
| TC | technical committee |
| TC68 | ISO/IEC Technical Committee 68 |
| TCP | Transmission Control Protocol |
| TCP/IP | Transmission Control Protocol/Internet Protocol |
| TDEA | Triple Data Encryption Algorithm |
| TDM | time division multiplexing |
| TDMA | time division multiple access |
| TEK | traffic encryption key |
| TERENA | Trans-European Research and Education Networking Association |
| TFT | thin film transistor |
| TFTP | Trivial File Transfer Protocol |
| TGS | ticket-granting service |
| TIA® | Telecommunications Industry Association |
| TID | tag identifier |
| TK | temporal key |
| TKIP | Temporal Key Integrity Protocol |
| TLD | top-level domain |
| TLS | Transport Layer Security |
| TMOVS | Modes of Operation Validation System for the Triple DES Algorithm |
| TOE | target of evaluation |
| *TOS* | trusted operating system |
| *ToS* | Type of Service |
| TPC | transmission power control |
| TPM | trusted platform module |

| | |
|---|---|
| TR | technical report |
| TRT | transport relay translator |
| TS | technical specification |
| TSA | time stamping authority |
| TSC | TKIP sequence counter |
| *TSIG* | Secret Key Transaction Authentication for DNS |
| *TSIG* | Transaction Signature |
| TSN | transitional security network |
| TSP | Time-Stamp Protocol |
| TT&E | test, training, and exercise |
| TTF | tag talks first |
| TTL | time to live |
| TTLS | Tunneled Transport Layer Security |
| TTP | trusted third party |
| TXT | text (record) |

**U**

| | |
|---|---|
| U.S. | United States |
| U.S.C. | United States Code |
| UAC | User Account Control |
| UART | universal asynchronous receiver/transmitter |
| UBR | Universal Description, Discovery and Integration (UDDI) Business Registry |
| UCC | Uniform Code Council, Inc. |
| UCE | unsolicited commercial email |
| UDDITM | Uniform Description, Discovery, and IntegrationTM |
| UDF | Universal Disk Format |
| UDP | User Datagram Protocol |
| UFS | UNIX File System |
| UHF | ultra high frequency |
| UI | user interface |
| UK | United Kingdom |
| UL | Underwriters' Laboratories® |
| ULA | unique local address |
| ULP | upper layer protocol |
| UML® | Unified Modeling LanguageTM |
| UMPC | ultra-mobile personal computer |
| UMTS | Universal Mobile Telecommunications System |
| UNII | Unlicensed National Information Infrastructure |
| UPC | Universal Product Code |
| UPnP | Universal Plug and Play |
| UPS | uninterruptible power supply |
| URI | Uniform Resource Identifier |
| URL | Uniform Resource Locator |

| | |
|---|---|
| USB | Universal Serial Bus |
| US-CERT | United States Computer Emergency Readiness Team |
| USIM | UMTS Subscriber Identity Module *or* Universal Subscriber Identity Module |
| UTM | unified threat management |
| UUID | Universally Unique Identifier |
| UWB | ultrawideband |

## V

| | |
|---|---|
| VB | Visual Basic |
| VB.NET | Visual Basic .NET |
| VBA | Visual Basic for Applications |
| VBScript | Visual Basic Script |
| VFD | variable frequency drive |
| VHD | virtual hard drive |
| VHF | very high frequency |
| VLAN | virtual local area network |
| VM | virtual machine |
| VMS | vulnerability management system |
| VoIP | Voice over Internet Protocol |
| VOIPSA | Voice over IP Security Alliance |
| VPN | virtual private network |
| VPNC | Virtual Private Network Consortium |
| VRRP | Virtual Router Redundancy Protocol |

## W

| | |
|---|---|
| W3C® | World Wide Web Consortium |
| WAN | wide area network |
| *WAP* | wireless access point |
| *WAP* | Wireless Application Protocol |
| WaSP | Web Standards Project |
| WAVE | Wireless Access for Vehicular Environment |
| WAYF | Where Are You From |
| WCCP | Web Cache Coordination Protocol |
| W-CDMA | Wideband Code Division Multiple Access |
| WDS | wireless distribution system |
| WebDAV | Web Distributed Authoring and Versioning |
| WEP | Wired Equivalent Privacy |
| WfMC | Workflow Management Coalition |
| WfMS | workflow management system |
| WG | working group |
| WIDPS | wireless intrusion detection and prevention system |

| | |
|---|---|
| WiMAX | Worldwide Interoperability for Microwave Access |
| WLAN | wireless local area network |
| WMAN | wireless metropolitan area network |
| WMM® | Wi-Fi MultimediaTM |
| WORM | write once, read many |
| WPA | Wi-Fi Protected Access |
| WPA2® | Wi-Fi Protected Access® 2 |
| WPAN | wireless personal area network |
| WS | Web services |
| WSDL | Web Services Description Language |
| WSH | Windows Script Host |
| *WS-I* | Web services interoperability |
| *WS-I* | Web Services Interoperability Organization |
| WSS4J | Web Services Security for Java |
| WS-Security | Web Services Security |
| WSUS | Windows Server Update Services |
| WVE | Wireless Vulnerabilities and Exploits |
| WWAN | wireless wide area network |
| WWW | World Wide Web |

## XYZ

| | |
|---|---|
| XACL | XML Access Control Language |
| XACMLTM | eXtensible Access Control Markup LanguageTM |
| XCBC | XOR Cipher Block Chaining |
| XCCDF | eXtensible Configuration Checklist Description Format |
| XHTML | Extensible Hypertext Markup Language |
| XKMS | XML Key Management Specification |
| XML | Extensible Markup Language |
| XOR | exclusive OR |
| XrML | eXtensible Rights Markup Language |
| XSD | XML Schema Definition |
| XSL | Extensible Stylesheet Language |
| XSLT | Extensible Stylesheet Language Transformation |
| XSS | cross-site scripting |
| ZSK | zone signing key |

# APPENDIX A—REFERENCES

Sources used in the development of the list of system and network security acronyms and abbreviations in this document include the following:

National Institute of Standards and Technology Publications, NIST Computer Security Division Resource Center Web site, http://csrc.nist.gov/

Internet Engineering Task Force (IETF), http://www.ietf.org/

Microsoft Hardware Developer Central, Glossary of Acronyms for PC and Server Technologies,

http://www.microsoft.com/whdc/resources

Organization for the Advancement of Structured Information Standards (OASIS), http://www.oasis-open.org/home/index.php

## APPENDIX B—FORMER ACRONYMS

Over time, as organizations, technologies, or other entities change, some acronyms associated with them may lose their definitions and thus no longer be considered acronyms. This appendix presents selected former acronyms related to system and network security. As additional acronyms in this publication lose their definitions, readers are encouraged to send notification of these, along with references to authoritative sources of information, to securityacronyms@nist.gov for possible inclusion in future releases of this report.

**IEEE** Originally defined as "Institute of Electrical and Electronics Engineers, Inc."
Definition dropped by the organization (http://www.ieee.org/web

**SOAP** Originally defined as "Simple Object Access Protocol."
Definition dropped as of April 2007 (http://www.w3.org/TR/soap12-part1/#intro).

# INDEX

## A



## B



## C

## D

## I



## J



## L

## M



## N



## O



## P

## Q



## R

## U



## V



## W



## X